THE COLONIAL LEGACY

THE
COLONIAL LEGACY

VOLUME II

Some Eighteenth-Century Commentators

Edited by

LAWRENCE H. LEDER

Lehigh University

A Torchbook Library Edition
Harper & Row, Publishers
New York, Evanston, San Francisco, London

CONTENTS

THE COLONIAL LEGACY

1.

Some Eighteenth-Century Commentators: An Introduction

Lawrence H. Leder

Although historians have long pondered the dimension and meaning of the American experience, we sometimes forget that eighteenth-century writers found themselves bemused by the same questions which have goaded each generation to reexamine its past. As eighteenth-century commentators looked back over their past in an effort to explain themselves, they created answers based upon situations through which they had lived or upon an oral tradition only a generation or so removed from the events. Thus they provided invaluable insights into both their past and their present.

These eighteenth-century commentators reflected the concerns and interests of their own time. Their predecessors had written ecclesiastical history because their society had a strong religious bent; eighteenth-century authors wrote secular history because their society was becoming increasingly secularized. As men's vision of God and His role changed, so too did their perspective on the past. Once clergymen had been the creators, guardians, and revisers of tradition; doctors, lawyers, and other educated laymen assumed those tasks in the eighteenth century.

These lay writers focused directly on man's political relationship with his fellow men. Ecclesiastical history had always examined man's condition, however cursorily, from the time of the

Garden of Eden; the newer secular history emphasized a narrower time span and a smaller geographical unit. Thus eighteenth-century Americans frequently saw provincial history as a microcosm in which to find answers to broad, basic questions. They did not have to deal with an ancient time or an alien people: they knew the events of which they wrote from first-hand experience, and they had at hand the documents and oral tradition. They also knew the importance of their story, their ability to tell it, and the interest of their audience.

Eighteenth-century Americans took pride in the stability and progress of their communities, honored their past, and confidently faced the future. They joyfully accepted their membership in the greatest political entity since the Roman Empire, and they sought to improve the relationship of its parts by making America and its inhabitants better understood by Englishmen. Thus, no matter how limited their geographical coverage, they wrote from an imperial and international perspective. Living in a turbulent era, they reflected the turbulence in their writings, even though their confidence in the outcome remained undiminished.

One theme permeated all the eighteenth-century colonial histories—the distinctiveness of this colonial experience. Americans knew they were different and prided themselves on that fact. Their pride extended over time from locality to province, from province to empire, and (after the sundering of Anglo-American ties in the 1770s) from empire to nation. Underlying their pride and sense of identification was an awareness of a continental unity that became increasingly important as the century wore on. Indeed, it shaped their gradual transition from an Anglo-American culture to an independent American one.

The cultural heritage of Americans relied heavily upon experiential factors. Americans, whether as dependent colonials before 1776 or as an independent people after 1776, were not devoid of ideas, but they predicated ideas on experience. This led to a critical and skeptical attitude in colonial writings. As commentators, Americans distilled the thoughts, attitudes, and experiences of their past and their present into a narrative which has become increasingly valuable as the time about which they wrote recedes into the past. As they ranged over their materials unhampered by scholarly apparatus or scientific pretension, they created a product marked by literary distinction. In this, too, they were children of the eighteenth century. Their products rank with those of the best of their English contemporaries.

Perhaps Thomas Clap best typifies the transition between the seventeenth and eighteenth centuries. His *Annals or History of Yale College* has a decidedly religious flavor, and Clap himself proclaimed Yale's purpose to be that of a seminary for the ministry. Yet he wrote about an institution which became increasingly secularized during the eighteenth century; indeed, he himself helped secularize it by introducing both Newtonian and practical sciences into its curriculum. Clap epitomizes seventeenth-century values challenged by eighteenth-century needs.

Regardless of Clap's personal biases, his *Annals* offers the first history of an American college and emphasizes the stresses felt by American higher education during the turbulent mid-eighteenth century. In many ways, Clap served his college well, transforming it into the precursor of the modern college. He forced the transfer of authority from the trustees to himself as president; he reformed the curriculum and thereby modernized the college; and yet he sought to keep the Great Awakening, the rise of the Church of England, and the growth of rationalism from endangering the college's purpose as a seminary for Congregational ministers.

Clap's own dichotomy of values created hostility and upheaval. His account of student discontent and violence in the mid-1760s suggests a pattern with some relevance for our own time. His *Annals* provides a documentary portrait of an institution in transition as it reacted to the changes being wrought in the mid-eighteenth century. His objectivity as a historian may be undermined by his religiosity and his personal involvement, but when viewed as a contemporary document the *Annals* underscores the uncertainty and tentativeness which afflicted a significant element of eighteenth-century American society.

A more self-assured though still highly critical interpretation of American society was that of Dr. William Douglass of Boston, whose *Summary* has an exceptional literary quality. The work is scrupulously accurate, witty, entertaining, and filled with aggressive and censurious comments on American practices. Douglass sought to inhibit change, but he focused on the development of the empire and condemned those things he believed to be inimical to its existence and prosperity.

Douglass attempted a work which would put all the North American colonies into an imperial perspective, but death prevented him from completing his task. However, the two volumes that he did publish adequately convey his outlook. His devotion to Boston, to New England, and finally to America was for him a total commitment. He bitterly criticized those things which he felt would lead to serious future difficulties. He charged that the rising democratic spirit in the colonies and the consequent leveling tendency in society stemmed directly from the inflationary results of paper money.

Douglass digressed frequently and indulged his personal whims and fancies. Thus his *Summary* became not only a history, but an excursion through American society under the guidance of a highly opinionated writer. In the process, Douglass revealed a good deal about the society in which he lived.

His writings both pleased and influenced his contemporaries. His imperial approach matched his generation's concern with the Anglo-French rivalry and its awareness that the colonies' future depended upon that struggle's outcome. Douglass was among the first to treat the colonies as a unity, to express their growing sense of continental self-consciousness.

Others shared Douglass's concern for the empire. These included Archibald Kennedy, who wrote a number of essays in mid-century dealing with such specific problems as Indian relations and military defense. He contended that the prime threat to the empire and to its future expansion was France's effort to gain continental hegemony. Moreover, Kennedy understood that New York was the key to British policy, because it contained the only practical water-level route to the interior and because it had a traditional and important role in Indian relations.

Kennedy involved himself in New York's domestic politics in order to forestall any alienation of the Iroquois. New Yorkers, he felt, had conceived of their relationship with the Iroquois only in a commercial sense. The Indians' importance, he argued, was strategic, not economic, for while they offered little of value in terms of imperial trade, they held the military balance of power. As a corollary to his interest in Indian affairs, Kennedy questioned the wisdom of policies determined by colonial assemblies, especially since they often reflected local rather than imperial interests. Kennedy stridently argued for imperial guidance, collective defense, and a unified control of Indian affairs.

To accomplish these objectives, he urged innovative policies: meaningful quitrents should be established and collected and the proceeds used for imperial defense purposes; frontier lands should be settled under Crown direction rather than possessed by absentee landlords; the colonial economy should be overhauled. Such an overhaul would have involved a complete reappraisal of British trade policies, of course, and Kennedy criticized the British unsparingly for not recognizing the empire's potential as a market for manufactured goods rather than a source of raw materials. If these policy revisions were not made, Kennedy predicted increasing British neglect, declining colonial prosperity, and growing American economic competition with England. From this, he forecast, could emerge a spirit of independence that would destroy the empire. Like Douglass before him, Kennedy glimpsed the reality of continental self-consciousness, and he urgently pleaded that the British use it for the benefit of the empire rather than its destruction.

One of Kennedy's contemporaries in New York, William Livingston, shared many of these concerns, though his solutions to imperial problems sometimes differed from Kennedy's. An active politician, William Livingston jumped into the fray and published an accurate account of the early years of the French and Indian War which was also a devastating attack on his political enemies and a laudatory analysis of the proposals of his friend William Shirley.

Livingston's *Review* analyzed the importance of the American colonies, deplored colonial disunity, and sought to stimulate colonial patriotism. Livingston's ardent imperialism at this stage of his career might seem incongruous when compared with his later revolutionary activity, but both were based on a sense of continental unity, on continental self-consciousness. The ideal of unity could still operate within the bounds of empire, at least until the empire became inimical to colonial goals.

William Livingston combined ardent imperialism with forthright partisanship. He analyzed New York politics in order to launch a diatribe against James DeLancey, Thomas Pownall, and William Johnson. Yet, though more outspoken than most, his work was history in the true sense of that term. Indeed, later historians, including Francis Parkman, Justin Winsor, and Lawrence Henry Gipson, recognized it as such. It incorporated more factual material on an event of immediate interest in both England and America than did any other contemporary publication.

The *Review*'s partisanship was but one of its eighteenth-century attributes; another was its literary merit. Trenchant and extravagant, vigorous and acerbic, it attracted as large a readership in

England as it did in America, partly because of its style and despite the efforts of Livingston's enemies to suppress the work.

The imperial wars with which Douglass, Kennedy, and Livingston concerned themselves seemed, to Americans, to have reached a satisfactory conclusion with the French defeat on the Plains of Abraham in 1759. However, new problems arose after 1759, especially over the disposition of the once-proud French Empire. An enterprising British publisher, Thomas Jefferys, jumped at the opportunity to shape public policy while selling his books; he put together the first full-scale analysis of the defunct empire in his *Natural and Civil History of the French Dominions*. In many ways a compendium of the best French sources translated into English, it appeared fortuitously as the British began an intensive debate over the future of the British Empire.

Jefferys's volumes proved most important in this debate, which centered on the fate of Canada—its retention by France or its acquisition by England. This decision would shape the future of the British Empire. If France retained Canada, Britain's North American colonies would continue to be self-contained and self-sufficient units, unable to expand because of the French presence to the North. England's acquisition of Canada, however, would necessitate a revamping of the entire imperial concept; unlimited geographical expansion would permit a rapid growth of potential markets, a greatly increased and dispersed colonial population, and possibly an eventual shift across the Atlantic of the locus of power within the empire.

While nearly one hundred pamphlets appeared arguing the merits of one approach or the other, Jefferys merely offered objective information to the English public and its officials. His straightforward approach probably became more influential than the multitudinous pamphlets, for government leaders leaned heavily on his work as a source of factual knowledge. In preparing his work, Jefferys had made extensive use of such French authors as

Charlevoix, whose enthusiasm for Canada seemed unbounded. His favorable statements about Canadian climate, geography, resources, and economic possibilities proved impressive, whereas his faint praise for the West Indian islands muted Englishmen's desires for their acquisition.

Jefferys also brought his English audience abreast of the French concept of *le bon sauvage* in its application to the American Indian. To Europeans, the most commonly known non-European was the Indian, but English and French attitudes toward him differed widely, perhaps because of their differences in utilizing him. Simply stated, the French embraced the native, while the English expelled him. Jefferys, who leaned heavily on Charlevoix, champion of the Indian, introduced to the English audience an idea which quickly captured its imagination and soon became a subject of intensive debate.

Jefferys's matter-of-fact approach may also have signalled the beginning of a decline in imperial enthusiasm, a mood that had peaked during the French and Indian War. Douglass, Kennedy, and Livingston had vigorously supported imperial policies; in the following years, particularly as crisis followed on the heels of crisis, American attitudes changed as the colonials began to question, to criticize, and finally to condemn. The criticisms and questions were broadly based, coming from both future revolutionaries and future loyalists. However, those who would become loyalists could never accept the condemnation of imperial policy and could never permit continental self-consciousness to supplant imperial loyalty, for continental self-consciousness would utimately lead to independence.

An initial imperial criticism is found in Samuel Smith's *History of . . . Nova Caesaria.* Keenly aware of imperial problems, although writing only about New Jersey, Smith took a dim view of the results of British control of the colonies. All too often, he argued, England forgot the advantages it derived from its empire and myopically neglected the welfare of its overseas possessions. Smith complained that England's view of empire had not altered since the days of Raleigh and Captain John Smith, even though the nature of its empire had changed drastically.

Smith wrote in the midst of mounting tensions between England and its colonies, which helped explain his jaundiced view of British hegemony in the New World. He reminded his readers that both England and the colonies had benefited by the New World experience, that the past record of the British as governors was at best spotty, and that British concern for the rights of individuals had never been exemplary. He applauded assembly aggressiveness as a recapturing of rights which had been vested in Americans from the beginning.

Just as Smith's politics were clear-cut and easily understood, so too was his concern for the Indians. Smith believed in the "noble savage," and he consequently found ample opportunity in New Jersey's history to criticize Anglo-colonial policy toward the Indians. He applied his Quaker conscience in his concern for the original inhabitants of the colonies, and he condemned Europeans who had aggressively deprived the Indians of their rights and had destroyed a native civilization. He constantly emphasized the benign attitude of the Indians toward the initial European settlers—an attitude the Europeans did not reciprocate. Increasingly, those critical of British management of the empire would question its treatment of the original inhabitants of the American colonies.

The entire British imperial system came under a searching analysis in the debates between John Adams and Daniel Leonard. Both men ardently believed in their positions, both enthusiastically endorsed the British constitution as the greatest governmental mechanism thus far devised, and both raised grave theoretical questions about colonial rights. Leonard denied the validity of Whig arguments, contending that they were merely self-serving devices to gain power and wealth. He charged that the pervasiveness of the Whig position resulted from its reiteration by newspapers, committees of correspondence, and pulpit speakers, as well as from the strength of mob action. The Whig viewpoint, he also suggested, flattered the nascent desire for independence, the continental self-consciousness which was becoming increasingly apparent. Leonard provided perhaps the ablest and most perceptive defense of the British position to be heard in the colonies.

John Adams realized the force of Leonard's arguments and sought to counter them, but he limited himself to a defense of colonial rights within an imperial context. For Adams, continental self-consciousness had not yet reached the point where it obviated imperial loyalty; it merely challenged imperial power. Americans resisted oppression and enslavement, not legitimate authority; if they were successful, they would guarantee the continuance of political liberty in England as well as in North America. If they failed, both would suffer an incalculable loss. The Americans had no option but to try, for their failure to do so would leave them in the same position as if they had not tried at all.

Adams and Leonard parted company most sharply on the role of Parliament in the government of the empire. Adams denied the political unity of the British Empire and the authority of the legislature of one part over the other parts, except insofar as the colonies had consented beforehand to heed parliamentary statutes. This Leonard could not accept. Neither could he agree to Adams's view that Parliament was subordinate to a constitution which had existed before government itself.

The debate between Leonard and Adams laid bare the essential problems of the British Empire in the 1770s. Their legalistic arguments had merit, but they can only be understood in the context of their time. The issue was really whether an existing system should be maintained or modified into something different. As Adams put it, British policy intended to replace simple republican virtues in the colonies with the corrupt class-ridden system which already dominated Great Britain. The basic conservatism of the Americans would not permit them to accept that alteration. The British government's insistence upon change caused it to lose credibility in the colonies and, consequently, all semblance of authority.

British efforts to maintain their authority over rebellious colonists led them into a prolonged and self-defeating military effort. Naked force could not create loyalty, nor could it turn the clock back. American loyalty, by force of circumstances, had shifted from the Crown of England to a combination of the states and the new nation. As the years passed, the focus of individual loyalty would come more and more to rest on the nation, until in our own day we sometimes view the states as little more than administrative conveniences.

As though to celebrate the repudiation of loyalty to the Crown and the emergence of republicanism, Mercy Otis Warren's *History of the Rise, Progress, and Termination of the American Revolution* appeared during Jefferson's administration. For Mrs. Warren, the American Revolution was merely a prelude to something greater, a worldwide triumph of republicanism. She dealt, therefore, with the principles of revolution rather than with its personalities.

Mrs. Warren began her investigation of the causes of the Revolution from a viewpoint similar to that of John Adams—that is, she followed the Whig theory. The controversy before 1776 thus became an effort by colonials to defend their rights, not a conspiracy by a handful devoted to independence. It shifted from controversy to conflict only when the English purpose became clearly defined as a conspiracy to impose a tyranny that Americans found repulsive.

She also correctly assessed the reasons behind America's victory in the revolutionary war. Both British and colonial military activity proved inadequate for a conclusive decision, but Americans had the advantage because of the weakness of England's political and social system. The Crown ended the war, she asserted, when it became obvious that conquest (if it were possible) would not restore the colonists to their former loyalty, that one nation could not maintain control over another that was determined to be free.

An integral part of the revolutionary movement, to Mrs. Warren, was the concept of republicanism. She believed that it depended on man's rational morality, while despotism depended upon his immorality. Her history traced the fortunes of this idea through the confederation period and the adoption of the Federal Constitution. Each step seemed to her a further departure from republicanism, but the amendment of the Constitution by the Bill of Rights restored the initial direction. Only that gave her hope for the future.

Mercy Otis Warren's history falls into no one school but draws from a number of them. She was not a Whig historian, though she recognized that the revolution was fought for liberty; she was not an "imperial" historian, though she recognized the international context of the revolution and its potential. For Mrs. Warren, the revolution did not end in 1783, but would continue indefinitely until the Last Judgment.

The changing attitudes demonstrated by these commentators provide an index to the changing views of colonial Americans during the eighteenth century. They were becoming something more than transplanted Englishmen, and the colonies were becoming something more than appendages of Britain. However, the British either failed to receive or to understand the message of these commentators. In retrospect, the warnings conveyed by these writers had a sense of the inevitable about them, but none of them ever envisioned the outcome of their arguments, for they were not prophets. Their message foretold the tragedy of the British Empire and the triumph of the American nation.

2.

Thomas Clap's *Annals . . . of Yale*

Louis L. Tucker

Someone once said of the elder William Pitt: "He never grew—he was cast." The same could be said of the Reverend Thomas Stephen Clap, president of Yale College from 1740–66.[1] Clap was molded in the crucible of Massachusetts Bay Colony Puritanism. Tempered by family heritage, parental training, and formal education, he emerged a "compleat" Puritan. His development was a common story in colonial New England.

Before Clap was born in the Plymouth Colony town of Scituate, Massachusetts, on 26 June 1703, three generations of his sturdy Puritan ancestors had established a tradition of dedicated service to church and state. There were no "shining lights" among this group, but collectively they left their mark on the political and religious history of Massachusetts. Pious, Godfearing, industrious, they quietly furthered the Puritan cause as deacons, representa-

---

1. Elaboration and documentation can be found in Louis L. Tucker, *Puritan Protagonist: President Thomas Clap of Yale College* (Chapel Hill, 1962).
   The complete title of Clap's work on Yale is: *The Annals or History of Yale-College, In New-Haven, In the Colony of Connecticut, From the first Founding thereof, in the Year 1700, to the Year 1766: With an Appendix, Containing the Present State of the College, the Method of Instruction and Government, with the Officers, Benefactors and Graduates* (New Haven, 1766) (hereafter cited as *Annals of Yale*).

tives to the General Court, and officers in local militia units.[2] They set a proper pattern for the "life style" of their progeny.

When Thomas Clap was born, his future was already determined: he was destined for the ministry, the highest of "callings" for a Puritan. In his thirteenth month Thomas was baptized in the church founded by his great-grandfather. His spiritual pilgrimage had begun. As he matured, his parents instructed him in the principles of Puritanism. The intensive indoctrination took effect. At age "7 or 8," as Clap recalled in later years, he prayed to God "in secret" and sought to penetrate his inner consciousness for evidence of grace—and sin.[3]

Formal education reinforced parental moral and religious teaching. Puritans believed that their ministers must be learned as well as pious. "Right reason" complemented piety. Grace alone did not make a preacher, for a minister must be a "Linguist, a Grammarian, a Critick, an Orator, a Philosopher, an Historian, a Casuist, a Disputant, and whatever Speaks Skill and Knowledge in any Learned Science. . . . He is to speak to all Subjects, and therefore must be made up of all Knowledge and Learning."[4]

The first stage for Clap in the realization of this ideal was grammar school.[5] It was an arduous experience, both physically and

2. See Ebenezer Clapp, *The Clapp Memorial, Record of the Clapp Family in America, Containing Sketches of the Original Six Emigrants, and a Genealogy of Their Descendants Bearing the Name* (Boston, 1876), pp. 105–6, and Harvey Pratt, *The Early Planters of Scituate* (Scituate, 1929), pp. 109–10, 126, 128, 137.

3. Clap described his early religious life, including parental influence, in "Memoirs of Some Remarkable Occurrances of Divine Providence Towards Me in the Course of my Life, Together With Some Reflections and Observations Upon them," Yale MS, Sterling Memorial Library, Yale University, New Haven, Conn.

4. John Edwards, *The Preacher*, 3 vols. (London, 1705–07), 1:268–69, quoted in Mary L. Gambrell, *Ministerial Training in Eighteenth-Century New England* (New York, 1937), p. 16.

5. The only evidence that Clap attended grammar school is in his funeral sermon delivered by Naphtali Daggett, *The Faithful Serving of God and Our Generation, the Only Way to a Peaceful and Happy Death. A Sermon*

mentally. The school day was long, the discipline stringent. A couplet in his *New England Primer* reminded the young Puritan that

> The Idle Fool
> Is whipt at School.[6]

It was not meaningless rhetoric.

While the grammar school curriculum contained a substantial body of secular instruction, it was suffused with Puritan dogma. Clap's teacher dispensed "Spiritual milk" at every opportunity. The young Puritan recited daily prayers, the Lord's Prayer, the Apostle's Creed, and the Westminster Shorter Catechism; he sang hymns and digested an assortment of Christian moral and theological precepts. He was taught that God was omniscient, omnipotent, and the contróller of the destiny of all human beings; that man was conceived in sin; that his corrupt nature caused him to commit transgressions and flout divine will; and that the "wages of sin" were death and eternal damnation. Learning became linked with living. His schoolmaster beat the constant refrain that the sole end of learning—and living—was the glorification of God. This was a proper grounding for all Puritans. It was the only grounding for a prospective minister.

The final years of Clap's grammar school education prepared him for college with a heavy concentration on the "tongues"—Latin principally, Greek to a lesser extent. This was the period when, as the satiric John Trumbull observed, a "Lattine Boye" spent many uncomfortable hours digesting "husks of Lily," "murd'ring Virgil's verse," "construing Tully into farce," and "blundering over a chapter in Greek."[7]

Occasioned by the Death of the Reverend Thomas Clap . . . (New Haven, 1767), p. 30.
   6. Numerous editions of this popular work appeared during the eighteenth century.
   7. *The Poetical Works of John Trumbull*, 2 vols. (Hartford, 1820), 2:13.

Harvard College provided the finishing educational touch. Clap entered Harvard in the fall of 1718 at the age of fifteen. His youthfulness was not unusual for the period; thirteen to fifteen was the average age of colonial youngsters entering college.

This was the critical period for the pious young Puritan. He had left the sedate, provincial village of Scituate and the watchful eye of his parents and minister and had entered the boisterous, magical world of Cambridge and Boston. Cambridge, the intellectual center of New England, teemed with high-spirited youngsters and with new and strange ideas about religion. Boston, the political and commercial capital of the colony, swarmed with worldly, cosmopolitan people, some of questionable moral character. Both communities were, for a rustic like Clap, windows to a larger world. Both were rife with opportunity for moral lapse.

But there was no moral lapse for Clap. His collegiate career revealed the depth of his prior conditioning. He remained pious and studious and resisted every temptation for wrongdoing. His name was absent from those college records which listed the normal student transgressions of "badgering" the tutors (this consisted of raiding their cellar lockers for food and drink, placing live snakes in their chambers, shattering the windows of their rooms, and committing "horrid abuses" upon their horses); "cutting" classes and slipping off to Boston to attend pirate hangings and horse races and to consort with ladies of easy or no virtue; playing cards; frequenting taverns; staging "great Debauches" in the College Hall at "unreasonable" times of the night; and stealing chickens from neighboring farmers and having a hen roast behind closed doors in the College Hall.[8]

8. The best account of colonial Harvard is Samuel E. Morison's delightful and scholarly *Three Centuries of Harvard, 1636–1936* (Cambridge, Mass., 1937). On student life, see pp. 101–32. Significant primary sources are: John Leverett's "Diary," Harvard University Archives; Harvard Faculty Records (photostats in Harvard University Archives); and "Benjamin Wadsworth's

Clap remained preoccupied with the salvation of his soul. During his sophomore year, he experienced "conversion," the acme of his religious life and the most memorable event of his collegiate career. He was ravished by the spirit of God. His soul was cleansed of all moral impurity. He sensed "new life." His spiritual pilgrimage was at an end. In his words: "I thought I was enabled by the Spirit of God to lay hold upon Christ, and to trust and rely wholly upon his merits, and receive Him as my Savior and Redeemer; and accordingly did seriously and solemnly give up myself to Him; promising by the Help and assistance of Divine Grace, to forsake all Sin, and to live a life of holiness and obedience to God's commands." Following his conversion, Clap joined the church in Cambridge Village, where he "found at times great delight and satisfaction in the ways of religion."[9]

In the classroom, he received the standard religious instruction which strengthened his ancestral bias. He studied the Bible in its Hebrew, Greek, and Latin texts, pored over works of the chief Protestant divines, and attended morning and evening prayers and sermons. Conjunctively, his tutor Henry Flynt[10] and Harvard President John Leverett directed him along the narrow path of religious orthodoxy.

Religion was important at Harvard, but it was not the sum and substance of the curriculum. Harvard was determined that Clap should leave Cambridge with his mind stocked with some-

---

Book, 1725–36," Colonial Society of Massachusetts *Publications* 31 (1835): 452–58.

9. Clap, "Memoirs of Some Remarkable Occurances," pp. 1–2, and *Records of the Church of Christ at Cambridge in New England, 1632–1830* (Boston, 1906), p. 86.

10. "Father" Flynt was one of the memorable characters of colonial Harvard and a competent teacher there for almost fifty-five years, from 1699 to 1754. See Clifford K. Shipton, *Biographical Sketches of Those Who Attended Harvard College in the Classes 1690–1700 with Bibliographical and Other Notes* (Cambridge, Mass., 1933–), 4:162–67.

thing more than religious dogma. As Samuel E. Morison, historian of Harvard College, has shown, the school did not function solely as a seminary for the Congregational Church. It was committed to a liberal arts education and it produced "learned gentlemen" as well as pious ministers.[11]

Among nontheological courses of study, two related secular subjects, mathematics and science, made a deep impression on Clap. This training would strongly condition his thinking on the teaching of these subjects when he served as president of Yale. In time Clap became so proficient in mathematics, physics, and astronomy that in those subjects he was held in "the first rank of Americans of his generation."[12]

Even before Clap entered Harvard, the teaching of mathematics and of natural philosophy (as science was then designated) had changed as a result of new currents of thought developed during the Enlightenment. Isaac Newton "entered" Harvard before Clap did. By the turn of the eighteenth century, Newtonian mathematical and scientific concepts began seeping into the curriculum, producing intellectual revolution.[13]

One might expect that the juxtaposition of Newtonian science and Puritanism would precipitate an intellectual crisis for Clap, that he would find it difficult to accommodate Newtonian celestial

11. On the Harvard curriculum see Samuel E. Morison's brilliant *Harvard College in the Seventeenth Century*, 2 vols. (Cambridge, Mass., 1937), especially chapters 7–13 of vol. 1. For the curriculum during Clap's tenure, see "Benjamin Wadsworth's Book," Colonial Society of Massachusetts *Publications* 31 (1835): 455–56.

12. Franklin B. Dexter, *A Selection From the Miscellaneous Historical Papers of Fifty Years* (New Haven, Conn., 1918), p. 197.

13. For material on scientific developments at colonial Harvard, see I. Bernard Cohen, *Some Early Tools of the Early Scientific Instruments and Mineralogical and Biological Collections in Harvard University* (Cambridge, Mass., 1950); Theodore Hornberger, *Scientific Thought in the American Colleges, 1638–1800* (Austin, Texas, 1945); Lao G. Simons, "The Adoption of the Method of Fluxions in American Schools," *Scripta Mathematica* 4 (1936): 209; and Frederick Kilgour, "Thomas Robie (1689–1729) Colonial Scientist and Physician," *ISIS* 30 (1939): 473–90.

mechanics with Puritan religion. Other Puritans, like Samuel Johnson and Charles Chauncy, had experienced such problems and their mental matrixes had been profoundly altered. But this was not the case with Clap. For him, science was linked with religion, but science had a subordinate value. It stood as a bulwark to theology and confirmed religious truths. Through astronomy, for example, one acquired a broader view of the wonderful design of creation and an incisive insight into the greatness and glory of God. Cotton Mather, Puritan of Puritans, spoke also for Clap when he wrote: "Philosophy [Science] is no Enemy, but a mighty and wondrous Incentive to Religion."[14] In this spirit Clap approached his scientific studies; in this spirit science was taught at Harvard. He experienced no inner conflict, no doubting of the "truths" of religion.

Only a few facts are known about Clap's activities between his graduation in 1722 and his assumption of a minister's post in Windham, Connecticut, in 1726. He apparently pursued academic studies for the master's degree he took at Harvard in 1725.[15] In the disputation exercise at commencement, he argued the negative of the question: "Is it possible to secure remission of sins through natural reason?"[16] Because New England Puritanism was beginning to feel the effects of rationalism, such a question had a pressing import. Later events demonstrated that Clap's argument was not an exercise in dialectics; it was grounded in deep-seated conviction.

Even before securing his second degree, Clap searched for a pulpit, but without success. After acquiring the degree, he learned of an opening in the First Congregational Church of Windham, a

14. Kenneth Murdock, ed., *Selections from Cotton Mather* (New York, 1926), p. 286.

15. Clap apparently left Cambridge during this period since his name does not appear in college financial accounts. One authority asserts that he served as schoolmaster in Scituate (Pratt, *Early Planters of Scituate*, p. 184).

16. *Harvard Commencement Sheet for the Year 1725*, Harvard University Library.

back-country community in rocky, northeastern Connecticut. He applied for the post and was invited to serve as a probationer. He was judged acceptable and was ordained on 3 August 1726.[17]

Clap remained with the First Church until early 1740. It was to be his only experience as a parish minister. His fourteen-year career in Windham was a conspicuous success; he displayed manifold talents, including those of an administrator. He instituted order and eventually developed his church into a model society. A man of prodigious energy, he worked incessantly at his task, directing his attention to every facet of church affairs. His dedication and concern for minutiae placed him in a special category as a minister. He quickly rose to a position of leadership in the County Association of Ministers, the high tribunal on intra- and inter-church disputes.

He also achieved notoriety as a disciplinarian. One commentator described him as a "terror to evil doers."[18] His influence as a guardian of public morality extended to the county at large. A commanding figure of the county ministerial association, he exercised his will on a broad front. In Clap's time, the association was referred to as the "County Watchdogs." Two of Clap's own brothers-in-law, both ministers, were haled before the association, one charged with immoderate drinking and the second with preaching without a license.[19]

Clap's activities as a "watchdog" carried over into the area of

17. Ellen Larned, *History of Windham County*, 2 vols. (Worcester, Mass., 1874), 1:104; Elijah Waterman, *A Century Sermon Preached Before the First Church in Windham, December 10, A.D. 1800* (Windham, 1801), p. 26; Connecticut Archives: Ecclesiastical Affairs 4:109, Connecticut State Library, Hartford; Eliphalet Adams, *Ministers Must Take Heed to Their Ministry to Fulfill it. A Discourse Delivered at Windham, at the Ordination of the Reverend Mr. Thomas Clap, August 3rd, 1726* (New London, Conn., 1726).
18. Waterman, *Century Sermon*, p. 28.
19. Franklin B. Dexter, *Biographical Sketches of the Graduates of Yale College with Annals of the College History*, 2nd ser. (New York, 1885–1912), 1:334, 342; Larned, *History of Windham*, 1:390–92.

religious deviation. As a "defender of the faith," he had few equals in all of New England. As a rock of orthodoxy, he insisted that other Congregationalists hew to the prescribed religious path. He accepted no compromise in matters of religion.

The Robert Breck controversy illustrated the point.[20] Breck, a bright Harvard graduate with a loose lip and a mind full of liberal religious notions, rode into Windham in 1733 to compete for a vacant pulpit. In his sermons, he stated doctrines which Clap branded heresy (the contemporary designation was Arminianism). One of Breck's favorite themes was: "That the Heathen that liv'd up to the Light of Nature Should be Saved." In addition, he questioned some foundational principles of Christianity, including the divinity of Christ. The young man's preaching became a stench in Clap's orthodox nostils. Clap met with Breck to convince him of his theological errors. "You are but a young Man," the thirty-year-old Clap cautioned, "and I would not have you set up to Reform the World too soon; least instead of Reforming of it, you should happen to corrupt it." But Breck was not prepared to change his theological vision. Clap applied pressure and ran him out of town.

Breck moved on to Springfield, Massachusetts, in the spring of 1734 and applied for another ministerial position. Clap alerted his Springfield colleagues to the theological outlook of the young candidate. Springfield conservatives soon began snapping away at Breck. He refused to withdraw his application, and the congrega-

20. All facets of the dispute are discussed in A *Narrative of the Proceedings of Those Ministers of the County Hampshire, That Have disapproved of the Late Measures Taken in Order To the Settlement of Mr. Robert Breck, in the Pastoral Office in the First Church in Springfield* (Boston, 1736), and *An Examination of and Some Answer To a Pamphlet, Intitled 'A Narrative and Defence of the Proceedings of the Ministers of Hampshire, Who Disapproved of Mr. Breck's Settlement at Springfield: With a Vindication of Those Ministers and Churches, that Disapproved of, and Acted in the Settlement of said Mr. Breck'* (Boston, 1736).

tion to whom he preached added fuel to the theological fire by voting to settle him, thus joining the issue for a major religious hassle. The dispute settled on the basic structure of the Congregational system of New England: where did final authority in ecclesiastical affairs reside—in individual churches or in ministerial associations? "Conservatives" and "liberals" drew up battle lines and began the inevitable war of words, an all too familiar scenario in Puritan New England. The controversy raged for three years and became a cause célèbre throughout New England. It provoked some bizarre highlights in that area's long history of religious strife, climaxed by Breck's arrest during a dramatic formal hearing at which all the disputants had gathered. The liberals were outraged and accused Clap of masterminding the "extraordinary interruption." Available evidence supports their accusation.

As a central figure in the dispute, and because of the pamphlet war and newspaper accounts it spawned from New York to Boston, Clap saw his reputation soar. He achieved instant fame in New England as a pillar of rigid orthodoxy. Throughout the dispute he had worked on a plane of equality with major religious figures who had been drawn into the controversy. One ally was the Reverend Jonathan Edwards; another was the Reverend Elisha Williams, rector of Yale College. The Breck affair set the stage for Clap's next and final position, rectorship of Yale.

Rector Williams resigned his post on 31 October 1739. The Yale trustees promptly appointed the thirty-six-year-old Clap as his successor. They were undoubtedly impressed with his credentials as an inflexible defender of the Congregational Way; a capable administrator and stern disciplinarian; a man of wide cultural interests, who helped establish subscription libraries[21] and engaged

21. Martha W. Hooker, "Booklovers of 1738—One of the First Libraries in America," *Connecticut Magazine* 10 (1906): 717–18.

in astronomical research[22]; and a competent sermonizer, not showy and given to rhetorical flourishes but articulate and forceful. Finally, he had exhibited special talents as a teacher. In his fourteen years at Windham, he had prepared twenty-six boys for entrance into Yale.[23] Considering the size of his congregation, the rural character of his community, and his busy schedule, this was an impressive record.

After the usual negotiations, Clap accepted the post. If he reflected upon his career in Windham, he may have regarded his domestic life as his only failure. It was a chronicle of repeated tragedy. In 1727 he had married Mary Whiting, fourteen-year-old daughter of the late minister of the First Church. She was a gentle, pious girl, and Clap loved her with a passion that may have disturbed his Puritan conscience. Of six children born of the marriage, four did not celebrate a first birthday. In 1736, the twenty-three-year-old Mrs. Clap, who once told her husband that "Bearing tending and Burying Children, was Hard Work," joined her four deceased youngsters in the village cemetery. Her death shattered Clap's Puritan equilibrium, but only momentarily.[24]

Clap served as titular head of Yale from 1740–66, an eventful and constructive era for the college. Clap can be credited with a number of major achievements. He left his mark on every area of the college, from administration to teaching. Perhaps his most

22. George Leon Walker, ed., *Daniel Wadsworth's Diary* (Hartford, Conn., 1794), p. 38.
23. *A Memorial Volume of the Bi-Centennial Celebration of the Town of Windham, Connecticut* (Hartford, Conn., 1893), p. 25.
24. On Clap's wife and domestic life, see Thomas Clap, "Memoirs of a College President, Womanhood in Early America," *Journal of American History* 2 (1908): 474–76. Shortly after becoming rector of Yale, Clap remarried. His second wife, Mary Saltonstall, was of high social standing and a two-time widow. See Chauncey Whittelsey, *A Discourse, Occasioned by the Death, and Delivered at the Funeral, of Mrs. Mary Clap, Relict of the Late Reverend President Clap* (New Haven, 1769).

significant administrative success was his Charter of 1745, which reconstituted the governmental structure of the college. The original Charter of 1701[25] had lodged administrative authority in the trustees, who held the power to "erect, form, direct, order, establish, impose, and at all Times in all suitable Ways for the future to encourage" the school. Their powers were absolute. The rector, little more than a glorified schoolmaster or resident agent of the trustees, was subject to peremptory dismissal with or without cause by majority vote, and his office could be abolished at pleasure.

Clap's charter created the position of president with executive responsibility. (Even as rector, he had been functioning in the fashion of his newly created president, since his was a "take charge" personality.)[26] After he became president, Clap's authority was paramount, his position unassailable. The shift in power from trustees to president constituted a "tremendously momentous revolution." As one authority has written, the revision marks "a turning point in the fortunes of the College."[27] The president now became the dynamic force in Yale's government. The new charter also incorporated Yale's governing body, thereby providing it with a legal base. When Clap wrote in his *Annals of Yale* that his charter "set the College in a much more perfect and agreeable State, than it was before,"[28] he understated the importance of his reform. For the college's future history, his charter was a monumental accomplishment which set a sturdy administrative and legal foundation for the university.

25. For the positive side of Clap's administration, see Louis L. Tucker, "President Thomas Clap and the Rise of Yale College, 1740–1766," *The Historian* 19 (1956): 66–81. Clap, *Annals of Yale*, pp. 5–8, 45–52.

26. Revealed by comparing the corporation records of Yale for Williams' tenure with those for Clap's first years as rector.

27. Franklin B. Dexter, "An Historical Study of the Powers and Duties of the Presidency in Yale College," *American Antiquarian Society Proceedings*, New Series 12 (1899): 34. This is a trenchant analysis of the changes Clap effected with his charter.

28. Clap, *Annals of Yale*, p. 52n.

The curriculum also showed Clap's zeal for reform. While he retained—even increased—the stress on religion, he moved Yale into the mainstream of secularism with some significant curricular adjustments.[29] He upgraded the quality of education by incorporating the new mathematics and science of the Enlightenment, particularly the Newtonian system. This process had begun even before Clap came to Yale, but he gave it a forceful impetus and converted Yale into a center of Newtonian science. He also instituted a program of experimental science and broadened the curriculum with such "practical" studies as surveying and navigation.[30]

Yale also expanded physically during the Clap era. While his building program may not have constituted a Periclean Age, it was an impressive accomplishment. When Clap arrived on the scene, the college proper consisted of one well-used building. In 1750–52, a second structure, Connecticut Hall, was built. In 1757–58, the college constructed a home for the professor of divinity (a chair Clap had established). The building program was completed in 1761 with the erection of a chapel, the upper floor of which served as a combination library and science laboratory.[31] Clap was involved in all these building projects to the finest detail.

With certain reservations, Clap succeeded in improving the college library. While he refused on occasion to accept donated books written by Deists and Freethinkers,[32] he did enlarge the library's holdings. From a collection of about twenty-five hundred

29. Ibid., pp. 80–84.
30. Louis L. Tucker, "President Thomas Clap of Yale College: Another 'Founding Father' of American Science," *ISIS* 52 (March 1961):55–77.
31. Clap, *Annals of Yale*, pp. 55–56, 68, 77–78.
32. Ezra Stiles to Jared Eliot, 24 September 1759, Yale Manuscripts, Yale University Library. On one occasion, Clap locked up Samuel Clark's deistic-tinged *Sermons*. See Thomas Darling, *Some Remarks on Mr. President Clap's 'History and Vindication of the Doctrines etc. of the New England Churches'* (New Haven, 1757), p. 127.

volumes in 1742, the library grew to four thousand volumes in 1766. During this time the library's holdings were catalogued for the first time, special collections were segregated, and rules governing the library were compiled.[33] In 1743 the library published its first catalog, a work of immeasurable value to bibliophiles.

Statistics on enrollment and graduates provide evidence of the "rise" of Yale College during Clap's presidency. For the decade 1753–63 (a period relatively free of student strife), yearly enrollment averaged 170, an increase of 90 students over the highest annual enrollment during Williams's rectorship. From 1754–63, Clap's most productive years, 505 students took degrees. From 1752–61, Yale for the first time produced more graduates than Harvard. The total number of graduates during Clap's era was over 750.[34]

Both quantitatively and qualitatively, Clap's Yale attained a par with its sister institution to the north by mid-century. Indeed, judged by any criterion, it compared favorably with all institutions of higher learning in North or South America, from the Jesuit college in Quebec to the Spanish universities in Mexico City, San Carlos, and Lima. Under Clap's dynamic leadership, a primitive school developed into a leading intellectual center of the New World. Clap's impressive record led the elder Timothy Dwight, a leviathan figure of early Yale, to state: "He was the greatest man who ever sat at the head of the institution." Charles Thwing, respected scholar of higher education, called him American education's "first greatly efficient president."[35]

This was the credit side of the ledger. There was also a negative

33. Thomas Clap, *A Catalogue of the Library of Yale College in New Haven* (New London, 1743); Clap, *Annals of Yale*, pp. 43, 86.

34. Franklin B. Dexter, ed., *The Literary Diary of Ezra Stiles* (New York, 1901), 2:226; Clap, *Annals of Yale*, pp. 77, 105–24.

35. Quoted in Theodore Woolsey, *Historical Discourse to Graduates of Yale College* (New Haven, 1850), p. 114. Charles Thwing, *A History of Higher Education in America* (New York, 1906), p. 85.

side, and it involved interminable controversy. Many contemporaries regarded Clap as a pigheaded, tyrannical, religious bigot—a characterization not without substance. In his effort to preserve orthodoxy, he engaged in a multitude of disputes. Most originated from three prominent issues which occupied his generation: the Great Awakening of the 1740s, growth of the Church of England in the colonies, and the spreading influence of rationalism.

In 1740, the Great Awakening broke over New England with hurricane force, splintering the established Congregational Church and introducing excessive emotionalism to religion.[36] Clap allied himself with opponents of the revival who condemned it as a manifestation of the devil. He emerged as a chief leader of the Connecticut "Old Lights," the conservative element. In the colony, he played a leading role in mitigating the effects of the revival through legislative action. Within the college, his anti-revival activities were even more effective. He banned itinerant preachers from the campus,[37] restricted students to college-sponsored religious exercises, and either censured or expelled those who refused to comply with his edicts. He even took disciplinary measures against students who participated in revival activities while at home on vacation.[38]

---

36. One of the best accounts of the Great Awakening is Edwin Gaustad, *The Great Awakening in New England* (New York, 1957). For its effect on Yale, see: George Whitefield, *A Continuation of the Reverend Mr. Whitefield's Journal, From a Few Days After His Arrival at Savannah, June the fourth, to His Leaving Stanford [Stamford], the Last Town in New England, October 29, 1740* (Philadelphia, 1741), pp. 114–19; "John Cleaveland Diary," photostat, Yale University Library; Chauncey Goodrich, "Narrative of Revivals of Religion in Yale," *American Quarterly Register* 10 (1838): 290–93; and Samuel Hopkins, *Sketches of the Life of the Late, Rev. Samuel Hopkins D.D., Pastor of the First Congregational Church in Newport, Written by Himself* (Hartford, 1805), pp. 31–34.

37. William Allen, "Memoir of Rev. Eleazar Wheelock, D.D.," *American Quarterly Register* 10 (1838):17, and Eleazar Wheelock to Mrs. Wheelock, 28 June 1742, Dartmouth College Manuscripts, Dartmouth College Library.

38. John Cleaveland, "Narrative of the Proceedings of the Government of Yale College in the Expulsion of John and Ebenezer Cleaveland," Essex Insti-

Since his ministerial days Clap had been waging war against the Church of England, historical enemy of Puritans.[39] As Anglican ranks swelled during and after the Great Awakening, Clap became increasingly alarmed and intensified his attacks. What particularly frightened him was the rise of Anglican enrollment at Yale and, irony of ironies, the demand by young Churchmen (and their parents) for freedom of worship. Fearing the destruction of orthodoxy at Yale, Clap refused these demands and insisted on compulsory attendance of all students at college-sanctioned religious services. As a result, he incurred the wrath of Anglicans, including the prominent Samuel Johnson, president of King's College, whose son was attending Yale. Clap's policy of repression against Anglicans was short-lived; it lasted less than half a year. He relented because Johnson threatened to appeal to the Crown for redress.[40] Clap had sufficient common sense to know that he would court disaster for Yale by rigid adherence to his policy. He capitulated on this issue, but he embedded his reputation as a religious tyrant in American historiography with granitic firmness by creating the impression that he refused liberty of conscience to Anglicans (and other non-Congregationalists) throughout his administration.

tute manuscript; Thomas Clap, *The Judgment of the Rector and Tutors of Yale College, Concerning Two of the Students Who Were Expelled: Together with the Reasons of It* (New London, 1745).

39. Waterman, *Century Sermon*, p. 28; Francis L. Hawks and William S. Perry, eds., *Documentary History of the Protestant Episcopal Church in the United States of America Containing Numerous Hitherto Unpublished Documents Concerning The Church in Connecticut*, 2 vols. (New York, 1863–64), 1:160–61.

40. On the Anglican issue at Yale see Louis L. Tucker, "The Church of England and Religious Liberty at Pre-Revolutionary Yale," *William and Mary Quarterly*, 3rd ser., 17 (July 1960):314–28. In his *Annals of Yale* (pp. 83–84), Clap pointed out that students of "all Denominations of Protestants" were admitted to Yale and were not questioned about their religious convictions either at entrance or later. He added, however, that if a student "should take Pains to infect the Minds of their Fellow-Students with such pernicious Errors, as are contrary to the Fundamentals of Christianity, and the special Design of founding this College, so that Parents should justly be afraid of venturing their Children here, it is probable that some Notice would be taken of it."

Rationalism represented a third major threat to the orthodoxy that Clap so stoutly defended. The president preached and wrote pamphlets against rationalists and their optimistic view of God and man. He ridiculed their belief that salvation could be achieved without the grace of God and that man was inherently good.[41]

When words failed to stem the twin "contagions" of Anglicanism and rationalism, Clap took more drastic measures. He instituted religious tests for college officers and tutors, created a professor of divinity chair, set up separate worship for the college congregation, and established the first independent College Church in America. He intended to preserve the Congregational character of Yale.[42]

Every action Clap took opened more controversy and produced more critics and outright enemies. Throughout the 1760s he was deluged with criticism. In 1763, a group of prominent Connecticut citizens (all of them Clap's avowed enemies) memorialized the General Assembly for an act which would permit aggrieved students to appeal college decisions to the governor and Council and would establish a "Commission of Visitation" to investigate Yale.[43] The ultimate objective of the memorialists was to oust Clap by legislative action. The issue centered on the legal point: Was the General Assembly the "founder" of Yale? If so, it could dispatch "visitors" to Yale and impose its will upon the college.

In a brilliant defense, which Justice Joseph Story later called "masterful,"[44] Clap convinced the Assembly that the "founders"

41. See, for example, Clap's pamphlet *A Brief History and Vindication of the Doctrines Received and Established in the Churches of New England* (New Haven, 1755).

42. Ralph H. Gabriel, *Religion and Learning at Yale: The Church of Christ in the College and University, 1757–1957* (New Haven, Conn., 1958), pp. 1–31. Thomas Clap, *The Religious Constitution of Colleges, Especially of Yale College in New-Haven, in the Colony of Connecticut* (New London, 1754).

43. Connecticut Archives: Colleges and Schools, 1st ser., pt. ii, 2:66–67, Connecticut State Library.

44. Charles H. Smith, "Early Struggles in American Education," *Connecticut Magazine* 8 (1903–04):183–84.

were the ministers who, as he affirmed, had conceived the college in the late 1690s, met formally in 1700 (a year before granting the charter), and donated forty folio volumes to the school. Yale was, therefore, an autonomous society beyond legislative reach. Clap's defense was a landmark in the history of governmental control over private colleges.[45] Practically the same theoretical argument in the Dartmouth College case of 1819 led the United States Supreme Court to uphold that college's independence from the New Hampshire state legislature, although the Yale precedent was not cited.

If Clap won an occasional battle, he continued to lose the war. He remained under heavy siege. In some cases it was a literal siege, since his own student body began to manifest physical displeasure of his autocratic rule. "Old Tom Clap," one student wrote in the margin of a library book, "you are quite wrong in your form of government."[46] The students did not restrict themselves to marginalia. In 1765, a group well fortified by wine assaulted Clap's home with stones and cattle horns, smashing his gates and breaking his windows. Clap was slightly wounded by flying glass.[47] Throughout 1765–66, turbulence and disorder pervaded the campus. The Stamp Act crisis of the same time also contributed to the unsettled character of the college.

In spring 1766, the students initiated a campaign of violence. All discipline broke down and anarchy prevailed. The tutors resigned *en masse* and rode out of New Haven; the students soon

45. Answer of President and Fellows of Yale College to the Memorial of Mr. Edward Dorr and Others Preferred to the General Assembly at Hartford, May 1763, Connecticut Archives: Colleges and Schools, 1st ser., pt. ii, 2:71, Connecticut State Library. See also Clap's summary account in his *Annals of Yale*, pp. 69–76.

46. Numerous other bits of anti-Clap marginalia are scattered among the pages of the books in the special collection "Yale Library of 1742," housed in the Sterling Memorial Library, Yale University.

47. Kenneth Scott, "A 'Dust' at Yale and a 'Blessing' for President Clap," Connecticut Historical Society *Bulletin* 23 (1958):46–49; Records of the Superior Court, New Haven Session, 1763–1765, XV, 27 August 1765, Connecticut State Library.

followed. An ex-Yale official wrote that the "good old Lady [Yale] seemed just to breath[e] but ready to expire."[48] The embattled president, now sixty-three years of age and in failing health, finally acknowledged defeat. Baffled and dispirited, he resigned on 1 July.[49] One of Yale's most creative—and destructive—eras ended. Six months later (7 January 1767) Clap succumbed to a pulmonary disorder.[50]

What caused Clap's downfall? Certainly his pugnacious personality was a prime "fatal flaw." A man of imperious will, he showed a unique talent for offending people. A more deep-seated cause of his demise was his intransigence in religious matters and his failure to gauge the temper of his time. In religious outlook, he was nearer the Middle Ages than the eighteenth century; to his enemies he was "Pope" Clap. He remained an apostle of philosophical gloom, a true son of John Calvin. While many Americans engaged in the "pursuit of happiness," he remained preoccupied with the old Adam in man. He stood fast on established Puritan values. He refused to adjust to the religious change sweeping over New England. Eventually he was engulfed.

A Historical First

In his years at Yale, Clap developed a yen to write history. Like most Puritan clerics of historical bent (Cotton Mather and Thomas Prince, for example), he was profoundly interested in the settle-

48. Chauncey Whittelsey to Ezra Stiles, 9 July 1766, Yale Manuscripts. Whittelsey also wrote: "I am almost ready to weep; Alma Mater is truly in a deplorable Situation, and I fear will be ruined."

49. Yale Corporation Records, 1:174, Yale University. He said his reasons were that he was "somewhat tired and fatigued," that his health was not as "firm" as formerly, and that he was "approaching towards the Decays of Nature."

50. For an account of Clap's final hours, see Naphtali Daggett, *The Faithful Serving of God and Our Generation, the Only Way to a Peaceful and Happy Death. A Sermon Occasioned by the Death of the Reverend Thomas Clap* . . . (New Haven, 1767), pp. 35–36.

ment and development of New England. His parochialism was easy to understand. His view of history was Puritan to the core: human history was the unfolding of God's plan, of which the settlement of New England was one grand chapter. The Puritans were His chosen people and they were carrying out His will.

One of Clap's ambitions was to write a history of Connecticut. He began assembling material for the project in the 1750s and requested prominent political leaders (ex-Governor Roger Wolcott, for example) to document their experiences and record reminiscences. After retiring from the Yale presidency, he set himself to the task in earnest and prepared an outline, or "proposed heads," of his projected study.[51] His opening section was predictable; it focused on "religion the Design of the first Planters." Other headings were more intriguing—for example, "The General Genius of the Inhabitants" and "The Advantages of their Privileges." Unfortunately, death came before he could apply himself to the writing. Had he completed this study, it would have been the first history of Connecticut.

Clap did complete one historical work, *The Annals or History of Yale College,* and it *was* an accomplished "first"—the first history of the college. Published in March 1766, the book was an updated version of two manuscript drafts, one developed in 1747 and a second in 1757.[52]

The book embodied many characteristic features of Puritan historiography: a pronounced religious point of view and flavor, a structure in the form of annals, a studding with source documents printed in entirety, and a ponderous style strong on fact and weak on interpretation and evaluation. From Clap's standpoint, the

51. "Roger Wolcott's Memoir Relating to Connecticut," Connecticut Historical Society *Collections* 3 (1895):325–36. The manuscript of the outline is in the Yale Library.

52. Both are in the Yale University Library. In his preface to *Annals of Yale,* Clap wrote that he developed his first draft in 1744. This is an error. The correct date is 1747.

"proper Province of an Historian" was the "just and simple Narration of Facts, without interspersing many Embellishments, Observations or Reflections; leaving them to be made by the judicious and candid Reader."[53]

The judicious and candid reader will observe that Clap's account of his own era, representing over half the book, does not measure up to current standards of "objective" history. He wrote didactic history aimed at showing that his administration was a chronicle of sustained progress. He constantly focused on achievement, accentuating the positive and eliminating the negative. He scarcely mentioned problems or difficulties. This account can lull one into thinking that all was bliss and calm on the campus. Nothing in the narrative suggests that this was colonial Yale's most turbulent era. Clap cavalierly ignored the Great Awakening, the Anglican issue, rationalism, and student disorders. When discussing an earlier era like 1716, however, he did not hesitate to discuss student and administrative turmoil and to cite the "broken and tottering State" of the college.[54]

The book should not be written off because it is not objective history. It would be asking too much to expect a main participant in a scenario, especially someone as contentious as Clap, to view events through an objective literary lens. Indeed, one of the book's primary virtues is its distinctive point of view.

If Clap slanted the presentation, he did not do so with stylistic verve, for his tone is restrained, his prose dispassionate. This is not surprising. In personal makeup Clap was not emotional, and reason was a powerful element in his thought structure. All his writings, including his polemical tracts, appealed to the mind rather than to the heart. He wrote history as he prepared and delivered sermons. As a contemporary noted, he was "not of the florid, showey sort: but solid, grave and powerful. . . . He was plain and

53. Clap, *Annals of Yale*, preface.
54. Ibid., pp. 16–17.

impressive, solid in his matter, but not eloquent in his manner; neither did he adorn his ideas with the ornaments of language. Having a confidence in the truth he left it to speak for itself."[55] Unlike Jonathan Swift, Clap could not wear a literary "mask." As a stylist, he was one-dimensional.

For a modern reader, the book lacks tension. Much of this can be attributed to the format in which events are strung together like so many boxcars. Each section stands in "splendid isolation," bearing no (or, at best, slight) relation to what goes before or comes after. Such critical and historically significant events as the founding of the school, establishment of the professor of divinity chair and the College Church, and Clap's 1763 appearance before the General Assembly are presented in a vacuum and lack genetic development.

Consider the founding of Yale, always a significant issue in institutional history. Clap totally ignored vital background information. What motivated the ministers to establish a college? Were these men, all Harvard graduates and extremely conservative in their religious outlook, disturbed by the growing latitudinarianism at their Alma Mater? Or were they activated by a desire to lower the cost of a collegiate education for the youth of Connecticut? Were they seeking to hoodwink the Crown by referring to the founders as "trustees, partners, or undertakers," to their institution as a "collegiate school," and to the president as a "rector"? Did they fear that the Crown would look with disfavor upon a Congregational school of higher learning? Why did they apply to the Connecticut General Assembly, rather than to the Crown, for a charter? Were they avoiding the problem Harvard experienced in 1684? (When the Crown revoked Massachusetts's charter, it also deprived Harvard of its legal base. During the first eleven years of King William's reign, Harvard authorities made five unsuccessful

55. Daggett, *Faithful Serving of God*, p. 30.

efforts to secure a new charter.) Clap remained silent on all these critical points. Surely he knew that these were salient issues in the early history of Yale. Yet he ignored them and thereby stripped his history of dramatic impact.

Notwithstanding these omissions, Clap's account of the founding is still important. In carefully measured words, he designated as "founders" the ten ministers who formulated plans for the college in the late 1690s and then met in "1700" and organized themselves into a "Body or Society, to consist of eleven Ministers, including a Rector, and agreed to Found a College . . . which they did at their next Meeting at Branford, in the following Manner, viz. Each Member brought a Number of Books and presented them to the Body; and laying them on the Table, said these Words, or to this Effect; 'I give these Books for the founding of a College in this Colony.'" In 1701, according to Clap, the "founders," doubting their legal right to hold property and receive private donations and contributions, applied to the General Assembly for a charter.[56] Clap's account implied that the charter had no relationship to the founding of the school. It came "after the fact" and merely solidified the legal base of the college.

Clap's version of the founding can be challenged, as can his credibility as an "objective" historian. Some curious facts surround this cardinal point. Two manuscript drafts of his history are extant. One carried the story to 1747. In this draft, Clap made no mention of a donation of books before the granting of the charter. He affirmed that the movement to found a college began in 1701 and that the trustees did not formally organize until after the charter was granted. When he reached 1702 in his exposition, he noted that several trustees had given some books to start a library.

56. Clap, *Annals of Yale*, pp. 2–8.

The second draft, prepared in 1757, contained a transcript of the earlier account plus an extension to 1757. The title page of the document read: "Annals of Yale College in New Haven, from the first founding thereof in the year 1701, to the present year 1757." When Clap extended this draft to 1765, he crossed out 1757 and inserted the new terminal date.[57] But he also changed the inceptive date. The final "1" in 1701 was covered by an "0" in ink of a different shade. The manuscript offered no explanation for this change, but Clap was probably responsible for it, and he ostensibly made it after 1763 when a legislative investigation threatened the college.

Two highly capable scholars have anatomized this issue with surgical skill.[58] In their judgment, Clap's account of the founding was not only inconsistent with available evidence, but represented a willful historical distortion. As one of these authorities put it: "1700 is an impossibly early date for the event, and . . . there is no likelihood that all the ten clergymen were ever present at or took part in such a contribution."[59] Clap's purpose was obvious. Whether for personal reasons (his fear of being fired, most notably) or out of genuine concern for the welfare of the college, he determined that Yale would remain free of legislative control. On this basis, he apparently felt no moral twinge in playing fast and loose with history. The proper province of the historian, he asserted in his preface, was to provide "a just . . . Narration of Facts," but he did not always adhere to this tenet. Nor does the modern University any longer adhere to Clap's founding date. In

57. In the title page of his published *Annals*, however, he listed "1766" as the terminal date.

58. Franklin B. Dexter, "The Founding of Yale College," New Haven Colony Historical Society *Papers* 3 (1882):1–31; Charles H. Smith, "The Founding of Yale College," New Haven Colony Historical Society *Papers* 7 (1908):34–64.

59. Dexter, "Founding of Yale," p. 23.

the late nineteenth century, Yale repudiated Clap's founding date in favor of 1701.[60]

In one of his most important and meticulously developed polemical writings, *Religious Constitution of Colleges, Especially of Yale College,* published in 1754, Clap presented a different chronological sequence for the founding. He first called attention to several acts of the Assembly and then added: "The Founders, at their first meeting, in 1701, make a Formal Foundation of the College, by an Express Declaration, and giving a Number of Books for a Library. . . ."[61] Thus he placed the book donation in 1701 and stressed the Charter of 1700 as the main element in the founding. But this was his view in 1754, a decade before the threat of legislative intervention.

Another notable feature of Clap's history was his concentration on Yale's function as a religious school and, more specifically, as a Congregational seminary. He opened with the statement that the "original and primary Design of the Institution of Colleges and superior Schools of Learning, was to educate young Men for the Work of the Ministry," and he then placed Yale within this historical framework.[62] This theme was threaded throughout his polemical writings.

Clap's historical reputation was that of a religious conservative, if not a reactionary. This reputation was based on his writings on the nature and purpose of Yale and on his illiberal religious policies. He was portrayed as a man out of joint with the times, one who sought to convert Yale into a Congregational seminary. Richard Hofstadter's judgment was typical: "Yale under the regime of

60. The exact date of the change cannot be determined. It was not effected by a Corporation action. According to a Yale official, "the matter underwent a gradual change between 1876 and 1901—and . . . no one year can be cited as *the* year." (Letter to author from Assistant to Secretary of Yale University, 26 January 1970.) Yale did celebrate its bicentennial in 1901.

61. Clap, *Religious Constitution of Colleges,* p. 9.

62. Clap, *Annals of Yale,* p. 1.

Thomas Clap as rector and president (1740–66) provides us with a case study of illiberalism. . . . There an attempt was made to reduce one of the major colonial colleges to the status of a severely sectarian agency. . . ."[63]

Considerable scholarly attention has been devoted to the question of whether Harvard and Yale were founded as theological seminaries or as liberal arts colleges. Scholars know that evidence exists to support both views. The founders and their immediate successors were not consistent on this issue and cluttered their statements with ambivalent sentiments. The curricula of both Puritan institutions were heavily weighted with religious content. The founders and most, if not all, of the subsequent governors of both schools were intent upon training ministers for the Congregational Church. But these men were also committed to the advancement of learning, and they did not regard religious purposes as all-inclusive. Moreover, they were aware that an annually increasing percentage of graduates were eschewing the ministry and entering "publick and important Stations in civil Life," to use Clap's phrase.

Clap certainly knew this. He may not have liked the development but he was forced to accept it. He could not require Yale graduates to become Congregational ministers. Indeed, Clap himself was not consistent in his own writings about Yale's fundamental nature and purpose. At times he found it politic to change his stress. In 1753, for example, appealing to the General Assembly for financial assistance in settling a professor of divinity, he began his memorial: "Whereas your Honors have been pleased to found, establish, and support a College in New Haven which by the Blessing of God, has been instrumental to qualifie many Persons to do public Service in the State, as well as to train up others for the great and

63. Richard Hofstadter and Walter Metzger, *The Development of Academic Freedom in the United States* (New York, 1955), p. 163.

important Work of the Gospel Ministry, for which it was principally designed."[64] Moreover, Clap accelerated secularism at Yale
by broadening and liberalizing the curriculum to reflect a growing
concern for useful and practical knowledge. At the time when
Clap began hammering away at the theme that Yale was a religious
institution (or "ministry factory," as his enemies derisively called
it) and began imposing "severely sectarian" policies and programs,
less than thirty percent of his graduates were entering the ministry
—and, to Clap's dismay and horror, some of these were taking
orders in the Church of England.[65]

Thus Clap's published statements on Yale's nature and purpose
must be recognized as propaganda. They became his main line of
defense, his primary rationalization for establishing separate worship and a College Church, among other "illiberal" acts. In
pleading his cause, he was compelled to assume this defensive
posture. But it would be unwise to regard his statements as a
true reflection of the educational process at Yale. Statistics prove
that Clap's Yale was not a theological seminary, that it fitted more
of its graduates for employment in secular professions than for
ministerial careers in the Congregational Church.[66]

Clap was not a secularist. His theory of education was based on
the medieval principle of directing knowledge toward moral ends.
In his view, religion was the serious business of the human race, and
the overriding purpose of education was to instill Christian morality in youth. As he informed his students in 1743, after outlining
Yale's curriculum: "Above all have an Eye to the great End of all

64. Connecticut Archives: Colleges and Schools, 1st ser., p. 319, Connecticut State Library.
65. In his *Annals of Yale* (p. 84) Clap noted that Yale had trained 400
ministers "of which 40 have been episcopally ordained."
66. For example, of the approximately 700 graduates of Yale for the
1741–65 period, 280 entered the ministry, 75 became lawyers, 79 followed
medical careers, 15 became educators and 24 pursued political careers. See
Bailey B. Burritt, "Professional Distribution of College and University Graduates," U.S. Bureau of Education *Bulletin* 19 (1912):83.

your Studies, which is to obtain the Clearest Conceptions of Divine Things and to lead you to a Saving Knowledge of God in his Son Jesus Christ."[67] Unlike provost William Smith of the College of Philadelphia, who led the secularist surge in the colonies, Clap remained committed to traditional educational values.[68]

Because Clap's book is studded with defects, the reader might mistakenly develop the view that it was a failure on all counts. The book does possess numerous positive virtues. Because Yale is a distinguished center of higher education, an account of its early life is significant. This is the *first* history of the school, and its author was Yale's *first* president. The second formal history of the college, published in 1841, relied heavily on Clap's effort, as have all subsequent accounts.[69] Despite its flaws, the book is *the* authoritative history of colonial Yale. In the words of an eminent specialist, it "is for many and most important particulars our only authority."[70]

The work's primary value is in its abundant factual and statistical data. It is a veritable encyclopedia of early Yale, providing information on a wide spectrum of college affairs: benefactors and their donations, including the famous Elihu Yale gift; financial dealings; physical expansion; library holdings, acquisitions, and policies; administrative policies and procedures; curricular content; and religious policies and programs. It contains the Charters of 1701 and 1745 and many other valuable documents. An appendix lists all rectors and presidents, trustees and fellows, tutors and students, and their dates of service or attendance. Of particular value to

67. Clap, *Catalogue of Yale Library* (New Haven, 1743), Advertisement.
68. Albert Gegenheimer, *William Smith: Educator and Churchman, 1727–1803* (Philadelphia, 1943).
69. Ebenezer Baldwin, *History of Yale College, From Its Foundation, A.D. 1700, To The Year 1883* (New Haven, 1841).
70. Franklin B. Dexter, *Sketch of the History of Yale University* (New York, 1887), p. 37.

educational history is Clap's extended discussion of the college in 1765, in which he delineates all aspects of the school's program. In sum, the book is an indispensable source for the history of higher education in colonial America. On this basis alone, its designation as a "classic" of early American history can be fully justified.

3.

William Douglass's *Summary*

David Freeman Hawke

I.

Dr. William Douglass's *Summary* is not one of these tomes resurrected from the past only to humor antiquarians, to satisfy librarians whose stacks lack a copy, or even to please historians who know its worth. The book seeks a wider audience, for with all its flaws—repetitious passages, errors of facts, confusing half-sentences with unfinished thoughts—it remains, some two centuries after first publication, one of the liveliest and most amusing and informative accounts of colonial America written in the eighteenth century. The *Summary*, so far as is known, was the first book specifically labeled by an author "this American history."[1] No one has since managed a narrower definition of the contents; it cannot be called a political, social, or economic history, though it contains much on all those subjects and more on medicine, Indians, science, and religion. Whatever occurred under the American sun, Douglass felt the need to include in his history. The result was a work at once encyclopedic, perverse, opinionated, witty, eccentric, and intensely personal.

The *Summary* is an odd book, like nothing else in American

1. William Douglass, *A Summary, Historical and Political, of the . . . British settlements in North America*, 2 vols. (Boston, 1755), 2:126n.

historiography, and that oddness makes it hard to resist a rash comparison: it resembles no other work in the English language so much as Lawrence Sterne's *Tristram Shandy*. It may do more harm than help to the reputation of the much-maligned Dr. Douglass to compare his work of history with a novel—some historians who find it filled with a "mass of misinformation"[2] suggest the book already edges close to fiction—but the risk is worth running, if only to underscore the *Summary*'s peculiar qualities and the delights it holds for the reader.

Compared with Sterne, Douglass was an artless writer, yet the two men shared a strikingly similar approach to their material. Each knew where he was going and took an incredibly circuitous route to get there. Like Sterne, Douglass meanders from one digression to another, sometimes slipping it in softly ("The following digression may perhaps be an agreeable amusement to some readers"), sometimes flaunting it ("A DIGRESSION"), occasionally confessing that "frequently I find some difficulty to restrain myself against [these] excursions." He concludes that a side trip now and then proves "more agreeable by its variety and turns, than a rigid dry connected account," thereby turning an inability to control his material into a virtue.[3]

Douglas writes history, yet his work, like Sterne's novel, revolves around a central character. The protagonist of the *Summary* is, of course, Douglass, who rarely steps offstage for even a page. His work is as much an autobiography as a history. When he spots a malfunction in a world he seeks to make better, he must speak out. ("I desire readers not affected with paper currencies, may excuse prolixity; when this vile chimera, or monster, comes in my way, I cannot contain myself.") He congratulates himself on a "laconick stile" while rambling through two fat volumes. He tells the reader

2. Michael Kraus, *The Writing of American History* (Norman, Okla., 1953), p. 56.
3. Douglass, *Summary*, 1:30, 234, 310n; 2:58n.

that "a little seasoning is sometimes used" in the story to be told, then proceeds to pepper virtually every page with sometimes shrewd, occasionally outrageous, but always firm opinions.[4]

He deludes himself in other ways. "My natural temper is rather to a fault backward and bashfull," he once told a friend, but any reader of the *Summary* knows differently. No bashful gentleman would dare, as Douglass did, to call Governor William Shirley the leader of "a party of fraudulent debtors"; to warn the clergy "never to intermeddle in the affairs of state"; to accuse the average physician in America of being "bold, rash, impudent, a lyar, basely born and educated"; or to dismiss all previous histories of Massachusetts as "credulous and superstitious . . . trifling" accounts written by a "succession of pious pastors, elders and deacons" who produced works that "in all respects are beyond all excuse intolerably erroneous." Douglass said he wrote "not as a snarling critick" but only because he believed mankind ought "upon occasion to be undeceived." His contemporaries wondered about that. He "is a man of good learning but mischievously given to criticism and the most compleat snarler ever I knew," said a colleague shortly after meeting him. "He is loath to allow learning, merit, or a character to anybody."[5]

Dr. Douglass was a prickly individual. But he was also something more. The fame of the *Summary* has obscured his reputation as one of the most distinguished American physicians of the day. He arrived in Boston still a young man, yet only a few years later colleagues in the city acknowledged him their spokesman and allowed him singlehandedly to take on the redoubtable Cotton Mather in their battle against inoculation. Even those who found

4. Ibid., 1:1, 499; 2:263.
5. William Douglass to Cadwallader Colden, 11 March 1728, in *The Colden Papers—1711–1729*, New York Historical Society *Collections* 1 (1917): 249; Douglass, *Summary*, 1:250, 361–62, 361n; 2:17; Carl Bridenbaugh, ed., *Gentleman's Progress: The Itinerarium of Dr. Alexander Hamilton 1744* (Chapel Hill, N.C., 1948), p. 116.

him a "compleat snarler" did not doubt the deep affection he held for New England—his "altera patria," as he called it. When the people of Boston ridiculed his broad Scots accent—"Maister," one parody went, "ye ken vary weel, that I canno spak Englis"[6]— they generally did so with good humor, knowing that none among them was more American than he, that none worked harder to promote their interests with the Mother Country. They also knew that the censures he sprayed forth against those who failed to measure up to his standards were invariably backed by a shrewd, highly intelligent, and extraordinarily well-informed mind. Men crossed his path warily, for Dr. Douglass never shied from a fight, and, as Boston learned soon after his arrival, he was not a man to be trifled with.

II.

Not all Douglass's troubles stemmed from his personality. He came into the land of Congregationalism a member of the Church of England—an institution for which he had "a great veneration." The quick respect he also showed for the Congregational Church (it "may be esteemed among the most moderate and charitable of Christian professions"), mitigated this handicap, but a second—his Scots background—proved harder to overcome. Thirty-six years in Boston did little to wash away the characteristics Americans had come to associate with his countrymen: clannishness, assertiveness, and hard practicality. Douglass cherished his membership in the Scots Charitable Society, which he joined soon after touching the Boston shore. Like most Scotsmen in America, he prospered. He rarely tarried when the time came to reduce "accounts into Bills

6. Quoted in Perry Miller, *The New England Mind: From Colony to Province* (Cambridge, Mass., 1953), p. 358.

and Notes for the improvement of my Purse." Occasionally his practicality took on a harsh note; one day during a smallpox epidemic he cut short a letter to a friend with the remark that his time must be guided by the maxim "of making hay while the sun shines." He could also be petty, as when he urged his friend Cadwallader Colden in New York to "contrive a Method of Franking our Letters" in order to make "our correspondence . . . more full and more frequent."[7]

Douglass talked and wrote fully about public affairs, but of his private life he had little to say. The facts about his years before emigration to New England are shadowy and few. He was born in the village of Gifford, but the date can be fixed no more exactly than about 1691. He came from a family sufficiently wealthy to assure him a superb education. He attended Edinburgh University, then traveled to the continent to finish his medical studies at the University of Leyden. He wrote his thesis under Hermann Boerhaave, the most renowned physician-teacher of the age, then went to Paris for practical experience in a city hospital. He arrived in America fluent not only in Greek and Latin (the mark of all educated men) but also in Dutch and French.[8]

The years in Paris and Leyden did not especially impress Douglass, mainly because his views on medicine—and possibly on life generally—had already been shaped at Edinburgh University by an overwhelming personality, Archibald Pitcairne, one of Scotland's greatest physicians and a notable maverick. Pitcairne had abandoned a lucrative practice in Edinburgh in 1692 to accept an invitation from Boerhaave and his colleagues to teach at Leyden. He remained only a year. Rumor long afterward had it that he left

---

7. Douglass, *Summary,* 1:441, 2:348n. Douglass to Colden, 20 February 1721, 28 July 1721, and 25 July 1722, in NYHS *Collections* 1 (1917): pp. 116, 144.

8. George H. Weaver, "Life and Writings of William Douglass," *Bulletin of the Society of Medical History of Chicago* 2(1921):229–59. This is the standard biographical work on Douglass.

bearing Boerhaave "a mortall grudge"[9] because the Dutchman expressed affection for the new English king, William III, who had deposed Pitcairne's hero James II. Actually, the reasons for the split went deeper. In an age when physicians were as eager to distinguish themselves from quacks as natural philosophers were from alchemists, Boerhaave had erected a medical "system" as neat and seemingly accurate as the one Newton had recently created for the universe. He did this by adapting to medicine the mechanical principles of Newtonian science. "The human body is undoubtedly an hydraulic machine through whose numerous orders of wonderfully variant vessels, or pipes, there is a constant motion of different fluids," was the way an eighteenth-century disciple explained Boerhaave's system, adding, "The encrease or declension of this motion from a due standard may be accounted the cause of disease. Perhaps the whole art of physic is little more than regulating, i.e. encreasing or retarding this motion in due time and order."[10]

Pitcairne would have none of this. He favored a clinical approach to medicine along the lines laid out by the great English physician Thomas Sydenham. Each disease must be treated by a therapy adjusted to the specific disease and to the individual. No theory, no generalized treatment for the variety of ills that plagued mankind would work. To that end Pitcairne pioneered the use of autopsies in Scotland in the hope that he and his students could learn more about the specific nature of disease.

To fellow Scotsmen, Pitcairne's medical views were the mildest of his heresies. He dared, in the hometown of John Knox, not only to mock the repressive rigidity of Presbyterianism but even to refuse to attend Sunday worship. To make sure no one missed the point, he joined the Church of England. He missed no chance to mock the conformist or the worshipper of tradition. No wonder,

9. Bridenbaugh, ed., *Hamilton's Itinerarium*, p. 132.
10. Dr. Thomas Young, "To the Public," *Pennsylvania Journal*, 5 July 1775.

then, that when an American learned "that Dr. D. had been a disciple of Pitcairne's" he thought he had found the answer to all Douglass's perverseness. When "Dr. D. talked very slightingly of Boerhaave" it was, of course, Pitcairne who had put such thoughts in his head. When Dr. D. expressed the shocking notion that he looked "upon empyricism or bare experience as the only firm basis upon which practise ought to be founded," Pitcairne again was speaking through his disciple.[11]

Apparently, however, Pitcairne also thought an enterprising student ought to hear the other side of an argument before committing himself, for it is hard to believe that Douglass set off for Leyden and enrolled in Boerhaave's classes without his master's approval. All that is known of the period in Leyden comes from a sentence out of the diary of a pro-Boerhaave acquaintance: "He braggs often of his having called Boerhaave a *helluo librorum* in a thesis which he published att Leyden and takes care to inform us how much Boerhaave was nettled att it; just as much, I believe, as a mastiff is att a snarling of a little lap-dog."[12] After Leyden and the practical experience in Paris, Douglass went to England and settled in the city of Bristol, where he had "the prospect of very good business." Just as his practice was getting under way, a friend who thought he had the next appointment for governor of Massachusetts sewed up, persuaded Douglass to pull up roots and travel to Boston, where close ties with the top royal official of that colony would assure the young physician a comfortable sinecure. This, Douglass later said, "was the inducement that brought me hither."[13]

When Douglass arrived in Boston in 1716, he was about twenty-five years old. He liked what he found, but when word came through that his friend's appointment as governor had fallen

11. Bridenbaugh, ed., *Hamilton's Itinerarium*, pp. 116, 133.
12. Ibid., p. 137.
13. Douglass to Colden, 20 February 1721, NYHS *Collections* 1(1917): 114.

through, he decided to explore the New World further before settling down. A year's tour of the West Indies convinced him that Boston looked better than ever. "I have resolved to fix here, and ramble no more," he wrote soon afterward. "I can live handsomely by the incomes of my Practice, and save some small matter." Though the town abounded with physicians, there was "no other graduate than myself." He adapted easily to the peculiarities of an American practice. In England medicines were concocted by apothecaries, but in Boston he found "all our Practitioners dispense their own medicines." English patients paid their physician an annual retainer fee, "but for the Native New-Englanders I am obliged to keep a day book of my Consultations advice and Visits, and bring them in a bill."[14]

New England winters pained Douglass—"Extremity of cold, may equally be called hell," he said, "as extremity of heat"[15]—but otherwise he enjoyed the country. He found time to visit the neighboring colonies and learned what he could about this strange new land. He followed Massachusetts politics closely and kept a full record of all he observed. Consciously or otherwise, he had begun to prepare himself for writing the *Summary* as he collected facts and attempted to understand America. This pleasant existence lasted four years, ending suddenly in the spring of 1721 when an epidemic of smallpox "broke loose" on Boston. Within a few weeks Douglass was embroiled in the first of his public disputes.

III.

The controversy began on 6 June, when Cotton Mather sent a letter to all practitioners in Boston (Dr. Douglass excepted), telling them of a way to limit the ravages of the epidemic of

14. Ibid., pp. 114, 115.
15. Douglass, *Summary*, 1:179n.

smallpox now at hand. Sometime earlier Douglass had lent Mather a volume of the *Transactions* of the Royal Society.[16] Mather had been struck by two reports that described a way of inducing a mild but immunizing case of smallpox in individuals. The accounts had reminded him of an earlier conversation with his slave Onesimus, who had told him of "an operation which had given him something of the smallpox and would forever preserve him from it." The operation or inoculation involved inserting live smallpox germs into an open incision. It was this procedure Mather recommended in his letter to the physicians of Boston.

Only one practitioner, a sometime minister named Zabdiel Boylston who had drifted into medicine, was persuaded to try out Mather's idea. He experimented on his child and two slaves; once satisfied they had survived the ordeal, he offered to inoculate all willing to take the risk. When word of the offer spread, the medical profession to a man condemned Boylston. The physicians were not reactionaries. As Perry Miller has remarked, "when Cotton Mather urged the physicians to try this device there was absolutely no reason to suppose, on any grounds which science or intelligence needed to respect, that his medical hypothesis was any more to be trusted than had been the theory of spectral evidence employed in 1692 by the Salem Court."[17]

Douglass had long regarded the contents of the *Transactions* as little better than trash, as most of it was; he had no doubt made his views on inoculation clear to Mather before the letter of 6 June (probably for that reason he did not receive a copy of Mather's letter). But he held his peace—publicly at least—for six weeks, perhaps assuming that the obvious absurdity of inoculation would

16. Two of a number of accounts of this famous controversy are Richard H. Shryock and Otho T. Beall, Jr., *Cotton Mather: The First Significant Figure in American Medicine* (Baltimore, 1954), which is pro-Mather, and Perry Miller's chapter "The Judgment of the Smallpox" in *From Colony to Province*, which is pro-Douglass.
17. Miller, *From Colony to Province*, p. 348.

soon cut short further experiments. (Douglass's low opinion of Mather's medical knowledge was not improved when he heard the cleric tell of cats who had caught the smallpox: "He had not discretion sufficient to observe, that the small-pox is a contagious distemper, peculiar to mankind. . . .")[18] But when Mather persuaded the bulk of the Boston clergy to put its prestige behind inoculation, Douglass could no longer remain silent. On 24 July he published an effective and, for him, moderate attack against the innovation. "I oppose this novel and dubious practice not being sufficiently assured of its safety and consequences," he told his friend Cadwallader Colden, also a physician and completely sympathetic to Douglass's stand; "in short I reckoned it a sin against society to propagate infection by this means and bring on my neighbour a distemper which might prove fatal [and] which perhaps he might escape (as many have done) in the ordinary way, [and] which he might certainly secure himself against by removal in this country where it prevails seldom."[19]

Through the summer and well into autumn the deaths from smallpox rose steadily—26 in August, 101 in September, 402 in October. The battle in the press over inoculation increased in warmth as the epidemic spread; the clergy, its reputation on the line, became as vituperative as the physicians. Douglass several times lost his temper in print, but at no time did he condemn inoculation outright. Privately, he even said that "to speak candidly for the present it [smallpox] seems to be somewhat more favourably received by inoculation than received the natural way." He condemned only Boylston's haphazard way of practicing it. Patients were not isolated while their open incisions were still discharging "a peculiar noisome fetor," but were allowed to go "abroad about their affairs." Douglass argued that the single "great

18. Douglass, *Summary*, 2:411.
19. Douglass to Colden, 1 May 1722, NYHS *Collections* 1 (1917): 143–144.

objection against inoculation" was permitting it to be "practised at random in a place whose greatest part of the People are liable to the distemper." In short, he said after the epidemic ended, "When a Man is not positive of a Practice, it is natural and consistent for him to be cautious in the rash and indiscreet Use of it."[20]

By January 1722 the epidemic had ended, but the controversy over inoculation had not. Douglass, now that he had time to spare, summarized his views in a pamphlet, *Inoculation of the Small Pox as Practised in Boston*, a balanced statement that still stands up well. A short while later came another, less calm report, *The Abuses and Scandals of some late Pamphlets in Favour of Inoculation. . . .* With considerable wit he attacked the clergy, those "vain self-conceited Men" who had stepped outside their rightful domain to impose upon "the Practitioners in their Rights and Priviledges." He paid particular attention to "the Hero in this Farce of Calumny," Cotton Mather, for whom he held a lingering bitterness that carried over to the final pages of the *Summary*.[21]

The clergy of Boston never forgave Douglass, and to some degree his reputation in history has been shaped by their hatred. "His prejudices were very strong," wrote one of the clan over a half-century after Douglass's death, "and such was the obstinacy of his temper, that he would never retract his errors, however palpable or unjust."[22] Insofar as Douglass had anything to retract in the inoculation controversy, he did so swiftly and gracefully. When smallpox hit Boston again in 1730, he published *A Practical Essay Concerning the Small Pox*, perhaps the ablest description of

20. Ibid., pp. 142, 143. Last quotation taken form Miller, *From Colony to Province*, p. 359.
21. Douglass, *Abuses and Scandals* (Boston, 1722), Introduction.
22. William Allen, *American Biographical Dictionary* (Cambridge, Mass., 1809). The quotation's harmful effect on Douglass's reputation was increased when a reputable physician, James Thacher, used the sketches of Allen and another clergyman, John Eliot, as the basis for his sketch of Douglass in the supposedly authoritative *American Medical Biography* (Boston, 1828).

the disease then published in America. In the same year he also came out with A *dissertation concerning inoculation of the small-pox* in which he cautiously recommended inoculation provided proper procedures were used. In 1752, when the disease again struck Boston, Douglass had this to say in the *Summary*: "The novel practice of procuring the small-pox by inoculation, is a very considerable and most beneficial improvement in that article of medical practice."[23] Once sensibly conducted experiments had been carried out—and this was all he had ever asked—Douglass withdrew his objections completely.

IV.

Douglass had entered the inoculation controversy something of an unknown to his medical brethren. He emerged from it the accepted leader of the profession in Boston, and during the remaining thirty years of his life he never lost that position. Colleagues regularly called him in on "difficult" or "extraordinary" cases. Newcomers to the profession listened to him so attentively that one disgruntled observer remarked that "most of the physitians here (the young ones I mean) seem to be awkward imitators of him. . . ."[24]

The acid judgments Douglass makes in the *Summary* about the quality of American medicine came after a lifetime of seeking to improve it. In an age when the rumor of an autopsy about to be performed could raise a mob against the offending physician, he dared to perform autopsies whenever he was puzzled by the cause of a patient's death. The plan laid out in the *Summary* for provincial legislation to regulate the profession and for a board of

23. Douglass, *Summary*, 2:406.
24. Bridenbaugh, ed., *Hamilton's Itinerarium*, p. 132.

physicians and surgeons to examine all men before they were allowed to practice was something he had fought to bring about for a quarter of a century. He took the lead in founding a Medical Society in Boston—the first in America—and though the volume of "Memoirs" he promised friends in 1736 never materialized, the Society continued to flourish. A visitor attended a meeting in 1744 where, he remarked, "Dr. D gave us a physical harange upon a late book of surgery published by Heyster, in which he tore the poor author all to pieces and represented him as intirely ignorant of the affair."[25]

Douglass's years of study in Europe did not, as might be expected, set him apart from home-trained physicians in Boston. He arrived, like most of his colleagues, "a blind follower" of Thomas Sydenham. Sydenham's name survives today because of his work as a clinician. He was the first to diagnose measles and (supposedly) scarlet fever, the first to distinguish between gout and rheumatism, the first to give an accurate description of St. Vitus' Dance, the first to establish the psychic character of hysteria. Before an American physician was satisfied with a diagnosis he inevitably checked his conclusions in Sydenham's *Medical Observations.*

Sydenham's influence was also great in the area of therapy. He held that disease resulted from the accumulation of "morbific matter" in the body; only when it had been drained off by bleeding, purging, or sweating would health return. Once the body had been cleansed, he called for mild therapy—rest, light foods, fresh air—to encourage nature's healing powers. Boston physicians accepted nearly all of this as gospel. "Blood-letting and anodynes are the principal tools of our practitioners," said Douglass. He added that they also "follow Sydenham too much in giving

25. Ibid., p. 137. The founding of the Medical Society and the prospective volume of "Memoirs" is mentioned in Douglass's letter to Colden, 17 February 1736, NYHS *Collections* 2(1918):146–47.

paregoricks, after catharticks, which is playing fast and loose," but that judgment came after he had ceased to be "a blind follower." The single but (in Douglass's eyes) crucial aspect of Sydenham's theory that Boston shunned was that "nature was never to be consulted, or allowed to have any concern in the affair."[26]

In the epidemic of 1721, Douglass later confessed, "I confided too much in the method of the celebrated Dr. Syden[ham], particularly his cold regimen, and frequent use of vitriolicks and opiates." In the epidemic of 1730 he began to part with the master, substituting "a moderately cool regimen," and when smallpox struck in 1752 he "depended almost intirely upon the fund or stock of my own observations."[27]

Dependence on his own observations did not imply a break with Sydenham, who emphasized the influence of climatic and atmospheric change on the cause and spread of disease and held that every season and each year had its peculiar "epidemic constitution" in which a particular disease with particular characteristics would prevail. It followed, then, that American diseases demanded a therapy adjusted to American conditions. The colleague who said Douglass "is of the clynicall class of physicians, crys up empyricism" got the point exactly: he refused to be tied down to a universal system of medicine. Astronomy has reduced the motions of planets "to equations or rules," Douglass said, "but it is to be feared that in our microcosm or animal oeconomy, there are so many inequalities as not to admit of any fixed rules, but must be left to the sagacity of some practitioners and to the rashness of others."[28]

As a clinician Douglass deserves to be ranked first among physicians in eighteenth-century America, if only because he was the first to diagnose a disease hitherto unknown to physicians. The mysterious illness struck Boston in the winter of 1735–36. Some

26. Douglass, *Summary*, 2:352.
27. Ibid., 2:394.
28. Bridenbaugh, ed., *Hamilton's Itinerarium*, p. 116; Douglass, *Summary*, 2:384.

four thousand people, about one-quarter of the population, caught it and over one hundred died from it. The severity of the onslaught and the feeling that this seemed "to be a new kind of epidemical disease" led Douglass to publish an account of it. He called it "an eruptive military fever" but medical scholars unhesitatingly accept what he described as America's first epidemic of scarlet fever. (Douglass might have used the name himself except that Sydenham had preempted it for a milder disease that has since been designated rubella.) After describing and giving the course of the disease, Douglass offered what had seemed to him a successful therapy for it: avoid excessive bleeding—"most of those who died of the physicians, died by immoderate evacuations"—and promote "the tendency of nature in our illness, by mercurials and gentle breaking sweats; which with good management seldom failed. . . ."[29] As the disease worked its way down the coast, Douglass's pamphlet was used by physicians everywhere as their guide to treatment.

Not only was his description of scarlet fever the first ever published—it antedated the better known and more widely publicized essay of Dr. John Fothergill in London by twelve years—but, as a later physician remarked, it remains "one of the best works extant upon the subject." Over a century and a half later another physician remarked that since Douglass's work little had been observed "in the clinical course of the disease which was not recognized and noted by him."[30]

A second clinical report by Douglass, published in 1740, has received little attention from medical scholars, though it had equally great influence on physicians of his day. In the autumn of 1749 the coastal towns of New England had been struck by what Douglass called "an acute malignant Fever." It centered mainly among children and appears to have been an epidemic of

29. William Douglass, *The Practical History of a New Epidemical Eruptive Military Fever with an Angina Ulcusulosa* (Boston, 1736).
30. Remarks on the scarlet fever paper by Walter Channing, Jr. and John Ware (1825) and Casper Wistar (1858) were found in Weaver, "Douglass."

diphtheria. Douglass visited the country towns to find out why the physicians there had a higher mortality rate than he and his colleagues in Boston did. He found they were using cathartics and "other hot driving medicines to expell the malignity as they express it, whereby they put nature in a greater fuss & confound or exasperated her." He deplored this therapy and urged the use of "mercurials with camphire," which promoted salivation and thus helped gently to rid the body of its "morbific matter." All this he wrote in a long letter to Cadwallader Colden in New York. Colden, impressed both by the description of the disease and by the therapy, turned the letter over to printer John Peter Zenger, who published it under the title *An Account of the Throat Distemper*.[31]

Douglass's use of mercury to treat the "throat distemper" and scarlet fever became, through these two publications, a standard part of therapy in eighteenth-century American medicine. In 1886 Dr. Oliver Wendell Holmes remarked: "I suspect that medicine in Boston owed the reform to its Materia Medica largely to Wm. Douglass."[32] This sounds like faint praise until one remembers that Holmes regarded Boston as the hub of the universe; reforms worked there radiated through the continent—or so Bostonians thought.

V.

While the furor over inoculation was still raging, Dr. Douglass found the energy to inject himself into another controversy, this one centering around paper money. In this debate he gave no

31. Douglass to Colden, 12 November 1739, NYHS *Collections* 2 (1918): 196–200. The Zenger publication of the essay-letter is referred to in Maurice Bear Gordon, *Aesculapius Comes to the Colonies* (Ventnor, N.J., 1949), p. 165.
32. Quoted in Weaver, "Douglass," p. 26.

ground; his zeal for the battle and his opposition's rancor increased rather than diminished with the years. Indeed, as the *Summary* reveals to the point of tedium, paper money had by the end of his life become a magnificent obsession, the touchstone by which he judged all America's current failings and predicted its collapse.

In 1727, when the issue first surfaced in Massachusetts politics, Douglass, unaccustomed though he was to fence-sitting, confessed that he had no judgment on "the merits of the case" for or against paper money. But it took only a few months for an opinion to congeal, and he set out at once to collect ammunition for battle. "Please favour me with some informations relating to your Paper money emissions & value for some years past," he wrote Cadwallader Colden early in 1728, "that I may be able to pass some judgement of the causes of your keeping its Standard & ours losing."[33]

From that time Douglass became "the oracle of the anti-paper party."[34] Several early essays served to plant the seeds of an argument that came to full bloom in 1739 with A *Discourse concerning the Currency of the British Plantations in America*, which has been called "one of the very best of the eighteenth century discussions of the money question."[35] That pamphlet failed to cleanse the spleen; bitterness accumulated steadily during the 1740s and boiled over so extensively in the *Summary* that if the remarks on paper money alone were excerpted they would make a fair-sized volume. A reader who scrupulously follows Douglass's discussion finds that somewhere past the line of boredom the obsession takes on an amusing aspect. "This accursed affair of plantation paper-

33. Douglass to Colden, 20 November 1727 and 1 January 1728, NYHS *Collections* 1 (1917): 238, 247.

34. Lawrence Shaw Mayo, ed., Thomas Hutchinson's *History of the Colony and Province of Massachusetts Bay,* 3 vols. (Cambridge, Mass., 1936), 2:335.

35. Charles J. Bullock, Introduction to A *Discourse,* reprinted in *Economic Studies* 2(1897):288.

currencies," goes a typical introduction to a heated passage, "when in course it falls in my way, it proves a stumbling-block, and occasions a sort of deviation." Long after confessing that when "the monster comes in my way, I cannot contain myself," he continues to fill pages with this "most disagreeable topick."[36]

Economists and economic historians, whether amused by Douglass's obsession or not, have on the whole given his arguments serious attention. In 1776 Adam Smith enhanced Douglass's reputation in Europe when in *The Wealth of Nations* he accepted his judgments and, in passing, honored him as an "honest and downright" gentleman. Charles J. Bullock, who thought enough of *A Discourse* to have it reprinted in 1897, praised Douglass's "firm grasp of fundamental facts and principles," adding that even today he may be "read with profit." Joseph Dorfman suggested that "he was none too careful in collecting his facts, and his knowledge of the literature was narrow," but then went on to give him a full and respectful hearing.[37]

Much of what Douglass said about paper money was perceptive and persuasive. Unlike many later historians, he saw that the demand for an inflated currency came not from farmers but from city-based speculators and shopkeepers who used mortgages and long-term credit to make their purchases in land and goods and later extinguished their debts with depreciated paper. A close reading of his writings reveals that Douglass's stand on paper money was more moderate than his language. To a degree it resembled his reaction to inoculation: he did not adamantly oppose the experiment but only the rash way legislatures performed it. Certain European nations, he observed, had managed safe and

36. Douglass, *Summary*, 1:499; 2:13n, 87n.
37. Adam Smith, *The Wealth of Nations*, 3 vols. (London, 1811), 2:78; Bullock, *A Discourse*, p. 238; Joseph Dorfman, *The Economic Mind in American Civilization 1606–1865*, 2 vols. (New York, 1947), 1:155.

sensible issuances of paper money by limiting it to a proportion of the silver then in circulation.[38]

But the validity of Douglass's arguments matters less to the modern reader than a point of more general interest—the passionate feeling he brought to the discussion. For a quarter century Douglass raged against paper money with a virulence that remained undimmed to the end. Why? Because to him the danger from paper money was greater than its effect on the colonial economy; he thought it sapped the underpinnings of American morality and ultimately endangered the stability of American society. Paper money, said Douglass, appealed only to the immoral among mankind: the idle, the improvident, the "fraudulent debtors." Most "men of substance" deplored its use, he said, and those few who favored it were known for their "natural improbity and depravity of mind."[39]

Douglass offered a moral rather than an economic solution to the perennial shortage of silver caused by a provincial economy's dependence on the mother country for manufactured goods: "Let us then lessen our Imports by our Frugality, and add to our Exports by our Industry; and we shall have no occasion for the chimerical ill founded Medium, Paper Money." Debt, he said, is a moral evil that undermines men's characters and will ultimately bankrupt the colonies, and paper money only promotes debt among the people.[40]

Douglass admitted more than once that his affection for America sometimes led him to speak forth with "passionate warmth and

38. Bray Hammond, *Banks and Politics in America From the Revolution to the Civil War* (Princeton, 1957), p. 16. Hammond has no respect for Douglass's views on paper money but is pleased that at least "he never attributes the issues to farmers." On the European experience with paper money, and Douglass's reaction, see Dorfman, *Economic Mind*, 1:155.
39. Quoted in Dorfman, *Economic Mind*, 1:157.
40. Bullock, *A Discourse*, p. 340.

indiscretion." As early as 1727 Douglass had worried about "a levelling principle" he saw taking shape in America, where through the indulgence of weak governors every man had "got a habit of doing . . . what is right in his own eyes." Since then "levelling and licentiousness" had increased and a "democratical spirit" had emerged, and Douglass believed these evils could be traced back to paper money. Debtors always outnumber creditors in any land, he said, but paper money increases their number; they elect their brethren to the legislatures and come to dominate political affairs. "The Debtor side has had the ascendant ever since anno 1741," he observed dismally, "to the almost utter ruin of the country." "A licentious people . . . a giddy people" refused to pay the salary of a governor who would not violate royal instructions that forbade the issuing of paper money. A more sinister evil had become apparent by 1750. Thanks to paper money, the Whigs in several colonies ("a genuine whig is for maintaining the ballance of power among the several orders or negatives of the legislature") had become outnumbered by a faction known as republicans ("a republican is for lowering or annihilating the prerogatives of a king, and for an unlimited extension of the privileges of the people in their representatives"). If this trend continued, Douglass saw no hope for the future of America.[41]

VI.

Fortunately there was more to Douglass's life than paper money and medicine, more than rancorous battles against an unenlightened community; otherwise the *Summary* would have been less than the marvelous and expansive work it is. He traveled widely

41. Douglass to Colden, 20 November 1727, NYHS *Collections* 1(1917): 238; Dorfman, *Economic Mind*, 1:157; Douglass, *Summary*, 1:535, 2:263.

through New England, visiting "the greatest part of our four Colonys" within a few years of his arrival in Massachusetts. During these trips he added some eleven hundred plants to the botanical collections he had begun in Leyden and Paris. He appears to have ended this "rural amusement" in the summer of 1729, when an epidemic of measles "devested me entirely from Botanical amusements." And the fine library that William Burnet brought from England when he assumed the governorship of Massachusetts "has not a little turned my head from my former Country Botanical perambulations." (In spite of these remarks, Douglass kept his interest in botany long enough to write a description of his collection for the Medical Society. His account somehow fell into the hands of John Bartram in Pennsylvania, who planned to incorporate the work in his own "description of our American plants.")[42]

Douglass's energy seemed as endless as his curiosity. He kept a daily record of the winds and the weather and also, once he had obtained a thermometer (there had been none in Boston when he arrived), of the temperature. Perhaps he sought to give Sydenham's generalization about the variance of disease with climate a scientific basis. In letters to Cadwallader Colden he tried to determine the cause of an earthquake that struck New England in 1727. Colden's request for information about distilling rum swung his interest in that direction. He reported that the business could "not be learned by writing, it is acquired only by Inspiration and practice" and that the distillers were intent on keeping the art a mystery. Later the tireless investigator reported: "The affair of distilling Rhum in hot Weather I think I have learnt to perfection, but am at a loss how the fermentation in very cold weather may be carried on to advantage, but this I hope to learn soon (our distillers

42. Douglass, *Summary*, 2:21; Douglass to Colden, 14 July 1729, NYHS *Collections* 1(1917):308; Bartram to Colden, 2 November 1744, NYHS *Collections* 3(1919):78.

continue to make a Mystery of their business) and shall freely communicate."[43]

Another request of Colden's, for a map of New England, sent Douglass off on another tangent. No decent map of the area existed; he decided to make one, though he knew nothing about cartography. He had an amateur's knowledge of mathematics and could handle a quadrant well enough to fix the latitude and longitude of a spot, and by 1739 he was busy reducing "our Province to an exact Map from the Several actual Surveys lodged in the Secretarys office." A decade later he had produced a map "about 3 and half feet square, by a scale of 5 miles to one inch," he said. "This plan, of many years collecting, and perfected at a considerable charge, is a free gift, for a publick benefit to the Provinces of New England. . . ."[44]

These activities had still not exhausted the range of Douglass's interests. In 1743 he published *Mercurius Nov-Anglicanus, or an Almanack* under the pseudonym "William Nadir, L.X.Q., student in the Mathematicks and a Lover of his Country." The presidency of the Scots Charitable Society, which he assumed in 1728 and held until death, gave him a chance to put into practice the firm views he held about charitable activities: "All charities, excepting to poor orphans, other impotent poor, and children of indigent parents, are charities ill applied," he said; "charities towards converting people from one mode of religion to another, where both are confident with society, are not laudable."[45]

Douglass delighted in the "promoting of children in town and country," and when the chance came to indulge this weakness and at the same time test out some of his ideas on education he seized it, taking in "a promising boy entirely at my own charge of subsistence and education, under my sole direction, to form a

43. Douglass to Colden, 11 March and 9 September 1728, NYHS *Collections* 1(1917):248, 270.

44. Douglass to Colden, 12 November 1739, NYHS *Collections* 2(1918): 196; Douglass, *Summary*, 1:404.

45. Douglass, *Summary*, 2:157.

practical (not notional) scheme of management and education
ob ovo, or rather ab utero." Douglass's detailed account of the
experiment is one of the most fascinating footnotes in the *Summary*.[46]

All these extracurricular affairs apparently interfered little with
his medical practice. The handsome income he boasted soon after
settling in Boston had a few years later declined to something "not
much above a competency," or so he said.[47] There is reason to
believe that, being a Scotsman, he prospered steadily. In 1723 he
bought a tract of "wild lands" in western Massachusetts, and in
later years he purchased three thousand more acres in the north-
western part of the colony. One of the townships carved from his
holdings was named after him. He acknowledged the honor by
donating $500—in "old tenor," he emphasized, not depreciated
paper money—"as a fund for the establishment and maintenance
of free schools, together with a tract of thirty acres of land with
a dwelling house and barn standing thereon." It would have pleased
the thrifty old gentleman to learn that 127 years after his death
the school fund still contained approximately $900.[48]

VII.

Dr. Douglass was fifty-five years old when he began to write the
Summary, but the project had been in his mind almost from the
time he settled in Boston. From the beginning he had regularly
made "observations and minutes of those [in Massachusetts] who
lead and of those who are led, of all the shelves and rocks on which
. . . our several parties and factions have ran foul." But he never
planned to focus solely on Massachusetts. This would be a history

46. Ibid., pp. 346–48n.
47. Douglass to Colden, 14 September 1727, NYHS *Collections* 1(1917):
167.
48. Weaver, "Douglass," p. 16.

of British America. As early as 1720 he began to pump his friend Colden about "the nature and constitution of this Country as a Body Politick; the history of our first grants and alterations of grants; limits of our Provinces; our Indians their different Tribes and numbers." The list of things he wanted to know seemed endless. "I have minutes of all these as they from time to time fall under my own observation, or from very good vouchers," he went on. "I expect from you returns of the same nature; but pray send nothing but what is exactly true and fact; take nothing from credulous people."[49]

Douglass never doubted his right to write a history of America. Although a Scotsman, he held that anyone who had studied the colonies as closely as he for some thirty years "may be said, as if born in the country." The work would be all his own, he said with a touch of arrogance, not built on borrowings from others. "No person can trace me as a plagiary," he said; "my own observations, hints from correspondents, and well-approved authors, and from public records are the materials of this essay." (The phrase "well-approved authors" meant little, for Douglass found virtually no one except Captain John Smith whose writings met his high standards.) It would seek to avoid petty squabbles; for that reason the early Puritan persecutions of Quakers and Anabaptists, of which previous authors had made so much, would be omitted "as being only local and temporary from the wrong-pointed zeal of the times, without any political wicked design." He would seek always to be entertaining and readable, but if along the way he felt the need to include some "dry accounts which are local" the reader was encouraged to pass them by "as being of no general concern."[50]

Originally the work was to be published in installments in the *American Magazine and Historical Chronicle*, and an announcement to this effect appeared there in January 1746. For some rea-

---

49. Douglass to Colden, 20 November 1727 and 20 February 1721, NYHS *Collections* 1 (1917): 116, 238.
50. Douglass, *Summary*, 1:91n, 109, 442, 459n.

son—did the editor object to the "honest and downright" Doctor's opinions?—the magazine reneged on the deal, but the plan for serial publication was nonetheless kept. The chapters came forth in the form of sixteen-page pamphlets. As they appeared, Douglass dispatched them to friends around the continent, promising that further installments would "be published in parcels as leasure time allows, and shall be remitted to you from time to time." He hoped the recipients would, as in the past, continue to help him out. "Please to contribute some hints concerning the legislature, Taxes, Quitrents, Exports of Furs, Skins, Flower, Copper-oar; and boundaris of New York & Jersies as also wherein consists the dispute between Maryld and Pensylvania, and what has been done in it," he asked Cadwallader Colden in what must have been a typical letter to scattered acquaintances. The first two "parcels" were sent out by early March 1747. The third was ready in mid-April. The flow continued through 1748 and 1749, when the pamphlets were finally collected and issued as a hardcover volume.[51]

The first volume of the *Summary* differed from the pamphlet editions in one notable aspect, to which Douglass refers in the opening note to the reader: a highly critical section dealing with Commodore Charles Knowles had been dropped. Knowles in 1747 had countenanced the impressment of a considerable number of New England seamen to fill out crews depleted by desertions. Douglass's account of the incident—written, he said, only with the intention of "setting the affair in a strong light"—had so angered the Commodore that when Governor Shirley refused to arrest the outspoken Doctor, Knowles instituted a libel action. Douglass retreated to the extent of dropping the offending passage from the hardcover volume and appending the apologetic note to his readers. But those who read the volume soon saw that Douglass

51. Lawrence C. Wroth, in *An American Bookshelf 1755* (London, 1934), discusses the publication history of the *Summary* in the Appendix, pp. 176–77. Douglass to Colden, 19 March and 16 April 1747, NYHS *Collections* 3 (1919):367–68.

had dissembled in his apology, for scattered throughout were a number of censorious remarks directed at Knowles. Their general tone was typified by the phrase "monster of wickedness."[52]

In the first volume Douglass rarely hesitated to cast judgments on any character who crossed the path of his narrative. An exception was Governor Shirley. A gentleman in office, Douglass explained, "is not to be used with freedom; it is a trespass against the subordination requisite in society: therefore I must defer the short account of this Gentleman's personal character and administration to the appendix. . . ." Shirley forced Douglass to change his mind. The governor had done his best to slow down if not dam up the stream of Douglass's pamphlets. Douglass opened Volume Two by revealing what "the great man of the province" had been up to, and from that point Shirley became fair game. The pamphlets continued to pour forth through 1750 and 1751. They stopped in 1752, when smallpox once again hit Boston, forcing Douglass to abandon history for medicine. What he thought would be a temporary pause became permanent; on 21 October 1752 Dr. Douglass died. The printer gathered the "parcels" together and issued the incomplete, much slimmer second volume in 1752. The set was reprinted in Boston and London in 1755 and again in London in 1760.[53]

VIII.

"The thing that matters in judging a book of the past," Lawrence C. Wroth has said, "is not whether it satisfies the standards of our own time, but whether it pleased, and possessed significance

52. John Noble, "Notes on the Libel Suit of Knowles *v.* Douglass in the Superior Court of Judicature," Colonial Society of Massachusetts *Publications* 3(1900):213–36.

53. Douglass, *Summary*, 1:482; 2:2n. Wroth, *American Bookshelf*, pp. 176–77.

for, the people for whom it was intended."⁵⁴ By that standard the *Summary* stands forth as a triumph: it was read and praised by contemporaries on both sides of the Atlantic.

Douglass made clear in the early pages that he wrote with a double audience in mind: "The people in Europe (the publick boards not excepted) have a very indistinct notion of these settlements, and the American settlers are too indolent, to acquaint themselves with the state of their neighbouring colonies." Both these ill-informed groups needed enlightenment, and both got it. William Smith, Jr., in his *History of New York*, censured the "immethodical" organization and the "often incorrect" facts, but in general he found the work useful.⁵⁵ Thomas Hutchinson, who knew Douglass and disliked him, in his own *History of Massachusetts Bay* found Douglass "erroneous" here and there but judged the work as a whole sound and sensible.

The loudest praise came from England. The *Summary* gave "a fuller and more circumstantial account of North-America, than is any where else to be met with," said the anonymous author of a long notice in the *Monthly Review* for October 1755. "The author appears to be a man of sound judgment, and extensive knowledge; he delivers his sentiments of persons and things with a blunt freedom, which is not always disagreeable; an air of integrity appears through the whole of his work." John Huske, in his *Present State of North America*, thought Douglass "very erroneous" in his remarks on Nova Scotia and "with respect to Limits between us and the French in general." (Curiously, Huske chose to criticize Douglass on his most prophetic point. "If the French," he wrote in one of several passages about the interior of America, "be allowed to become masters of the river St. Laurence, of the great inland lakes, and of the great river Mississippi; they are in conse-

54. Wroth, *American Bookshelf*, p. 88.
55. Douglass, *Summary*, 1:1. Smith is quoted in Wroth, *American Bookshelf*, p. 88.

quence masters of all the inland trade of North-America; an incredible prejudice to the British nation.") Otherwise, however, Huske had only praise for the *Summary*, calling it "the best Collection of facts in general for a future Historian, that was ever published. For of all the crude indigested works that were ever submitted to the Public, I believe this excels them therein."[56]

Douglass's high standing as a historian faded with the eighteenth century. According to one turn-of-the-century critique, the *Summary* "can only be considered as a strange medley of affairs relating to his family, his private squabbles, and public transactions, without judgment or sound discretion. He would not take pains to arrange his materials, nor to inform himself of particular facts." Justin Winsor in 1887 found the book "suggestive" but "an unsafe guide to the student." A few years later Moses Coit Tyler, a notably sound critic of colonial literature, found Douglass "essentially a journalist and pamphleteer. He is hot, personal, caustic, capricious; and his history is only a congeries of pungent and racy editorial paragraphs."[57]

The twentieth century, if it bothered to glance at the *Summary*, dismissed it as "a curious work," "a work that survives as the revelation of a personality rather than as history," a book filled with a "mass of misinformation."[58] *The Harvard Guide to American History* did not bother even to list the volume. The charge of misinformation has been leveled so consistently at the *Summary* that

56. Both the *Monthly Review* and Huske quotations appear in Wroth, *American Bookshelf*, pp. 88–89. Douglass's quote on the French is from the *Summary*, 2:226.

57. Thacher, *American Medical Biography*, p. 256; Justin Winsor, *Narrative and Critical History of America*, 8 vols. (Boston, 1884–89), 5:159; Moses Coit Tyler, *A History of American Literature, 1607–1765*, 2 vols. (New York, 1878), 2:391.

58. Kraus, *Writing of American History*, p. 56; David Hawke, *The Colonial Experience* (Indianapolis, 1966), p. 457. Not all modern readers have been so hard on Douglass; Lawrence C. Wroth is kinder in *American Bookshelf* and Jarvis M. Morse gives an excellent summary of Douglass's work in *American Beginnings* (Washington, D.C., 1952), pp. 196–200.

Charles J. Bullock's balanced statement on the issue deserves to be given in full:

That Douglass was a man of strong prejudices, always inclined to espouse one side of any question and unable to see the other, must be apparent to any reader of his *Summary*. That his information could not be always accurate on all the multifarious subjects which he treated is equally evident. His style is usually careless, his taste is sometimes bad, and his arrangement of his materials is far from satisfactory. These defects of the *Summary of the British Settlements* are only too patent. Moreover, his conception of historical method is entirely inadequate. But the critics of Doctor Douglass have often gone too far. It is certain that his errors are not so numerous as sometimes represented, while in not a few cases the critics have forgotten that more accurate information was nearly or quite inaccessible for him. In most respects he is no more deserving of criticism than the majority of early American historians. Finally, in some cases, it is the critics who err, not Douglass.[59]

IX.

Anyone who doubts that Douglass is worth reading should start with the chapter on Connecticut in his second volume. If those pages prove boring, uninformative, devoid of humor, or too digressive, read no farther, for here Douglass is at his best. The chapter on Connecticut illustrates an aspect of the *Summary* that historians, who tend to take their classics too seriously, rarely refer to: the work makes excellent bedside reading. It can be dipped into at almost any spot with profit and pleasure. The reader never knows what to expect from one page to another. On one he will find a eulogy to the coal fire ("A wood fire is more pleasant to the sight and smell than that of pit coal, but it is not so steady and lasting, its smoke and vapour is more offensive to the eyes, it

59. Bullock, *A Discourse*, p. 277.

discolours and dry-rots paper prints more than pit-coal."), and on the next a "Short account of Dr. Berkley's tar water used as a medicine."[60] The chapter on New Hampshire, though heavily padded and one of the weakest in the book, offers a fascinating digression on the lumber industry. A mention of whales early in the first volume sends Douglass off on an intriguing discussion of colonial whaling, perhaps the first such circumstantial account in American history.

So much has been made of Douglass's addiction to digressions that the *Summary* may seem to resemble a junkyard of historical facts. Actually, Douglass wrote with a clear plan in mind of where he was going, and he adhered to it. After one hundred pages of introductory material, he moves to the West Indies, then back to the continent to discuss in full the American Indians. After some fifty pages of general discussion about the continental colonies, he takes up each colony individually, starting with the northernmost.

Much about the *Summary* will not appeal to the modern reader. Douglass could boast in one breath that "a TOLERATION for all Christian professions of religion, is the true ecclesiastical constitution of our American colonies" and in the next say that from this toleration all Catholics "ought to be excluded," for "they have an indulgence for lying, cheating," and so forth. He views slavery with cold-blooded practicality in the chapters on the West Indies and in his few brief comments about Georgia, a colony "too much Utopian" whose exclusion of slaves was "the principal reason of the settlement coming to nothing."[61]

Douglass was a man of his time, and he would have been puzzled and infuriated by much of the political literature that began appearing within two decades of his death. His affection for America never led him to forget that he and the colonists owed

60. Douglass, *Summary*, 2:70, 72.
61. Ibid., 1:224–25, 225n. On Georgia, see 1:119, 2:6n.

their ultimate allegiance to Great Britain. The colonists in his eyes had no "rights"—the word is not used in the *Summary*—but only "privileges": the privilege of raising their own taxes, the privilege of enacting their own laws. Nor, curiously, does he speak of allegiance to the king, but only to Parliament. "The parliament of Great-Britain may abridge them of many valuable privileges which they enjoy at present; as happened in an affair relating to Ireland," he says at one point. At another he reminds readers, "In gratitude, we ought not to forget the compassionate goodness of the Parliament of Great-Britain, the parent of all our Colonies."[62]

But given Douglass's prejudices and his ties to the times, it is surprising how often he rises above both. He remains to the end his own man, judging men and events by his own lights. Previous historians elaborated on the disastrous Indian wars in New England. Douglass had another view. "Upon good enquiry it will be found," he said, "that our properly speaking Indian wars have not been so frequent, so tedious, and so desolating, as is commonly represented in too strong a light"—a judgment closer to the modern view than any other advanced in the eighteenth century. His understanding of the uniqueness of American life was extraordinary. Long before Tocqueville observed the American love for titles, he said: "In all our plantations, colonies, and provinces; they abound with civil and military titles of judges, squires, colonels, majors, and captains; gratifications for being of a governor's party, or by a pecuniary interest." He may or may not have coined the phrase "voluntary associations" but he was one of the first to recognize their importance in America and to say they "ought to be encouraged" in order to promote such institutions as libraries and academies. Douglass's plea for a system of public schools in all the colonies and a series of provincial colleges culminating in an American university to serve the continent antedated a similar

62. Ibid., 1:212–13, 528.

proposal of Benjamin Rush's by some thirty years. The plan he offered in the *Summary* for reorganizing the empire along lines more equable to the colonies as well as more profitable and efficient for the Mother Country was, as far as it went, as sensible as anything put forward before the revolution.[63]

Dr. Douglass took the title of his work seriously: his aim was to write of British America as a whole. The inordinate amount of space given New England misleads some readers into thinking the *Summary* is only another parochial history. Even when immersed in local issues, Douglass always has one eye trained on British America and seeking to relate the parts to the whole. Douglass, Max Savelle has remarked, was the first author "to present the American colonies as a unity," the first to see "the colonies as one." It was this vision that made the *Summary* "the first important literary and documentary expression to an American continental self-consciousness." For that reason, if for no other, Dr. William Douglass deserves the epitaph Perry Miller gave him: "a historian to whom all historians are indebted."[64]

---

63. Ibid., 1:191, 2:194–95.
64. Max Savelle, *Seeds of Liberty* (New York, 1948), pp. 382, 425, 567. Perry Miller, *From Colony to Province*, p. 350.

4.

Archibald Kennedy: Imperial Pamphleteer*

Milton M. Klein

Archibald Kennedy, one of colonial New York's most durable royal officials, served the Crown from his arrival in the province in 1710 until his death in 1763. Kennedy held both military and civil offices, including a thirty-four-year tenure on the New York Governor's Council. A confidant of virtually every governor under whom he served, Kennedy still maintained cordial relations with the most important colonial politicians who opposed those chief executives. He was also one of the colony's most prolific writers, penning between 1750 and 1755 no less than six tracts on government and colonial defense. Two of his tracts were republished in England, and one was reprinted twice in America. His literary and scientific confreres included New Yorkers like Cadwallader Colden, one of the colony's leading savants, and James Alexander, dean of its bar, as well as Benjamin Franklin and physician-historian William Douglass of Boston.

Despite these numerous claims to fame, Kennedy's life and career remain shrouded in obscurity. No biography of him exists, and the few biographical sketches are either incorrect or incomplete.[1] His early life baffled even those diligent and indefatigable

* Acknowledgement is made to the Faculty Research Fund, University of Tennessee, Knoxville, for assistance in the preparation of this essay.
1. William H. MacBean, *Biographical Register of Saint Andrew's Society of the State of New York*, 2 vols. (New York, 1922, 1925), 1:13–14; New

compilers of the directories of the British peerage: they could not determine his birthdate, his children's identity, or very much about his first wife.[2]

Kennedy's historical unobtrusiveness resulted from the absence of any significant collection of his papers. Despite his vigorous expression in public prints, Kennedy was not loquacious in his private correspondence. His friend Colden complained of Kennedy's "Laconick Stile," and this plus his temperamental reserve may account for the paucity of his personal papers. Another hindrance to Kennedy biographers is the confusion created by references to "Captain Archibald Kennedy" which do not distinguish between father and son, who bore the same name and held, at times, the same rank. That both men married Schuylers adds further to the bafflement.[3]

Kennedy was one of a group of talented Scotsmen who immigrated to New York during the administration of Governor Robert Hunter (1710–19), himself a Scot and one of the colony's ablest and most successful chief executives, and who joined

York Historical Society *Collections* 30(1897):287–88; Charles W. Spencer's sketch in the *Dictionary of American Biography*, eds. Allen Johnson and Dumas Malone, 22 vols. (New York, 1928–44), 10:332.

2. See, for example, John Burke, *A General and Heraldic Dictionary of the Peerage and Baronetage of the British Empire*, 4th ed., 2 vols. (London, 1833), 1:17–19; see also the 104th ed. (London, 1967), p. 34; George E. Cokayne, *The Complete Peerage . . .*, ed. Vicary Gibbs, 13 vols. (London, 1910–40), 3:80. See also *Archives of the State of New Jersey*, ed. William A. Whitehead, 42 vols. (Newark and Trenton, 1880–1949), 20:460; NYHS *Collections* 30(1898):285–88, 61(1928):x–xi; Neil R. Stout, "Captain Kennedy and the Stamp Act," *New York History* 45(1964):44–58.

3. Colden to James Alexander, 23 July 1729, *The Letters and Papers of Cadwallader Colden, 1711–1775*, 9 vols. (NYHS *Collections* 50–56, 67–68 [1918–24, 1937]), 1:290 (hereafter cited as *Colden Papers*). On the relationship of the Kennedys and the Schuylers, see George W. Schuyler, *Colonial New York: Philip Schuyler and His Family*, 2 vols. (New York, 1885), 2:193–94, 212–15; *New Jersey Archives*, 9 (1885):460; Edmund B. O'Callaghan, comp., *New York Marriages Prior to 1784* (Albany, 1860, reprinted Baltimore, 1968), p. 211.

Hunter's political circle. They included James Alexander, surveyor-general of New Jersey, and Cadwallader Colden, named to the same post in New York by Hunter's successor; they were joined by still another countryman who had been in the province for three decades, Robert Livingston, speaker of the Assembly during Hunter's administration.[4]

Archibald Kennedy may have arrived in June of 1710 in Hunter's entourage, but in what capacity is unclear. The twenty-five-year-old immigrant would surely have come to the new governor well recommended. The son of Alexander Kennedy, a justice of the peace in Craigoch, Ayrshire, young Archibald descended from a junior member of the noble family of Cassilis. His ancestry and his connections with Hunter undoubtedly explained why New York City's Common Council complimented "Archibald Kennedy, Gentleman," with the freedom of the city on 25 July 1710, little more than a month after his arrival.[5]

Kennedy's activities during the next two years are not clearly known. He may have assisted Hunter's ill-fated naval stores project along the Hudson River which employed several thousand German Palatine redemptioners. "I was a witness of the indefatigable Pains he took, and had some Share in the fatigue," Kennedy observed cryptically forty years later. His experience may have shaped the views he would express in 1750 in his first public tract about the importance to New York of a staple commodity besides furs. In 1711, Kennedy commanded a contingent of these Palatines re-

4. Of all these prominent figures, only Livingston has received adequate biographical treatment, in Lawrence H. Leder, *Robert Livingston, 1654–1728, and the Politics of Colonial New York* (Chapel Hill, 1961). Henry Noble MacCracken's *Prologue to Independence: The Trials of James Alexander, 1715–1756* (New York, 1964) is unsatisfactory, as is Alice M. Keys, *Cadwallader Colden: A Representative Eighteenth Century Official* (New York, 1906).

5. *The Burghers of New Amsterdam and the Freemen of New York, 1675–1866* (NYHS *Collections* 18[1886]), pp. 90, 464.

cruited as part of an army to invade Canada during Queen Anne's War. Hunter had commissioned Kennedy on this occasion as "Lieutenant of Fuzileers" in the New York militia.[6]

The Canadian expedition was recalled before it set foot on enemy soil, but the experience whetted Kennedy's appetite for military service. On 14 April 1712 he secured a regular army commission as third lieutenant of the Independent Company of Foot at New York. At the same time Governor Hunter named him adjutant of all four companies of British regulars in the province.[7]

New York was the only mainland colony to have British regulars stationed within its borders during the entire colonial period, a recognition of its strategic importance. However, in one of those many anomalies of administration in the old colonial system, Britain negated the troops' usefulness by steady neglect. Underpaid, undersupplied, and undercommanded, the troops were inadequate to guard the frontier from French or hostile Indian incursions. As adjutant for ten years, Kennedy shared the frustration of both Hunter and his successor, Governor William Burnet, with the niggardliness of the home government in maintaining the establishment. Hunter sent repeated and fruitless appeals to Whitehall; Burnet made his representations via Kennedy, whom he sent to England late in 1721 to plead the case. In a forceful memorial to the Board of Trade, Kennedy asked for two additional companies to garrison the frontier, erection of a fort at Niagara Falls,

6. Archibald Kennedy, *Observations on the Importance of the Northern Colonies under Proper Regulations* (New York, 1750), p. 16. On the Palatine venture, see Walter A. Knittle, *Early Eighteenth Century Palatine Emigration* (Philadelphia, 1937), chs. 6–7; Leder, *Robert Livingston*, ch. 13; Archibald Kennedy, *The Importance of Gaining and Preserving the Friendship of the Indians to the British Interest* (New York, 1751), pp. 9, 22; and E. B. O'Callaghan, ed., *Calendar of New York Colonial Commissions, 1680–1770* (New York, 1929), p. 16.

7. Charles Dalton, ed., *English Army Lists and Commission Registers, 1661–1714*, 6 vols. (London, 1960), 6:189.

provision for sick and invalided enlisted men, and bedding, which was in outrageously short supply.[8]

Kennedy's representation to the Board of Trade was more than an appeal on behalf of his suffering troops. It was an integral part of an imperial defense program that had originated with New Yorkers like Robert Livingston, engaged the support of governors Hunter and Burnet, and ultimately occupied much of Kennedy's time and attention. The heart of the program was the Iroquois alliance and, through it, the allegiance of the Indians of the Great Lakes region and the Ohio and Mississippi valleys. The political affections of the natives were governed by economic considerations. They preferred British trade goods to French, for the former were cheaper and better-made. The traditional entrepôt for British-Indian trade was Albany, which since 1686 had held a monopoly of the traffic in furs in New York. At Albany, a group of Dutch dealers conducted the business, but by the time of Hunter's administration they found it more convenient to secure pelts in bulk from Montreal, whence they arrived via the French *coureurs de bois*, who trapped, lived, and traded with the natives on their own hunting grounds.

To imperial-minded New Yorkers, the Albanians' conduct smacked of treason, which indeed it became when the Dutch traders trafficked with Canada during Queen Anne's War. While the Albany policy supplied England with furs, it lost the Crown

---

8. Stanley M. Pargellis, "The Four Independent Companies of New York," in *Essays in Colonial History Presented to Charles McLean Andrews by His Students* (New Haven, 1931), pp. 96–123; "Memorial of Archibald Kennedy to the Lords Commissioners for Trade and Plantations," [24 January 1722], in Shelburne Papers (William L. Clements Library, Ann Arbor, Michigan), 45:254; *Calendar of State Papers, Colonial Series: America and West Indies*, 43 vols. (London, 1860–1963), 33:11 (hereafter cited as *Calendar of State Papers*); *Journal of the Commissioners for Trade and Plantations, 1704–1782*, 14 vols. (London, 1920–1938), 4:338–40 (hereafter cited as *Journal of the Board of Trade*).

the political loyalty of the natives. The far western tribes sold to the French, who paid for the furs with their Albany-secured British goods. In the process, the French gained political influence over the natives. The Iroquois, conversely, who had made their profits by serving as middlemen between the western tribes and Albany or by trapping furs themselves, found themselves bypassed by the Great Lakes-Montreal-Albany axis.[9] The Iroquois, a brave and proud people, were disturbed by a British-tolerated policy which substituted profits for patriotism. The French willingly sent soldiers into the woods to protect and assist the natives; the British expected the Iroquois to defend their interests, but the British did not exert themselves militarily against the French.

The 1722 Burnet-Kennedy application to the Board of Trade to strengthen the British garrisons in New York served a political as well as a military purpose. A fort at Niagara Falls would give the British command of "the Pass where all Nations stop," intercept the trade between the western tribes and Montreal, and also prevent the French from acquiring "the very Key of that fine Country." New frontier forts would also encourage the peopling of western New York by assuring protection to settlers. Of greater importance, the expansion of British military influence into the Great Lakes would constitute the "only effectual security against the Designs of the French and the only sure means to keep the Indians true to us."[10]

With less vision than the New Yorkers, officials at Whitehall

9. Historians disagree about the Iroquois' role. See Charles H. McIlwain, ed., *An Abridgment of the Indian Affairs . . . by Peter Wraxall* (Cambridge, Mass., 1915), pp. xl–li; Arthur H. Buffinton, "The Policy of Albany and English Westward Expansion," *Mississippi Valley Historical Review*, 8 (1922): 327–66; and Allen W. Trelease, "The Iroquois and the Western Fur Trade: A Problem in Interpretation," ibid., 44 (1962):32–51.

10. Kennedy to the Lords of Trade, [24 January 1722], Shelburne Papers, Clements Library; Burnet to the Lords of Trade, 2 December 1721, *Calendar of State Papers*, 32:496–97; E. B. O'Callaghan, ed., *Documents Relative to the Colonial History of the State of New York*, 15 vols. (Albany, 1853–87), 5:644–45 (hereafter cited as *N.Y. Col. Docs.*).

rejected Kennedy's plea, despite a strong endorsement by the Board of Trade. The Board of Ordnance even declined to supply the existing four companies, placing that responsibility on the colony, and ignored the request for the two additional companies. Undeterred by London's shortsightedness, Burnet, supported by Kennedy, Livingston, Colden, Alexander, and Lewis Morris, sought to achieve the objective by local action. A series of New York laws between 1720 and 1726 prohibited outright direct trade between Albany and Montreal and, when this proved difficult to enforce, imposed instead a heavy tax on the trade. A British trading post was begun in 1722 and completed in 1727 at Oswego on Lake Ontario to intercept trade from the West. Pressure from the Albany traders in the Assembly, reinforced by British merchants who supplied them with goods, led to a royal disallowance in 1729 of the prohibitory legislation. A shift in control of the Assembly to an antigubernatorial party headed by Adolph Philipse and later by James De Lancey reduced expenditures for the frontier trading posts and ultimately neglected them. New York returned to the Albany policy of benign neglect of the Iroquois.[11]

While most officials during the next three decades relegated Indian policy and imperial defense to a secondary role, these matters obsessed Kennedy and his friends Colden and Alexander. Kennedy soon found other grounds for concern about the shortcomings of British colonial policy. While in England requesting troop reinforcements, Kennedy traded his army commission for appoint-

11. *Journal of the Board of Trade*, 4:342, 6:73; *Calendar of State Papers*, 33:20, 44, 84; Pargellis, "Independent Companies," pp. 104–05, 112–13; *The Colonial Laws of New York from the Year 1664 to the Revolution*, 5 vols. (Albany, 1894), 2:8–12, 98–105, 197–98, 248–51, 281–94, 372–403; McIlwain, ed., *Wraxall's Abridgment*, pp. lxv–lxxxi; Buffinton, "Policy of Albany," pp. 358–63; Leder, *Robert Livingston*, pp. 251–56, 267–68; and *N.Y. Col. Docs.*, 5:897–99. For an account of Indian policy in New York politics, see Milton M. Klein, "Democracy and Politics in Colonial New York," *New York History* 40(1959):221–46 (especially pp. 223–25).

ments as receiver-general of the province of New York and as collector of customs for the port.[12] Kennedy held both offices until his death, and he performed his duties with the same fidelity and concern for the empire that he had demonstrated during his military service. He soon saw a connection between the collection of quitrents and the problems of imperial defense. So long as speculators acquired tracts of land virtually rent-free, the border areas would remain unsettled and undefended. Worse, the ease and informality of land grants encouraged chicanery in defining their limits, and the victims of these frauds were often the Indians. This was still another cause for the natives' disaffection from the Crown.[13]

In his concern for the land problem, Kennedy again found himself in close agreement with councilors James Alexander and Cadwallader Colden, now also surveyor-general of the province. Shortly after assuming office as receiver-general, Kennedy asked his friends for assistance. They prepared a comprehensive list of all the land grants in the colony and the rents due under each grant. The survey confirmed cases of extravagance and fraud already suspected: some large tracts paid rents as trifling as "a lamb if Demanded," one tract of more than two million acres owed £3 a year, others paid no rent at all, boundaries were so vaguely defined that one

---

12. *The Army List of 1740* (Sheffield, N. Y., 1931), p. 57; O'Callaghan, *Calendar of New York Colonial Commissions*, p. 33; *Calender of Council Minutes, 1668–1783* (New York State Library *Bulletin* 58 [1902]):286; and James Sullivan and Alexander C. Flick, eds., *The Papers of Sir William Johnson*, 14 vols. (Albany, 1921–65), 1:539–40.

13. On Indian complaints concerning land grants, see Georgiana C. Nammack, *Fraud, Politics, and the Dispossession of the Indians: The Iroquois Land Frontier in the Colonial Period* (Norman, Okla., 1969), especially chapters 2, 4, 5; Douglas E. Leach, *The Northern Colonial Frontier, 1607–1763* (New York, 1966), pp. 168–71; Ruth L. Higgins, *Expansion in New York, with Especial Reference to the Eighteenth Century* (Columbus, Ohio, 1931), pp. 83–86; and Oscar Handlin and Irving Mark, "Chief Daniel Nimham v. Roger Morris, Beverly Robinson, and Philip Philipse—An Indian Land Case in Colonial New York, 1765–1767," *Ethnohistory* 2 (1964):193–246.

three hundred-acre grant became twenty thousand acres and another was extended by fifty thousand acres.[14]

During his long tenure as receiver-general, Kennedy tried valiantly to reverse this trend. He made the first serious effort to collect quitrents, and, as a result of Colden's systematic survey, Kennedy added more to the treasury than any of his predecessors. However, his 1724 proposal to convert nominal rents into specified sums passed the Council but failed in the Assembly. The landlords feared for their purses, and the "popular party" sought to prevent a "permanent support" which would free royal officials from dependence on Assembly-fixed salaries. In 1742, when the Assembly did pass a strong collection bill, the Privy Council disallowed it for barring chancery proceedings against delinquents. A similar bill was finally approved both in New York and London in 1755 and renewed in 1762 and 1768. The laws promised more than they produced, however. By 1768, rents were still £19,000 in arrears, and Kennedy annually collected £800 instead of the £40,000 due upon enforcement of the two shillings, six pence per hundred acre legal rate. Despite Kennedy's best efforts, the quitrent system in colonial New York remained a failure, and Kennedy continued to lament the large, vacant tracts that were "of great Prejudice to the settling and improving" of the colony.[15]

Kennedy's disillusionment with British colonial administration was heightened by his experience as customs collector. Charged with enforcing the Acts of Trade, he found himself frustrated by

14. "Representation of Cadwallader Colden . . . to Governor William Burnet," November 1721; Colden to Kennedy [September 1722 ?]; Colden to Kennedy [1727–28 ?]; *Colden Papers,* 8:160–64, 166–70, 186–90.

15. *Journal of the Legislative Council of the Colony of New York* [1691–1775], 2 vols. (Albany, 1861), 1:509, 513; Beverly W. Bond, Jr., *The Quit-Rent System in the American Colonies* (New Haven, 1919), ch. 9; *N.Y. Col. Docs.,* 6:273–74, 928, 7:369; William Smith, Jr., *The History of the Late Province of New-York from Its Discovery to the Appointment of Governor Colden in 1762,* 2 vols. (New York, 1829), 2:188n; Kennedy, *Observations on the Importance of the Northern Colonies under Proper Regulations,* p. 19.

his inability to prosecute lawbreakers in the Vice-Admiralty Court. Merchants whose goods were seized objected to the court's jurisdiction because the collector's actions took place close enough to land to try the alleged offenses within the province's common law courts with benefit of jury. In a classic case, *Archibald Kennedy, Esq. qui tam v. The Sloop Mary and Margaret, Thomas Fowles Reclaimant* (1739–43), the issue went to the Privy Council, which ruled against Kennedy. This considerably weakened enforcement of the Navigation Acts and provided New York's merchants with a ready handle against the zealous customs collector.[16]

Still another of Kennedy's frustrations in his customs job was the province's failure to provide him with an official place of business. The building set aside as a customs house—a store built by the Dutch West India Company—fell into such disrepair that it was demolished as a public nuisance. Kennedy did business in a variety of places until he personally purchased two buildings on lower Broadway in 1745 and set up one as a customs house and the other as his residence.[17]

However irritating the improvisation of a customs house, Kennedy could afford the expense by mid-century. His second marriage in 1736 to Mary Walter Schuyler allied him to a "Gentlewoman of a Plentiful Fortune," who by the death of her first husband had inherited £4,000. In addition, Kennedy, like other royal officeholders, took advantage of his intimacy with governors and councilors to ease through the complicated land patent process; his own elevation to the Council in 1727, upon Burnet's recommendation,

16. Charles M. Hough, ed., *Reports of Cases in the Vice Admiralty of the Province of New York* (New Haven, 1925), pp. 16, 82–83, 181–83; Justin H. Smith, *Appeals to the Privy Council from the American Plantations* (New York, 1950), pp. 515–17; Bernhard Knollenberg, *Origin of the American Revolution, 1759–1766* (New York, 1960), pp. 267–68; and George Clarke to the Lords of Trade, 15 December 1739, N.Y. *Col. Docs.* 6:154–55.

17. I. N. Phelps Stokes, *The Iconography of Manhattan Island*, 6 vols. (New York, 1915–28), 4:564, 584, 587, 634, 683–84.

gave him an even more favored position for land acquisition. Three years after his arrival in the colony, Kennedy joined in the rage for land, as much for its symbolic social and political significance as for its monetary returns. Between 1713 and 1739, Kennedy patented some five thousand acres in his own name and some twenty-two thousand more which he shared with others in Ulster, Orange, and Albany counties and in the Mohawk Valley. Kennedy's land-grabbing, however, appears positively slothful compared with that of Colden, De Lancey, Lewis Morris, and George Clarke—the latter managing, as secretary and lieutenant governor, to acquire more than one hundred thousand acres.[18]

Kennedy made more profitable deals in New York City lands. He acquired Bedlow's Island (site of the Statue of Liberty) in 1746 for £100 and in 1758 sold it to the city for a pest house at the handsome price of £1,000. He persuaded the Common Council that the lot on which the unused customs house stood was of no value to the city and likely to become "a Dunghill and a Nuisance," and as a result he acquired it for himself. When he made his will in 1745, Kennedy listed lands in upper New York, two farms in New Jersey, his two houses in New York City, Negro slaves, plate, books, furniture, a chaise, and several boats—all of which made him comfortably well-to-do but not one of New York's wealthiest citizens.[19]

His moderation in business ventures was paralleled by his

18. Ibid., 4:550; Schuyler, *Colonial New York*, 2:193–94; *Calendar of State Papers*, 34:409, 35:57, 59; *Journal of the Board of Trade*, 5:226, 270; *N.Y. Col. Docs.*, 5:766, 779, 817; *Calendar of N.Y. Colonial Manuscripts Indorsed Land Papers . . . , 1643–1803* (Albany, 1864), pp. 105, 119, 126, 127, 129, 174–75, 184, 214–15, 219, 236, 239; *Calendar of Council Minutes*, pp. 250, 252, 259, 260, 269, 288, 293, 298, 303, 322, 325; and Edith M. Fox, *Land Speculation in the Mohawk Country* (Ithaca, N. Y., 1949), pp. 3–7, 50.

19. Stokes, *Iconography*, 4:309, 634, 690, 696–97; *Calendar of · Council Minutes*, p. 385; "Bedlow's Island," *Magazine of American History* 13(1885):502–03; *New Jersey Archives*, 1st ser., 9(1885):460; NYHS *Collections*, 30(1898):285–86.

cautious path in politics. Perhaps Kennedy's experience as an outspoken supporter of the Indian policy of governors Hunter and Burnet and the vigorous local opposition it engendered soured his taste for further politicking—or at least moderated his political energies. Perhaps he simply sought to preserve his seat on the Council from factional pressures. The security of his customs and revenue-collecting positions could hardly have concerned him, since those salaries were paid from the returns of the offices and were not controlled by the Assembly. More likely Kennedy's natural temperamental reserve kept him from veering to either extreme in the colony's heated political contests.

During Governor William Cosby's hectic administration (1732–36), which was capped by the famous Zenger trial, Kennedy remained precariously but successfully on the fence, personally intimate both with Cosby and with the Zengerites, who included his Scottish cronies Colden and Alexander. Kennedy could not have been enthusiastic about Cosby's personal land-grabbing, but he felt obliged, as an instinctive "governor's man" and upholder of prerogative, to support the chief executive against the "popular party." As the Zengerites' leader, Lewis Morris, put it, Kennedy was "willing" enough to join Cosby's opponents but "dare[d]" not do so. Officially, Kennedy aided Cosby; unofficially, he informed his opposition friends of the governor's activities.[20]

Kennedy also miraculously maintained his neutrality during colonial New York's most acrimonious partisan feud, that between Governor George Clinton (1743–53) and Chief Justice James De Lancey. With fellow Scotsmen like Colden, Alexander (who served alternately as Clinton's "prime minister"), and William

20. *Colden Papers*, 2:50, 86, 143; Stanley N. Katz, *Newcastle's New York: Anglo-American Politics, 1732–1753* (Cambridge, Mass., 1968), pp. 79, 87–88, 88n; Livingston Rutherfurd, *John Peter Zenger . . .* (New York, 1904; reprinted 1941), pp. 22–23; Cosby to the Duke of Newcastle, 3 May 1733, Council to Newcastle, 17 December 1733, *N.Y. Col. Docs.*, 5:942–50, 979–85.

Smith, Sr., Kennedy became one of the "Governor's Club," which met to socialize and to plot political strategy. Kennedy edited the state papers that Colden drafted for the governor and kept both informed of the De Lancey faction's maneuvers in the Council. Yet Kennedy did not demonstrate the same intransigent hostility to the De Lanceys as his friends did, and in 1750 he even tried to negotiate a truce between the factions. By 1752, Governor Clinton, who secured an army commission for young Archibald Kennedy, Jr. as an expression of respect for the elder Kennedy's political "Interest," indicated his irritation with the latter's "timorous Temper" and with his lack of "resolution enough" to make him a reliable political ally. Other New Yorkers who enjoyed partisan politics were equally baffled by Kennedy's "squeemishness," his scrupulous attention to official regulations, and his preference for a quiet rather than an active role in the factional struggles.[21]

Whatever his vacillation and timidity in local politics, Kennedy demonstrated neither when involved with his favorite issues: Indian policy, imperial defense, and the advancement of the British Empire. Between 1750 and 1755, his pen publicly warned New York and its neighbors of the danger posed by French aggression. Kennedy wrote six essays: *Observations on the Importance of the Northern Colonies under Proper Regulations* (1750); *The Importance of Gaining and Preserving the Friendship of the Indians to*

21. *Colden Papers*, 3:215, 310–11, 335, 357–58, 4:307, 314; *N.Y. Col. Docs.*, 6:460–63; Beverly McAnear, "Politics in Provincial New York, 1689–1761" (Ph.D. diss., Stanford University, 1935), pp. 634–35, 642–44, 693 699; Katz, *Newcastle's New York*, p. 179; Clinton to John Catherwood, 18 February 1752, George Clinton Letter Book, Clements Library, Ann Arbor, Mich. For other examples of Kennedy's squeamishness, see George Clarke to Goldsbrow Banyar, 15 February 1750, 10 May 1751, 5 March 1752, 2 July 1753, and Banyar to Clarke, 23 December 1752, in Goldsbrow Banyar Papers, New York Historical Society; James Duane to Robert Livingston, Jr., 21 April 1761, Duane Manuscripts, New York Historical Society, quoted in McAnear, "Politics," p. 727.

the British Interest, Considered (1751); An Essay on the Government of the Colonies (1752); Serious Considerations on the Present State of the Affairs of the Northern Colonies (1754); A Speech Said to Have Been Delivered Some Time before the Close of the Last Sessions, By a Member Dissenting from the Church (1755); and Serious Advice to the Inhabitants of the Northern-Colonies on the Present Situation of Affairs (1755). The last five were published when written; the first was printed in 1750, circulated privately, but not published until 1765. Of the six, Kennedy acknowledged the 1750, 1751, and 1754 publications as his when they appeared. The other three appeared anonymously and have been recently identified as Kennedy's.[22]

The pamphlets represented Kennedy's extended thinking about and experience with the problem of British power in North America and of the northern colonies' utility to the empire. The prime threat to the British, he said, was France's military posture. Kennedy had arrived in the New World in the midst of the second war between the two European powers. Neither that conflict nor King George's War, which followed, proved more than a duel; both led to indecisive results and armistice rather than to peace. By 1750 the tenuous nature of that armistice had been made apparent by France's claim to the Ohio Valley, which was dramatized in 1749 by a French expedition down the river. Between that time and the appearance of Kennedy's last pamphlet, the two powers resumed unofficial but genuine hostilities. In 1752, a French-led party of Indians destroyed the British trading post at Pickawillany on the Great Miami River (now Piqua, Ohio); in 1753, the French completed a string of forts on the western border of Pennsylvania. When Virginia militia tried to oust the French from the forks of the Ohio the next year, George Washington was compelled to sur-

22. Lawrence C. Wroth, An American Bookshelf: 1755 (Philadelphia, 1934), pp. 118–26; Nicholas Varga, "New York Government and Politics during the Mid-Century" (Ph.D. diss., Fordham University, 1960), p. 11n.

render Fort Necessity and retreat to Virginia. By 1755, Britain's effort to roll back French power on the Ohio with regular troops ended ingloriously in Braddock's defeat.

In the face of this threat to Britain's North American possessions, Kennedy witnessed in New York—a lynchpin of the empire —only inaction or, at best, lukewarm reaction. Governor Clinton had become involved in a conflict with the De Lancey-controlled Assembly that had political and economic overtones and military repercussions. The Assembly refused appropriations unless it could control their disbursement; the governor insisted on his prerogative power of spending the money by his warrant. Clinton sought long-term support for the administration; the Assembly preferred annual appropriations. The governor wanted the conduct of Indian affairs under his office; the De Lanceys preferred to keep it in the hands of Albany officials who had directed relations with the Iroquois as a "Board of Commissioners for Indian Affairs."[23]

While Clinton urged the commissioners to enlist the Indians actively in hostilities against the French, the Albanians preferred to keep the Iroquois at peace, to protect Albany and its environs from Indian warfare, and to permit uninterrupted trade with Montreal. Albany sought to maintain its 1686 monopoly of the fur trade; Clinton's advisers urged opening the trade to all New Yorkers. In retaliation for Clinton's hostility and in pursuance of the Albany-favored policy, the Assembly refused adequate funds to supply the northern forts or to mollify the Iroquois.[24]

Clinton dismissed James De Lancey, leader of the Assembly-

23. Allen W. Trelease, *Indian Affairs in Colonial New York: The Seventeenth Century* (Ithaca, N.Y., 1960), ch. 8, and McIlwain, ed., *Wraxall's Abridgment*, pp. liii–lxi.

24. Buffinton, "Policy of Albany," pp. 348–52; Berne A. Pyrke, "The Dutch Fur Traders of Fort Orange and Albany," *Yearbook of the Dutch Settlers Society of Albany*, 18–19(1942–44):5–19; Alice P. Kenney, "Dutch Patricians in Colonial Albany," *New York History*, 49(1968):249–83 (especially pp. 265–68). See also A. C. Flick, ed., *History of the State of New York*, 10 vols. (New York, 1933–37), 2:225–32.

Albany coalition, as his chief adviser and turned in mid-1746 to Colden and his coterie for political advice. At the same time, Clinton turned over the management of Indian affairs to William Johnson, a successful fur trader who had gained Iroquois confidence by establishing his home on the frontier, extending his hospitality to the natives, learning the Mohawk language, and taking one (or more) of their maidens as his mistress. Johnson, commissioned "Colonel of the Warriors of the Six Nations," got the Iroquois to take up the hatchet against the French, but by 1751 he had resigned in disgust because of the Assembly's failure to compensate him for gifts to the natives. Indian policy in New York returned to its older and more lackadaisical state, and Clinton complained bitterly that "the Faction in this Province continue Resolute in pursuing their Schemes of assuming the whole executive powers into their Hands, and . . . they are willing to risque the Ruin of their Country in order to carry their Purposes." The Iroquois responded by informing Clinton, at a conference in 1753, that only Johnson's restoration to office would mend the "covenant chain," symbolic of the ancient alliance between the Six Nations and the British. The Indians would have nothing more to do with the Albanians, who cheated them in trade, defrauded them of land, and then sat comfortably at home expecting the natives to protect them from the French.[25]

Kennedy firmly advocated the Clinton-Colden-Johnson policy; in his publications he defended it and roused New Yorkers to its support. His persistent theme was the danger of neglecting the Iroquois alliance. The natives "cast the Balance" in the military

25. Ibid., 2:188–91; Keys, *Colden,* pp. 132–43; James T. Flexner, *Mohawk Baronet* (New York, 1959), chapters 3 and 5; Clinton to the Board of Trade, 19 November 1751, Colonial Office Papers, 5:1064, pp. 47–51, Public Record Office, London; Clinton to the Duke of Newcastle, 8 June 1746, Clinton to the Duke of Bedford, 15 November 1748, in George Clinton Papers, Clements Library, Ann Arbor, Mich.; Nammack, *Iroquois Land Frontier,* pp. 31–38.

scales of North America, he said; if the French became "absolute Masters of the Indians, adieu to our *English* settlements." Kennedy regarded Indian friendship as more important strategically than commercially. At one time he expressed willingness to surrender the entire fur trade to the French. Its profits to New Yorkers he regarded as minimal, scarcely enough to pay for a fraction of the colony's British imports. Sensible, however, of the De Lancey group's direct interest in the trade, he stressed the economic as well as the military benefits of the Indian connection in *The Importance of Gaining and Preserving the Friendship of the Indians* (1751), the fullest exposition of his views on this subject. A well-managed Indian trade could be entirely engrossed by the British within twenty years, he said, because of the natives' preference for British goods. It would be necessary only to cut off the trade between Albany and Montreal, to remove duties on British goods destined for the Indian trade, and to insure fair dealings with the natives.[26]

Like Governor Clinton, Thomas Pownall (a recent arrival to New York from England), and Peter Wraxall (New York's Indian Secretary after 1750), Kennedy denounced the Albany Indian Commissioners as a "Tribe of Harpies" who had "abused, defrauded, and deceived" the natives for years.[27] Kennedy particularly criticized the Albanians' dual role as both public officials and private traders, which often led them to cheat those they should protect and to sell privately to the Indians the goods they were

26. Kennedy: *Serious Advice* (1755), p. 16; *Observations* (1750), pp. 6, 9; *The Importance of . . . the Indians*, pp. 12–13, 22; see also *An Essay* (1752), pp. 39–40.
27. Kennedy, *The Importance of . . . the Indians*, pp. 5–6. Pownall virtually duplicated Kennedy's criticism of the Albany Commissioners in his "Notes on Indian Affairs, 1753–1754," Loudoun Papers, no. 460, Huntington Library, cited in Nammack, *Iroquois Land Frontier*, p. 31; see also John A. Schutz, *Thomas Pownall, British Defender of American Liberty* (Glendale, Calif., 1951), pp. 39–40. Wraxall's denunciation of the Albanians appears in his *Abridgment of the Indian Affairs*, pp. 61n, 66n, and 132n.

commissioned to give them officially. In contrast, Kennedy pointed to the Massachusetts system of public trading posts ("truck-houses") operated by state officials who traded at fixed prices and thereby set a standard for Indian dealings by private traders.[28]

Kennedy's most original proposal was for the designation of a single "Superintendent of Indian Affairs," appointed and paid by the Crown and assisted by interpreters and gunsmiths. The latter would be stationed in Indian villages to repair firearms, teach the English language, and serve as official fur traders at prices fixed by law. The Superintendent would make annual tours of the Indian country to receive complaints and correct injustices and would report to the Crown through the governor and Council of New York. In place of the Albany monopoly, Kennedy proposed a wide-open trade in the hope of raising a corps of English "bushlopers" to compete with the French *coureurs de bois*. To strengthen the frontier and provide protection for Britain's Indian allies, Kennedy suggested a string of forts, manned by additional regular troops (preferably rugged Scottish Highlanders), and a series of new townships to be settled by Irish, Scotch, and Dutch immigrants attracted by rent-free land grants.[29]

Kennedy's plea for centralized direction of Indian policy reflected his larger disillusionment with provincial assemblies, either as reliable instruments for managing Indian affairs or as bulwarks of imperial defense; he reiterated this theme in virtually all of his publications. "From Assemblies, by Experience," he wrote in 1750, "we have little to hope for." They were uninformed and, worse, preoccupied with local issues, the gratification of "particular Resentments," and "grasping at more Power than may be consistent with a proper Ballance." The strength of the British con-

28. Kennedy, *The Importance of . . . the Indians*, pp. 15–16; Ronald D. Macfarlane, "The Massachusetts Bay Truck-Houses in Diplomacy with the Indians," *New England Quarterly* 11(1938):48–65; and Leach, *Northern Frontier*, pp. 147–49.

29. Kennedy, *The Importance of . . . the Indians*, pp. 7–10, 13–15.

stitution—the envy of "every State and Power on Earth"—was its "regular Mixture" of the elements of monarchy, aristocracy, and democracy. The "due Poise" of the colonial constitution lay in the balance among governor, Council, and Assembly, and the most persistent challenge to it came from the assemblies' encroachment on the royal prerogative. Kennedy went so far as to assert the extreme Tory theory that the colonies were fiefs of the Crown, "no more than a little Corporation," their powers no more than privileges as "Tenants at Will."[30]

In place of local control, Kennedy urged a collective defense and unified management of Indian affairs. From the Crown he asked the appointment of a single Indian superintendent and two additional companies of British regulars for duty on the frontier. From the colonies Kennedy sought an intercolonial defense force and the forts and supplies required to house them. Troop quotas and financial levies would be fixed at an intercolonial meeting of commissioners held annually at Albany or New York City. The meeting would also apportion contributions toward subsidizing the importation of immigrants for the new frontier townships: each colony could perhaps sponsor a single settlement. Kennedy suggested a liquor excise or a duty on furs and goods used in Indian trade as appropriate revenues to finance the Indian program. Such a "confederated" effort, he believed, would not only relieve New York of its excessively heavy defense burden but also awe the Indians and "strike Terror into the French."[31]

By 1755, Kennedy stridently favored united colonial action. France, he stressed, was more than a match for any single colony,

---

30. Kennedy, *Observations* . . . , p. 7. Kennedy, *An Essay* . . . , pp. 10–15, 17–20, 22, 32–33. William Smith, Jr. observed in 1757 that the "contradiction of sentiments" between Kennedy and most New Yorkers—who held that they were "entitled to all the privileges of Englishmen" as a matter of right—naturally produced "contentions." (Smith, *History*, 1:307–08.)

31. Kennedy, *The Importance of . . . the Indians*, pp. 8–11, 17–18, 22; Kennedy, *An Essay*, p. 39.

as Fort Necessity had demonstrated. Even though Washington's surrender placed New York's "most inveterate hereditary Enemies, actually in view upon our Backs," the Assembly dallied over the nature of the new college (King's) and ignored Virginia's appeal for assistance. Incredulously, Kennedy exclaimed: "When a Neighbor's House is a Fire, every one runs." Self-interest no less than humanity dictated collective action. The business would "admit of no longer Delay." To quibble over the precise contribution of each colony invited disaster. On a more positive note, he assured the colonists of victory in view of their respective thousand-to-one and twenty-to-one superiority in materials and men. Only "Want of Unanimity and Spirit" were lacking. A single military commander, headquartered at Albany and advised by an intercolonial war council, and a general fund fixed by Parliament and raised within the colonies by quotas, along the lines of the Albany Plan of 1754, would insure Indian participation and bring certain success. The alternative was a French-Indian alliance, French seizure of Albany and the Hudson Valley, and dissection of the mainland settlements. Such a defeat at the hands of the French would "convert rich, flourishing free People" into "mean slaves to a *French* King."[32]

Kennedy knew of the home government's disinclination to add to its own expenses on the colonies' behalf ("let us not at this Time burden too much our Mother Country, she probably may have enough upon her Hands, and that too chiefly on our Accounts") and he carefully pointed out that his proposed program could be achieved at minimal cost to Britain. The salary of the new Indian superintendent could be secured by eliminating one of the two American surveyor-general positions. Although he more than once mentioned the possibility of returns from duties on Indian trade goods, Kennedy's own experience with customs collections

32. Kennedy, *A Speech* (1755), pp. 33–37; Kennedy, *Serious Advice*, pp. 3, 5–7, 15, 16–17.

gave him little hope that such a source would raise enough. In 1750 he estimated that the returns from customs in all the northern colonies could not support the four independent companies in New York for a single year. His more practical substitute was a high quitrent on royally-granted lands. This would not only produce a significant revenue but also discourage the retention of large, speculatively acquired tracts which remained unpeopled and hence weakened the frontier. Kennedy would rather grant frontier lands without rents or fees to bona fide settlers than see the land remain vacant while owned by absentee proprietors.[33]

Kennedy paralleled his blunt admonitions to the colonies with some equally forthright advice to the mother country. Once the French menace was eliminated, he said, Britain must bind the northern colonies by ties more durable and beneficial than the existing Acts of Trade. Kennedy had some harsh words for the Wool, Hat, and Molasses Acts. While the first compelled New Yorkers to buy their woolens from England, the last barred them from a source of the hard cash they needed to pay for such imports. And the Hat Act foolishly denied New Yorkers a legitimate industry which did not compete with Britain's, since American hats were made from waste furs not suitable for export. Nor did Kennedy have high regard for the enumerating of specified articles of colonial production for export to England. Such a practice he called "a Solecism in Trade, and the Bane of Industry"; the colonists properly resented any restraining laws which they had had "no hand in . . . contriving or making."

Kennedy dismissed the foodstuffs upon which New Yorkers concentrated so much of their productive energies as unsound and inadequate bases for the colony's prosperity. Only the West Indies used New York's wheat and flour; Britain could obtain beef and butter more easily from Ireland; the rum industry depended on

33. Kennedy, *Serious Advice*, p. 6; *The Importance of . . . the Indians*, pp. 8, 13; *Observations*, p. 20; *An Essay*, pp. 37–39.

French and Spanish sugar and molasses imports. Even furs and flaxseed exports gave New York returns no greater than needed to pay the cost of "the Apparatus of our Tea Tables."[34]

In place of "Violence and oppressive Laws," Kennedy urged "Liberty and Encouragement" to make the northern colonies prosperous and consequently advantageous to the mother country. Specifically he proposed that Britain aggressively and systematically encourage shipbuilding and naval stores in the northern colonies, taking advantage of their timber and iron and their hemp-growing soil capacity. The colonists should be encouraged by cash prizes to engage in pitch, tar, and hemp production. Iron production should be encouraged by removal of all British duties on iron importation. Shipbuilding should be promoted by attracting skilled workers from England. Master craftsmen from abroad should train the colonists in logging, shipbuilding, potash manufacture, and pitch and tar extraction; the newcomers should be rewarded by liberal grants of land and by freedom from taxes and the obligation of military service for seven years. An export tax on foodstuffs and a more energetic collection of quitrents would pay for the prizes and the bounties.[35]

Unless the northern colonies were thus "usefully employed," Kennedy foresaw only a combination of increasing British neglect, declining colonial prosperity, and, in self-defense, channeling of American energies into industries directly competitive with the home country. Kennedy did not rule out the possibility of a movement for colonial independence. His own preference was truly mercantilist—a symbiotic relationship between colony and mother country that would benefit both:

34. Kennedy, *Observations*, pp. 8–10, 19. L. H. Gipson has called Kennedy's criticism of the Acts of Trade "courageous" in view of his position as a royal officeholder in *The British Empire before the American Revolution*, rev. ed., 15 vols. (New York, 1936–71), 3:240n.
35. Kennedy, *Observations*, pp. 11, 14–18, 27–28.

. . . it is infallibly true, that whatever Wealth the Plantations gain, by any Article of Trade that doth not directly interfere with the Trade of Great-Britain, is so much Gain to Great-Britain, since every such Acquisition is sure to center there at last; and therefore, it is the Interest of Great-Britain to encourage and promote the Industry and Labour of the Plantations; which never fails to increase the Wealth and Power of Great-Britain; and is the Case of all distant Provinces, with respect to their Mother Countries, which always increase in Power in Proportion as their Colonies flourish.[36]

Virtually every argument and almost all the evidence Kennedy presented in his other pamphlets were included in his *Serious Considerations on the Present State of the Affairs of the Northern Colonies*, which appeared in 1754, shortly after the Albany Congress. This essay was apparently written while the conference was in session, although Kennedy himself was not invited by Lieutenant Governor De Lancey as one of New York's four representatives. Nonetheless, Benjamin Franklin must have kept Kennedy informed of the Congress's deliberations. (The two had already conferred about Franklin's plan of union.) William Smith, Sr., one of the New York delegation, must also have advised Kennedy of the proceedings.[37]

The 1754 pamphlet endorsed the work of the Congress and urged approval of its recommendations upon both colonists and British officials. Kennedy found such a public plea easy to make, since many of the Congress's suggestions echoed views he had

36. Ibid., Preface, pp. 10, 20–23, 30, 31. Kennedy's thoughts along these lines had been outlined earlier in a memo to Clinton, 27 November 1744, George Clinton Papers, Clements Library.

37. The Albany Congress ended on 11 July, and Kennedy's pamphlet was advertised for sale in the *New-York Gazette, or Weekly Post-Boy* on 12 August. Robert C. Newbold, *The Albany Congress and Plan of Union of 1754* (New York, 1955), p. 41; Franklin to Alexander, 8 June 1754, Alexander to Colden, 9 June 1754, in *The Papers of Benjamin Franklin*, ed. Leonard W. Labaree, 13 vols. to date (New Haven, 1959—), 5:337–41; Colden to Franklin, 20 June 1754, Alexander to Colden, 26 July 1754, Colden to Alexander, ? August 1754, in *Colden Papers*, 4:449–51, 459–61, 9:140.

already expressed publicly in his own writings: vigorous, united action against French encroachments; centralized and honest management of Indian affairs; maintenance of Indian friendship; preservation of public as well as private interest in the fur trade; erection of forts in Indian country; prevention of fraud in land transactions with the natives; settlement of large tracts of unoccupied land. The Congress also stressed the necessity of a colonial union to achieve those ends. Colden found these proposals "just and impartial," and Kennedy appealed to the colonial assemblies for "a hearty and generous Concurrence" in the Congress's recommendations.[38]

In his *Serious Considerations*, Kennedy criticized Britain for failing to prevent the erection of a French fort at Crown Point on Lake Champlain, for missing the opportunity of fortifying Niagara Falls, for returning Louisbourg at the end of King George's War, and for "total Neglect of Indian Affairs." The Indians, he reemphasized, were the key to British military success. The tactics of regular European-trained troops were of far less value in an American campaign than were those of the natives. Should the French recruit the Indians in their cause, woe to New York, besieged by French regulars and the French navy at the mouth of the Hudson and by French-led tribes at the northern end. Kennedy reiterated his suggestions for retaining the allegiance of the natives: extending the Massachusetts "truck-house" system to other colonies, assuring Indians fair prices for their furs, erecting forts in Indian country to protect the tribes and the smiths and ministers settled in their villages, and augmenting the British garrisons with companies of rugged Scotch Highlanders and Indian-style rangers.[39]

Two of the Albany conference's recommendations Kennedy found especially praiseworthy: the centralization of Indian policy

---

38. Newbold, *Albany Congress*, pp. 80–86; Colden to Alexander, ? August 1754, *Colden Papers*, 9:140; Kennedy, *Serious Considerations*, p. 14.
39. Kennedy, *Serious Considerations*, pp. 4–6, 9–13.

and the formation of an intercolonial union. Both had been his own ideas; through Franklin, they had been passed on to the conferees. The first was incorporated into policy by the British government when, in 1756, it created two Indian superintendencies and named William Johnson to head the northern and Edmond Atkin the southern departments.

Many claimed the honor of fathering the Indian superintendencies, and it may be easier to apportion credit among them all than to assign it exclusively to any one of them. As early as 1748 Governor Clinton and Governor William Shirley of Massachusetts had recommended replacing the Albany commissioners with "one or more suitable persons," but the proposal went no further. Peter Wraxall's *Abridgment of the Indian Affairs*, written in 1754, became a report to the home government and was forwarded that same year to Lord Halifax. Wraxall, a friend of William Johnson, studded his "objective" account of Indian affairs with footnote criticism of the Albanians; his report may have influenced the final official action. Thomas Pownall, an observer of the Albany Congress and a person of influence at home through his brother, the secretary of the Board of Trade, later stated that a report he prepared for the Board on the Albany proceedings produced Johnson's appointment. Yet Pownall acknowledged that he based his report largely on Kennedy's 1751 pamphlet, which expressed its position so cogently, Pownall conceded, that "nothing can be added to what Mr. Kennedy has said."[40] Edmond Atkin, a South Carolina merchant and Indian trader and a member of that colony's Governor's Council, sent a report on Indian affairs to the

40. Sullivan and Flick, eds., *Johnson Papers*, 2:434–35; Wilbur R. Jacobs, ed., *The Appalachian Indian Frontier: The Edmond Atkin Report and Plan of 1755* (Lincoln, Neb., 1967), p. xxiin; Clinton and Shirley to the Lords of Trade, 18 August 1748, in *N.Y. Col. Docs.*, 6:437–40; McIlwain, ed., *Wraxall's Abridgment*, pp. xcv, xcvii–c; Schutz, *Thomas Pownall*, pp. 41–43; and Pownall, "Notes on Indian Affairs, 1753–1754," Loudoun Papers, Huntington Library, quoted in Nammack, *Iroquois Land Frontier*, p. 39.

Board of Trade in 1755 in which he proposed the appointment of "two fit Persons" to conduct relations with the northern and southern tribes. John R. Alden, in our own day, has attributed the creation of the Indian superintendencies to the recommendations of the Albany Congress.[41] However, none can assert priority over Kennedy's public proposal in 1751 of a single office for the management of Indian affairs. The lines of influence cannot be drawn precisely, but Kennedy's recommendations became publicly and privately known in England shortly after their appearance in New York.

The essay on Indian affairs was republished in an English edition in 1752 and received favorable notice in London for "judiciously" pointing out a method of preserving Indian friendship and maintaining British power in America against "the superior arts and assiduous encroachments of our politic neighbours, the *French*." Three years later, the pamphlet was cited approvingly and quoted liberally by the unknown author of *The State of the British and French Colonies in North America*.[42] Kennedy himself did not direct his views to the attention of any British officials, but Cadwallader Colden, after seeing a draft of Kennedy's essay, incorporated its principal ideas in a memorandum for Governor Clinton in August 1751, and the latter transmitted it to the Board of Trade in October of the same year.[43]

In a less direct way, Kennedy was also an architect of the 1754

41. Jacobs, ed., *Appalachian Frontier*, pp. 77–78; John R. Alden, "The Albany Congress and the Creation of the Indian Superintendencies," *Mississippi Valley Historical Review* 27(1940):193–210.

42. *Monthly Review* 6(1752):150. See pp. 69, 74, 88–89, 93–94, 96, 101 of the *State of the British and French Colonies in North America* (London, 1755).

43. Kennedy to Colden, 15 April 1751, and "The present state of the Indian affairs . . . in North America . . . ," 8 August 1751, in *Colden Papers*, 4:264, 271–87; Clinton to the Lords of Trade 1 October 1751, N.Y. *Col. Docs.*, 6:738–47. For the only disparaging comment, see Shuckburgh to Johnson, 14 May 1751, in Sullivan and Flick, eds., *Johnson Papers*, 1:332.

Albany Plan of Union. The origins of this colonial federation have been controverted by modern historians, notably Lawrence H. Gipson and Verner Crane, who respectively hold for Thomas Hutchinson and Benjamin Franklin.[44] Whatever the merits of each case, Kennedy played a role in both. His *Importance of Gaining and Preserving the Friendship of the Indians* first publicly proposed an intercolonial approach to imperial defense and Indian policy and specifically suggested an annual meeting of colonial commissioners to fix troop quotas, apportion the expense of erecting forts, and jointly subsidize the importation of immigrants to settle new frontier townships. Hutchinson was probably familiar with Kennedy's publication, although the evidence is inferential rather than direct. Franklin read Kennedy's essay in draft form, and his endorsement of it appeared as an appendix to the publication. Franklin had nothing to offer "for the improvement of the Author's Piece," but expressed some reservations about the use of German settlers in frontier townships and the propriety of a Crown-initiated union as against a "voluntary Union entered into by the Colonies, themselves." Franklin also preferred rotating the site of the annual congress to fixing it permanently in New York. Inspired by Kennedy's rather general suggestion for a colonial confederation, Franklin's endorsement spelled out a more detailed scheme. The latter then became the nucleus of Franklin's "Short Hints towards a Scheme for Uniting the Northern Colonies," composed in 1754 and presented to the Albany Congress. Kennedy's influence again appeared when Franklin sent his "Short Hints" to Kennedy's colleagues Colden and Alexander for their re-

44. Gipson, *British Empire before the American Revolution*, 5:128–29, and "Thomas Hutchinson and the Framing of the Albany Plan of Union, 1754," *Pennsylvania Magazine of History and Biography* 74(1950):5–35. Crane challenged in the same journal, 75(1951):350–53; Gipson responded on pp. 129–36 of the same magazine and in another article, "Massachusetts Bay and American Colonial Union, 1754," *Proceedings of the American Antiquarian Society* 71 (1961):63–92.

view prior to the Albany meeting and showed the paper personally to Kennedy in New York City early in June, before the opening of the conference.[45]

Kennedy, like Colden, was less concerned with the details of the plan adopted by the Congress than with the urgency of some confederation. In his *Serious Considerations,* he stressed the close connection among the French threat, Indian affairs, and colonial union. The logic of his exposition was simple: France was Britain's "implacable and most inveterate" enemy, whose goal could be accomplished in America only by seducing the Indians and splitting the colonies. In both methods the English had unwittingly aided the French. Years of "cheating and abusing" the natives had taken their toll of Indian good will; the Albany commissioners and the direct trade with Montreal had undermined Indian friendship. Then, far from meeting the challenge, the English colonies had quibbled over the expenses of a military effort and declined to aid each other. Kennedy especially criticized New Jersey for failing to send a delegation to Albany, an indefensible action he attributed to the "Caprice of a few Assemblymen."[46]

Kennedy reminded New Yorkers of their myopia in failing to heed Virginia's appeal for aid, and he warned them of the "fatal Effects" of provincialism and of a "parsimonious Disposition" by the Assembly. Mixing emotionalism with reasoned argumentation, Kennedy concluded with an appeal to the patriotism as well as the good sense of the colonists. Indolence and disunity would dissolve the British Empire in North America, he said; public spirit

45. Kennedy to Colden, 15 April 1751, in *Colden Papers,* 4:264; Franklin to Alexander, 8 June 1754, Alexander to Colden, 9 June 1754, in *Franklin Papers,* 5:337–38, 339–41, 381n; *The Autobiography of Benjamin Franklin,* ed. Leonard W. Labaree (New Haven, 1964), p. 210.
46. Colden to Kennedy, ? August 1754, *Colden Papers,* 9:140; Kennedy, *Serious Considerations,* pp. 3, 6, 8, 10, 18–19, 22–23; Donald L. Kemmerer, *Path to Freedom: The Struggle for Self-Government in Colonial New Jersey* (Princeton, 1940), pp. 240–41; Newbold, *Albany Congress,* pp. 38–39.

and union would preserve "our Religion, our Liberties and our Properties, and upwards of a Hundred Years Labour in these wild Desarts [sic], for the sake of our Posterity." Kennedy closed with one of the many classical quotations which studded his pamphlets: "In peace, like a wise man, provide for the needs of war."[47]

Kennedy's forceful appeal for colonial union had no more effect than did those of other partisans of the Albany Plan. The confederation proposed in 1754 fell victim to the suspicions of colonial assemblies and the shortsightedness of British officialdom. Kennedy himself continued to sound the alarm for a vigorous united policy against the French in the two pamphlets he published in 1755, but these new entreaties were no more successful than the earlier one. The 1754 essay, republished the same year in a British edition, was well received for its "important and useful hints" toward checking French expansion and "retrieving our declining credit with the *Indians.*" Franklin had the pamphlet reprinted in Philadelphia, and two years later a second New York printing appeared.[48]

Kennedy's last three pamphlets were published in New York anonymously, although he acknowledged authorship of *Serious Considerations* in the British edition. The reason for the half-hearted attempt at anonymity is unclear. Perhaps, as a Council member, Kennedy preferred not to be known for publications so critical of the Assembly. Whatever the reason, contemporary readers seemed to identify the author readily, since many wrote the name "Archibald Kennedy" on the title pages of their copies.

One almost immediate effect of the appearance of *Serious Considerations* in New York was political and partisan. In two places

47. Kennedy, *Serious Considerations,* pp. 15, 17. The Latin is "*In pace, ut sapiens, aptarit idonea bello*" (Horace, *Satires,* 2:2, 111).
48. Alison G. Olson, "The British Government and Colonial Union, 1754," *William and Mary Quarterly* 17(1960):22–34; *Monthly Review* 11(1754):316.

in the pamphlet, Kennedy scoffed at the young lawyers William Livingston, William Smith, Jr., and John Morin Scott for using their reform journal, *The Independent Reflector* (published 1752–53), to expose municipal corruption and the vices of the clergy and for using their professional talents to serve as legal counsel to New Jersey farmers engaged in a bitter land squabble with the proprietors of that province. In Kennedy's view, these advocates of civic virtue might better expose the New York Assembly's delinquency in defense matters and criticize the Jerseyites for nonattendance at the Albany Congress. The triumvirate took up Kennedy's challenge, and in two New York newspapers they argued more fervidly than Kennedy for colonial union and concerted action against the French.[49] They leveled charges of apathy and inaction against Lieutenant Governor De Lancey, their political foe, as well as against the New York Assembly.

Having burst onto the historical scene in the mid-1750s after some forty years of relative obscurity, Kennedy seems to have faded into that same historic concealment thereafter. He remained on the Governor's Council until 1761, when he asked to be relieved. A few years earlier, he had had the satisfaction of issuing the formal declaration of war against France in the Governor's absence. Kennedy continued to associate with his Scottish friends, both socially and politically, and in 1756 helped found the New York Saint Andrew's Society.[50]

By avoiding active participation in most of the heated political

49. Kennedy, *Serious Considerations* pp. 7, 22–23; Milton M. Klein, ed., *The Independent Reflector* (Cambridge, Mass., 1963), pp. 378–79, 434–35; "The Watch-Tower," *New-York Mercury*, 13 January, 20 January, 24 February, 21 July, 4 August, 11 August, 18 August, 22 September 1755; *The Instructor*, 6 March–8 May 1755.

50. Moncton to the Lords of Trade, 10 November 1761, in *N.Y. Col. Docs.*, 7:471; *Journal of the Legislative Council*, 2:1445; Stokes, *Iconography*, 4:682; David B. Morrison, *Two Hundredth Anniversary of Saint Andrew's Society of the State of New York* (New York, 1956), p. 8.

controversies of his day, Kennedy escaped factional criticism from his contemporaries. He differed with the Livingston triumvirate on the establishment and operation of Kings' College, but his temperate arguments spared him that trio's characteristically caustic rejoinder. At worst, politicians regarded Kennedy as cautious or indecisive. Few, however, could gainsay the "Honour and Fidelity" of his service to the Crown during his half-century residence in New York. Upon his death on 14 June 1763, he was eulogized as "a Gentleman who always sustain'd a fair and amiable Character" and whose passing was "universally lamented by all his Acquaintance[s]." Thomas Jones, New York's Tory historian of the revolution, praised Kennedy as one of those "sensible, honest, worthy men, of opulent fortunes, unblemished characters and fair reputations" who had adorned the Governor's Council during the colonial period. The portrait is overdrawn. Kennedy was never entirely disinterested in his public efforts, but on the larger issues his focus was always on the British Empire and on the advantages it brought to the colonies and to the mother country. As "that loyal and comfortable servant of the crown," Kennedy merits more historiographic visibility than he allowed himself.[51]

51. Beverly McAnear, "American Imprints concerning King's College," *Papers of the Bibliographical Society of America*, 44(1950):301–39 (especially p. 326); Moncton to the Lords of Trade, 10 November 1761, in *N.Y. Col. Docs.*, 7:471; Weyman's *New-York Gazette*, 20 June 1763; *New-York Mercury*, 20 June 1763; Edwin F. De Lancey, ed., *History of New York during the Revolutionary War*, 2 vols. (New York, 1879), 1:12n; Richard E. Day, "A Summary of the English Period," in Flick, ed., *History of the State of New York*, 3:112.

5.

William Livingston's A Review of the Military Operations in North-America*

Milton M. Klein

The Anglo-French wars that began in 1689 and lasted for almost a century involved all the British colonies in America, but none more so than New York. It stood in closest proximity to Canada, commanded the land approaches to Montreal and Quebec, and, via the Great Lakes, controlled the water passage between the French settlements on the St. Lawrence and the Ohio and Mississippi rivers. Albany was Montreal's principal rival in the fur trade, and New York was Canada's competitor for the friendship and alliance of the Six Nations of the Iroquois Confederacy. New Yorkers always harbored a special fear of France, for conflict between the Bourbon monarchy and England exposed the New York frontier to the horrors of Indian warfare. New York always considered itself a special target of French military strategy.[1]

New York did not always translate its perception of its crucial position in Anglo-French relations into commensurate military or political action. The disparity is explained by economic and practical considerations. Albany's fur traders, having long ago ex-

* Acknowledgement is made to the Faculty Research Fund, University of Tennessee, Knoxville, for assistance in the preparation of this essay.

1. The best account of New York's role in the Anglo-French wars is Arthur H. Buffinton, "The Colonial Wars and their Results," in A. C. Flick, ed., *History of the State of New York*, 10 vols. (New York, 1933–37), 1:ch. 6.

hausted the local supply of skins, had come to depend on two sources for beaver: the western Great Lakes and Mississippi Valley region, and Montreal. The latter was both convenient and profitable, since it saved the Albanians the effort of either trapping or engaging in retail trade with individual Indians, but it was of doubtful political desirability. The French wanted British manufactures for their own dealings with the natives, and the wholesale traffic with Albany permitted them to exchange their furs in bulk for British cloth and other products. That such a commerce strengthened French ties with the Indians seemed not to trouble the Albany traders; indeed, they continued it even in wartime, negotiating an informal truce with Canada during Queen Anne's War that kept the Indians neutral and trade uninterrupted. These objectives were readily achieved since the colony's official agency for dealing with the Iroquois, the Board of Indian Commissioners, was made up of men who were themselves traders or related to dealers in furs. A second and more personal advantage to the Albanians was that such a neutrality spared their homes from surprise French and French-Indian attacks.[2]

Not all New Yorkers were as solicitous of the personal and financial interests of the Albany traders. Those with imperial rather than provincial outlooks were horrified by the Montreal-Albany fur traffic, which strengthened France's hold on the very tribes whose loyalty the British were trying to maintain. Those engaged in retail trade with the Indians resented the easy profits of the Albany wholesalers and their New York City merchant

2. On the Albany-Montreal trade, see Buffinton, "The Policy of Albany and English Westward Expansion," *Mississippi Valley Historical Review* 8(1922):327–66; Charles H. McIlwain, ed., *An Abridgment of the Indian Affairs . . . by Peter Wraxall* (Cambridge, Mass., 1915), pp. xxxv–lxxxv; Allen W. Trelease, *Indian Affairs in Colonial New York: The Seventeenth Century* (Ithaca, N.Y., 1960), ch. 8; Douglas E. Leach, *The Northern Colonial Frontier, 1607–1763* (New York, 1966), pp. 149–56; Lawrence H. Leder, *Robert Livingston, 1654–1728, and the Politics of Colonial New York* (Chapel Hill, 1961), chapters 15 and 16.

suppliers. And those who aimed at driving France out of North America considered the Albanians veritable traitors for sacrificing long-term political interests to short-term private gains.

The long and protracted conflict between the two groups became entangled in New York's already complicated local politics.[3] An effort by Governor William Burnet (1720–28) to interdict the Montreal-Albany commerce and to establish British trading posts on Lake Ontario was defeated by the influence of the Albany traders and their British suppliers. Future governors abandoned the effort and concentrated on strengthening New York's frontier and securing control of Lake Ontario, hoping thereby to assure the colony's security and weaken French influence with the natives. The "neutralists" used their control of the New York Assembly to haggle over gubernatorial requests for funds for frontier posts and to obstruct every effort to transfer Indian affairs from the Albany commissioners to the chief executive. Political considerations again intruded as the assembly insisted on maintaining control over the disbursement of funds for military purposes while the governor claimed these matters as a royal prerogative.

During King George's War (1744–48), the interplay of local and imperial politics reached a climax. Governor George Clinton, who arrived in New York in 1743, ardently advocated a vigorous war policy, but, as a naval officer without political experience, he was poorly equipped to cope with the intricacies of factional alignments and to manage astute politicians.[4] He early allied himself

3. On the connection between the fur trade and New York local politics, see Milton M. Klein, "Democracy and Politics in Colonial New York," *New York History* 40(1959):221–46 (especially pp. 223–28) and Stanley N. Katz, *Newcastle's New York: Anglo-American Politics, 1732–1753* (Cambridge, Mass., 1968), pp. 171–73.

4. On Clinton's administration and his frustrations, see Katz, *Newcastle's New York*, chs. 7 and 8, and Nicholas Varga, "New York Government and Politics during the Mid-Eighteenth Century" (Ph.D. diss., Fordham University, 1960), chs. 2 and 3. As even Cadwallader Colden, his later confidant and supporter, put it, Clinton "was educated in the Sea Service and was little

with James De Lancey, a member of the council and chief justice of the Supreme Court. Clinton naïvely failed to recognize in De Lancey an ambitious future political rival and also a leading merchant specializing in goods for the Indian trade between Albany and Montreal. In 1744 Clinton generously offered De Lancey a new judicial commission "during good behaviour" rather than at the customary "pleasure" of the Crown—thus effectively freeing him from Clinton's control—and appointed four of De Lancey's friends to the council. De Lancey also cajoled the governor into violating his instructions by accepting both an annual salary instead of a long-term support and an appropriation bill which allocated funds to individuals named by the assembly rather than allowing the monies to be expended upon the governor's warrant. Still unaware of the power he had already entrusted to De Lancey, Clinton offered him command of the New York forces raised for an expedition against Canada; and when De Lancey declined the appointment for personal reasons, Clinton named a replacement proposed by the chief justice.[5]

Clinton's confidence in his political adviser was shaken when the De Lancey-dominated Assembly declined to appropriate funds for the attack against Canada or to fortify posts such as Oswego

conversant in any other publick affairs." William Smith, Jr. described Clinton's principal weakness as his tendency to associate with "a little trifling circle," a "manner of living . . . the very reverse of that requisite to make a party or make friends." Colden to Dr. John Mitchell, 6 July 1749, *The Letters and Papers of Cadwallader Colden*, 9 vols. (New York Historical Society *Collections*, 1917–23, 1934–35 [New York, 1918–37]), 9:20 (hereafter cited as *Colden Papers*); William Smith, *The History of the Late Province of New-York from its Discovery to the Appointment of Governor Clinton in 1762*, 2 vols. (New York, 1830), 2:158.

5. Katz, *Newcastle's New York*, pp. 168–69. There is no biography of De Lancey other than Edward F. De Lancey, "Memoir of James De Lancey," in E. B. O'Callaghan, ed., *Documentary History of the State of New York*, 4 vols. (Albany, N.Y., 1849–51), 4:1037–59. Clinton to De Lancey, 24 August 1746; De Lancey to Clinton, 30 August 1746; Clinton to Captain [John] Roberts, September 1746, in George Clinton Papers, William L. Clements Library, Ann Arbor, Mich.

on Lake Ontario. A new house elected in 1745 proved somewhat more cooperative, but it irritated Clinton by insisting on naming the distributors of army supplies and on seeing the governor's entire war plan before voting money for an expedition against the French fort at Crown Point on Lake Champlain. Embittered, Clinton blamed De Lancey for his difficulties. The two men parted company early in 1746 over De Lancey's refusal to aid passage of an amendment to a Militia Bill providing for punishment of deserters. "The altercations ran so high," historian William Smith, Jr. recorded, "that Mr. De Lancey left the table with an oath of revenge, and they became thenceforth irreconcilable foes." By 1747 the break between the two men was complete and open. De Lancey refused to aid Clinton in preparing his state papers, he criticized the governor's messages, and his supporters spread rumors that Clinton would be replaced by De Lancey's brother-in-law, Sir Peter Warren. Clinton, for his part, wrote a long and tedious series of letters complaining of the "faction" formed to "distress" him and make his administration "uneasy."[6]

The personal animosity between Clinton and De Lancey had its military repercussions. While the governor sought a vigorous prosecution of the war, De Lancey now openly advocated the old-style neutrality and continuation of the Albany-Montreal trade. Since the Albany Indian commissioners were, in Clinton's words,

6. Beverly McAnear, "Politics in Provincial New York, 1689–1761" (Ph.D. diss., Stanford University, 1935), pp. 585–94; Clinton to the Duke of Newcastle, 18 November 1745, in E. B. O'Callaghan, ed., *Documents Relative to the Colonial History of the State of New York*, 15 vols. (Albany, N.Y., 1856–87), 6:281–85 (hereafter cited as *N.Y. Col. Docs.*); Colden to Dr. John Mitchell, 6 July 1749, *Colden Papers*, 9:21–32; Clinton to the New York Council, 18 October 1746, Miscellaneous manuscripts, Clements Library; Varga, "New York Government," pp. 88–89; Katz, *Newcastle's New York*, pp. 169–71; Smith, *History*, 2:83; Clinton to the Duke of Newcastle, 9 December 1746 and 22 June 1747, *N.Y. Col. Docs.*, 6:312–14, 352–57; "State of . . . Geo[rge] Clinton's Case with regard to his Admin[istration] in New York . . ." [1747?], George Clinton Papers, Clements Library, Ann Arbor, Mich.

"well wishers" for neutrality, the governor transferred control of Indian affairs to William Johnson, a young Irishman and independent trader. For political advice, Clinton turned to a veteran councilor, Cadwallader Colden. Johnson managed to enlist the Iroquois in the war, but Colden failed to secure money from the assembly to prosecute it. The executive and legislative branches continued to engage in bitter partisan strife, leaving New York little energy for the war with the French.[7]

Clinton's allies in maintaining the royal prerogative and promoting a strong war policy included Johnson, Colden, royal receiver-general and customs collector Archibald Kennedy, and James Alexander, a member of the New Jersey Council and a prominent lawyer in New York City. These men could not muster sufficient political strength, however, to counter the De Lancey forces. Colden retired as "prime minister" in 1748, Johnson gave up his Indian agency in 1751 when the assembly refused to reimburse him for his expenditures, and Kennedy retreated to a discreet neutrality. Clinton spent the last years of his governorship entreating the Lords of Trade to recall him or to allow him to displace De Lancey and his henchmen from their appointive positions. The home authorities offered the governor a dubious escape: he could leave the province and turn over its administration to his enemy De Lancey, who late in 1747 was named lieutenant governor of New York! The dumbfounded Clinton expostulated that "nothing could be so unhappy" than delivering the colony into the hands of his archenemy.[8]

7. Clinton to the Duke of Newcastle, 8 June 1746 and August 1747; to the Duke of Bedford, 15 November 1748, George Clinton Papers, Clements Library, Ann Arbor, Mich.; James Sullivan and Alexander C. Flick, eds., *The Papers of Sir William Johnson*, 14 vols. (Albany, N.Y., 1921–65), 1:54, 59–61, 86–88; A. C. Flick, *History of the State of New York*, 10 vols. (New York, 1933–37), 2:189–90, 226–29; McAnear, "Politics," pp. 595–607 and ch. 14.

8. Newcastle to Clinton, 27 October 1747, George Clinton Papers, Clements Library, Ann Arbor, Mich.; Clinton to Newcastle, 9 November 1747 and 13 February 1748, *N.Y. Col. Docs.*, 6:409–10, 416–18; Clinton to Colden, 31 January 1748, *Colden Papers*, 4:10–11.

Clinton deferred his departure from the province as long as he could, always hopeful that the Crown would vacate De Lancey's commission, but in October 1753, when these hopes proved futile, Clinton departed. Only then did he surrender to De Lancey the commission which had been withheld for six years.[9]

Clinton's difficulties were not entirely due to his own personality. The brief and tragic career of his successor, Sir Danvers Osborne, demonstrated this. Osborne arrived on 7 October 1753, armed with ample royal instructions—the strictest ever issued—to free himself from financial dependence upon the legislature, to curb Assembly powers, and to restore executive control of expenditures. After a five-day analysis of the realities of New York politics, Osborne hanged himself. De Lancey thereupon became acting governor.[10]

On the horns of the dilemma posed by his simultaneous leadership of an assembly determined to maintain its financial powers and his governorship with royal instructions to retrieve those powers, De Lancey was saved by the advent of the fourth intercolonial war. Whitehall willingly abandoned some of its prerogative claims in favor of colonial support of the war. The ministry surrendered its demand for permanent salaries and accepted temporary support bills; the Assembly, in turn, expended money upon the governor's warrant while specifying the amounts to be paid. This arrangement continued during De Lancey's administrations

9. Katz, *Newcastle's New York*, ch. 8; Clinton to the Board of Trade, 26 November 1749, Colonial Office Records, CO 5:1064, pp. 1–6, Public Record Office, London; [John Catherwood], "Memorandum on behalf of Governor Clinton" to the Earl of Lincoln, 20 June 1750; "Reasons for Suspending of James De Lancey, Esqr from the Execution of the office of Lieutenant Governor . . ." July 1750, both in George Clinton Papers, Clements Library, Ann Arbor, Mich.; Clinton to the Lords of Trade, 8 April 1752, *N.Y. Col. Docs.*, 6:759–60.

10. Smith, *History*, 2:151–60; Flick, *History*, 2:191–92. The thirty-ninth article of Osborne's instructions specifically mandated permanent salaries for all the important royal officials and disbursements of funds only upon the warrant of the governor and council. The press quickly reproduced this. See *New-York Mercury*, 12 November 1753.

(1753–55, 1757–60) and that of Sir Charles Hardy (1755–57), who relied on De Lancey as lieutenant governor to manage the province while he participated actively in the French war.[11]

The harmony between legislature and executive produced by De Lancey's clever strategem did not, however, assure him an "easy" administration. Local politics, religion, and the French war proved such contentious issues that De Lancey found himself in partisan controversy almost as violent as that of his predecessor. As an enemy of Clinton's, De Lancey could expect the enmity of the former governor's supporters—Colden, Alexander, and William Smith, Sr.—but by 1756, De Lancey's "incaution" about the founding of King's College and his lukewarm support of the war added to his opposition the Livingston family and a trio of young lawyers: William Livingston, William Smith, Jr., and John Morin Scott.[12]

The coalescence of these groups into a formidable anti-De Lancey party involved the tangled and often elusive elements typical of colonial New York's history, but a few stand out starkly. The founding of a college, nonpartisan in its origin and an aspect of the "college enthusiasm" after 1745, became a heatedly sectarian issue as Anglicans sought to establish it under Church of England auspices. In 1752 the triumvirate began an active campaign to prevent an "Anglican seminary." They insisted that a "free college" should properly be instituted by legislative enactment rather than by royal charter, and they enlisted not only religious dissenters, al-

11. Flick, *History*, 2:194–95.
12. On the triumvirate, see Dorothy R. Dillon, *The New York Triumvirate: A Study of the Legal and Political Career of William Livingston, John Morin Scott, William Smith, Jr.* (New York, 1949). For biographical treatments, see also: Theodore Sedgwick, Jr., *A Memoir of the Life of William Livingston* (New York, 1833); Leslie F. S. Upton, *The Loyal Whig: William Smith of New York and Quebec* ([Toronto], 1969); and Brother Harry M. Dunkak, "John Morin Scott and Whig Politics in New York, 1752–1769," (Ph.D. diss., St. John's University, New York, 1968).

ways fearful of the Church of England's power, but also anti-prerogative men who would join any movement to curb gubernatorial power.[13]

De Lancey himself did not originate the Anglican college scheme, nor did the Livingston group intend to campaign against him. The triumvirate planned the crusade against the college as early as 1749. As a Church of England man, however, De Lancey supported the Anglicans; as acting governor, he granted the college its charter on 31 October 1754. For the next two years, the triumvirate fought to deny the college funds already raised by public lottery or to create a "free college" in opposition. A compromise in 1756 left the Anglicans with their seminary but with only half the funds raised for higher education in the colony. A press war over the issue hardened the lines between Anglicans and Presbyterians, the latter attacking De Lancey and the former defending him.[14]

De Lancey's enemies saw political capital in the college controversy. The Presbyterians were joined by "another sort . . . the most able, active and Cunning who are for dividing the present Power of the De Lancey Family, and make their Opposition to the College subservient to this view." The most prominent of these was James Alexander, a veteran anti-De Lanceyite, who wished to revenge his old patron George Clinton. Alexander was not particularly disturbed by the Anglican complexion of the college, but he joined the Presbyterian opposition in order to weaken De Lancey politically. As De Lancey himself became the focus, Alexander

13. Beverly McAnear, "College Founding in the American Colonies, 1745–1755," *Mississippi Valley Historical Review* 42(1955):24–44; on the King's College controversy, see Milton M. Klein, "Church, State, and Education: Testing the Issue in Colonial New York," *New York History* 45(1964):291–303.

14. The triumvirate's view of the controversy is presented in Milton M. Klein, ed., *The Independent Reflector* (Cambridge, Mass., 1963), and Smith's *History*, 2:190–92, 199–201, 230–31, 238–39; the Church side, in Herbert and Carol Schneider, eds., *Samuel Johnson, President of King's College: His Career and Writings*, 4 vols. (New York, 1929), vol. IV.

used his seat on the New York Council—to which he was named in 1750—to aid the triumvirate.[15] An ally of Alexander's on the council was William Smith, Sr., who like Alexander had been disbarred by De Lancey during the preliminaries of the famous Zenger trial. Smith's Presbyterianism reinforced his personal antipathy to the lieutenant governor, and he saw the Anglican college as a forerunner of a full church establishment in the province.[16]

The addition of other Livingstons to the anti-De Lancey party has a more varied and complex explanation. The founder of the Livingston dynasty in America had opposed De Lancey's father in the 1720s, but this disagreement did not determine the political affiliation of succeeding generations. Philip Livingston, the second manor lord and a personal friend of both James Alexander and William Smith, Sr., had incurred the wrath of Governor Clinton and was thereby forced reluctantly into the De Lancey camp. Philip Livingston was the colony's Secretary for Indian Affairs and an Albany fur trader. Somewhat inexplicably, Governor Clinton considered him a leading neutralist and Montreal trader in King George's War when, in fact, Livingston supported an aggressive anti-French policy, as had his father before him.[17]

More substance existed for Clinton's conviction that Livingston's shady Indian land purchases made the task of retaining

15. Goldsbrow Banyar to George Clarke, Jr., 23 November 1754, Banyar Papers, New York Historical Society; Alexander to Colden, 2 February and 19 April 1753, *Colden Papers*, 6:369, 386; "The Independent Reflector" to Alexander, 8 March 1753, Rutherford Papers, 3, New York Historical Society; Samuel Johnson to William Samuel Johnson and William Johnson, 10 June 1754, in Schneider and Schneider, eds., *Samuel Johnson*, 4:15.

16. Livingston Rutherford, *John Peter Zenger: His Press, His Trial, and a Bibliography of Zenger Imprints* (New York, 1904, reprinted 1941), ch. 2; and James Alexander, *A Brief Narrative of the Case and Trial of John Peter Zenger*, ed. Stanley N. Katz (Cambridge, Mass., 1963), pp. 17–20.

17. On Robert Livingston's position, see Leder, *Robert Livingston*, pp. 138–39, 250–53; Livingston's Memorial to the Board of Trade, 13 May 1701, N. Y. *Col. Docs.*, 4:870–79, and his letters to William Blathwayt, 23 May and 3 September 1701, BL 149 and 217, Huntington Library, San Marino, Calif.

Iroquois loyalty more difficult. Livingston, for his part, castigated both Clinton and the Assembly for the political infighting which inhibited New York's war effort. He wanted to conquer "our Troublesome neighbour be the Expence ever So much," and he was "fully persuaded that nothing should be left undone in our power to promote the Reduction of Canada" and "free ourselves of the charges and trouble in defending our frontier from a heap of murderers. . . ." Clinton nevertheless wrote off all the Livingstons as "a vile family"; Livingston responded that the governor had so "abuzd me that I have no Concern with him for I find nobody can be his friend but those who will do, say, and think, as he doth, which I would not do for his Governm[en]t and all he has."[18]

Philip Livingston's death in 1749 did not immediately end the feud between that family and the governor. Clinton made certain that none of the late manor lord's public offices went to his sons; they, in turn, campaigned actively against Clinton's friends in 1750, William Livingston emerging as the chief penman. But the young firebrand of the clan was in an awkward position as an intimate of William Smith, Jr., and William Alexander, both of whose parents were Clinton confidants. By the end of 1753, circumstances moved William Livingston into the Clinton camp and into opposition to De Lancey. The De Lancey Assembly had refused to protest the impending Iron Act, which would hurt the manor family's iron works, and it refused to assist Livingston

18. "Petition of Mohawk Indians to Governor Clinton," 1 December 1746, Clinton to Henry Pelham, 8 December 1746, George Clinton Papers, Clements Library, Ann Arbor, Mich.; Clinton to the Duke of Newcastle, 18 November 1745 and 9 December 1746, to the Lords of Trade, 30 November 1747, *N.Y. Col. Docs.*, 6:286, 315, 412–13; Philip Livingston to Robert Livingston, 13 March 1745, Livingston-Redmond Collection, Franklin D. Roosevelt Library, Hyde Park, N.Y.; Philip Livingston to Jacob Wendell, 14 January, 5 April, and 14 June 1746, and 13 February 1747, Livingston Papers, Museum of the City of New York.

Manor in its boundary dispute with Massachusetts because it was a private rather than a public affair. William Livingston was indignant. As for De Lancey, Livingston avowed to his brother, "he cares not a Groat for you nor your Manor, nor any Man living. That always was my Opinion about him; now is so; and ever shall be, world without End. . . . He knows no such thing as friendship abstracted from political Views, and the purposes of Trimming and popularity."[19]

The rapprochement between the Livingstons and Clinton developed slowly, with mutual suspicions gradually giving way to a recognition of identical anti-De Lancey interests. By 1753, Clinton wrote solicitously to Robert Livingston about the manor's troubles with Massachusetts and assured him of "my best Endeavours for your protection," at the same time writing a personal recommendation for the manor lord's brother, who was settling in Jamaica as the family's West Indian representative. Instead of a "vile" family, he now described the Livingstons as "one of the best in this Place."[20] Clinton's departure in late 1753, De Lancey's assumption of the governorship, and the latter's involvement as an Anglican partisan in the college controversy completed the Livingston-Alexander-Smith coalition and made William Livingston more comfortable as the lieutenant governor's political foe. The

19. Klein, ed., *Independent Reflector*, pp. 12–13; Katz, *Newcastle's New York*, pp. 190–91; Smith, *History*, 2: 136–37; William Livingston to Robert Livingston, 25 November 1751 and 4 February 1754, Livingston-Redmond Collection, F. D. R. Library. William's brothers, John and Philip, expressed similar views about De Lancey. See John Livingston to Robert Livingston, 25 November 1751, and Philip Livingston to Robert Livingston, 29 November 1751, ibid. On the New York-Massachusetts border controversy, see Oscar Handlin, "The Eastern Frontier of New York," *New York History* 18(1937): 50–75.

20. "Petition of Robert Livingston, Jr., To the Honourable George Clinton . . . ," 16 April 1752, Livingston Family Papers, New York Public Library; Clinton to Robert Livingston, 29 January 1753, Clinton to Governor Charles Knowles, 16 January 1753, George Clinton Letter Book, Clements Library, Ann Arbor, Mich.

outbreak of the French war in 1754 gave Livingston additional grounds for his enmity toward the De Lanceys.

William Livingston, like his father and grandfather, was a militant imperialist. Although more Dutch than Scottish—his mother was a Van Brugh and his paternal grandmother a Schuyler—Livingston did not share the Albany fondness for neutrality or even for a mere defensive posture against the French. During King George's War, Livingston was but a law clerk and in no position to air his views publicly. He did express them amply in private correspondence with a Yale classmate, Noah Welles, then a minister at Stamford, Connecticut; his views paralleled his father's sentiments. Philip Livingston confided his admiration for the expedition Massachusetts organized in 1745 against the French fortress at Louisbourg and hailed Governor William Shirley of the Bay Colony as the architect of that victory. He contrasted New York's "Spirit of Indolence and Envy" with its neighbor's united war effort and blamed Governor Clinton for New York's failure. "We want here a Shirley," he wrote in 1746, to revive his "drooping Languishing Spirits" and a legislature with as much "Publick Generous Spirit to defend and secure our frontiers" as the Massachusetts government had demonstrated.[21]

The younger Livingston also praised the "Gallant thunderbolts" of New England, whose valor was "justly celebrated thro' all Europe" by the capture of Louisbourg. He satirized New York's assemblymen for frivolous legislation—"proclaiming war against Cows and rattlesnakes"—instead of attending to serious combat with the French. In any case, New York's politicians had a pen-

21. With profits in view as well, Livingston tried to secure the contract to supply the garrison at Cape Breton for his son Henry. Philip Livingston to William Pepperell, 29 August 1745, Massachusetts Historical Society *Collections*, 6th ser., 10(1899):369–70. Philip Livingston to Jacob Wendell, 14 January, 2 June, and 27 August 1746, Livingston Papers, Museum of the City of New York.

chant for squandering money, and they could not accomplish with a thousand pounds what New Englanders could do with half the sum. Because of his conviction that Louisbourg was the "DUNKIRK of North-America" and the key to all of France's American possessions, Livingston was shocked by the peace settlement which returned that fortress to the enemy.[22]

From 1748 to 1754, William Livingston was absorbed in launching his legal career and in the fight against the Anglican college proposal, but when the contest between France and England in America resumed in 1754, Livingston again turned his attention and his pen to imperial relations. The New York papers were filled with news of French advances in the Ohio Valley, Washington's unsuccessful demand that the French decamp, the appeals of governors Dinwiddie of Virginia and Shirley of Massachusetts for war funds, and, in July 1754, Washington's surrender at Fort Necessity. In the face of this danger, New York took only half-measures. Two of the four companies of British regulars in the province were dispatched southward, but a dispute between the Assembly and the Council blocked funds to transport and supply them. De Lancey received a sharp reprimand for New York's delinquency, but the assembly responded that guarding its own frontiers had already overburdened the colony.[23]

The famous Albany Congress, held between June and July 1754, offered Livingston further evidence of New York's passivity in the imperial crisis. De Lancey was the official host of the conference,

22. William Livingston to Noah Welles, 9 December 1745, 24 January 1746, Johnson Family Papers, Yale University; William Livingston, *Review of the Military Operations in North-America* (London, 1757), p. 3.
23. *New-York Gazette*, 18 February, 4, 25 March, 1 April, 6, 13 May 1754; *New-York Mercury*, 25 March, 1 April, 6, 13 May, 22 July (Supplement), 26 August, 2 September 1754; *Journal of the Votes and Proceedings of the General Assembly of the Colony of New-York*, [1691–1765], 2 vols. (New York, 1764–66), 2:383–88; *Calendar of Council Minutes, 1668–1783* (New York State Library *Bulletin* 58 [Albany, N.Y.], 1902):392, 395–97; Smith, *History*, 2:172–76; N.Y. *Col Docs.*, 6:827–28, 834, 844–45.

but only New York's delegates attended without official commissions. De Lancey concentrated his efforts on securing intercolonial financial contributions for a chain of forts on the New York frontier. When the commissioners ignored this proposal, De Lancey refused to support their plan of union. He did not vote against it at the Congress, since he presided, but he made no effort to secure Assembly approval for the plan in New York, withheld publication of the project, and even failed to send the plan to the colony's agent in London.[24]

Livingston and his colleagues were of a far different mind. Both the elder Smith and James Alexander, advisers to the triumvirate in their political campaign against De Lancey, were strong partisans of the Albany Plan of Union. Smith, as a New York delegate, had voted for its adoption; Alexander was, in a sense, one of its architects, Franklin having discussed the scheme in advance with him and secured his advice and endorsement. William Livingston and William Alexander both appeared at the Congress to assist in mollifying the Indians by publicly surrendering their claims as heirs to certain lands that the Mohawks had insisted were obtained by fraud.[25] Livingston and his associates now attacked De Lancey for his obstructionism with regard to colonial union.

On 23 September 1754, a long essay titled "A Summary View of the Present State of this Continent" appeared in both of New York's newspapers. Undoubtedly authored, although not signed, by William Livingston, it appealed strongly for colonial union on strategic as well as patriotic grounds. It urged the colonies to cease "impolitically and ungenerously" considering themselves as "dis-

24. Robert C. Newbold, *The Albany Congress and Plan of Union of 1754* (New York, 1955), pp. 23–24, 40–42, 77–79, 117n, 166–67; Smith, *History*, 2:187n, 216n; Beverly McAnear, "Politics in Provincial New York, 1689–1761" (Ph.D. diss., Stanford University, 1935), p. 859.

25. Newbold, *Albany Congress*, pp. 34, 167; Smith, *History*, 2:185n; Lawrence H. Gipson, *The British Empire before the American Revolution*, 15 vols. (New York, 1936–71), 5:125–26; *N.Y. Col. Docs.*, 5:850, 879–80.

tinct States, with narrow, separate and independent Views," it
requested Heaven's interposition to further the Albany Plan of
Union, and it implored the colonists to pledge their honor and
fortunes to crush France and thereby insure "the inestimable
Blessings of Civil and Religious Liberty, and the uninterrupted
Possession and Settlement of a great Country." Privately, Livingston believed that unless the colonies united, they would be easily
picked off one by one. He had little faith in the dependability of
the Indians. While they inclined toward the British, "our Indolence about defending our Frontiers . . . have given them such
disadvantageous Impressions of our Conduct . . . that it wo[uld]
not have surprized me had they long since utterly abandoned us."
In any case, rum and liquor so debilitated the natives that they
were "pusillanimous and weak." The colonies had better look to
their own resources. A union, supported by the home government,
would enable the colonists to "repel the encroachments of an ambitious and barbarous Foe."[26]

News of the dispatch to America of British regulars under Major General Edward Braddock encouraged Livingston to appeal
again to New Yorkers for aggressive support of a war against the
French. He used his "Watch-Tower," a newspaper column nor-
mally devoted to fighting the college issue with the Anglicans, to
"sound the Alarm" against the "unwarrantable Encroachments of
the *French* King" and to urge colonial union in defense of "our
priceless Freedom . . . and the Glory of the *British* Name."
When the contest with churchmen monopolized that organ of
propaganda, a new paper was launched to carry on the anti-French
campaign.[27]

Braddock's disastrous defeat in July 1755 on the banks of the

26. *New-York Gazette*, 23 September 1754; *New-York Mercury*, 23 September 1754; Livingston to Rev. David Thompson, 28 October 1754, Letter
Book A, Livingston Papers, Massachusetts Historical Society.
27. *New-York Mercury*, 13, 20 January, 24 February 1755. The paper was
titled *The Instructor*, and it ran from 6 March to 8 May 1755.

Monongahela—"a day never to be forgotten in the annals of North-America"—Livingston attributed to the general's failure to employ French-Indian military tactics and "an obstinate Self-Sufficiency in his own way." The defeat in the South turned Livingston's attention even more closely to the northern half of the British war plan for 1755. Braddock's orders had been to drive the French from the forks of the Ohio, take the French post at Crown Point on Lake Champlain, and secure Lake Ontario by seizing Fort Niagara. While Braddock himself had assumed direction of the Ohio campaign, he had designated Governor William Shirley of Massachusetts to lead the Niagara expedition. Command of the Crown Point forces was given to William Johnson with a direct commission from Braddock as Superintendent of Indian Affairs for the northern tribes.[28] The relations between Johnson and Shirley became politically entangled and fiercely partisan and constituted the immediate occasion for publication of the *Review of the Military Operations in North-America*.

The Livingstons had no special reason to dislike Johnson, and they were enthusiastic about both the Crown Point and the Niagara expeditions, but they had a special interest in the latter. Shirley, a personal friend of the Livingstons, had been a guest at the manor during his campaigns in King George's War and was admired by the family as a leading advocate of colonial union. They viewed his able leadership of Massachusetts in that conflict as a striking contrast to Clinton's ineptness in New York. The relationship was strengthened by Shirley's appointment of William Alexander as his secretary and by Shirley's assignment of the supply contract for the Niagara campaign to the firm of Livingston and Morris, headed by William Livingston's brother Peter and

28. *Review of the Military Operations*, p. 40; Livingston to Rev. David Thompson, 12 January 1756, Letter Book A, Livingston Papers, Massachusetts Historical Society; Gipson, *British Empire*, 6:137–39.

Lewis Morris, Jr. Livingston, in turn, shared his interest in the firm with William Alexander.[29]

By his links with the Livingstons, Shirley almost inevitably aroused the hostility of the De Lanceys, who also had other reasons for opposing the Massachusetts governor. Oliver De Lancey, brother of the New York lieutenant governor, had hoped for the Niagara supply contract, and he was furious to have lost out to the Livingstons. He threatened to make his rivals "jump most high," and brother James gladly lent his aid to engineer the acrobatics. The lieutenant governor himself suspected Shirley's advocacy of colonial union because he believed the Massachusetts governor sought to head the proposed confederation himself.[30]

De Lancey's hostility to Shirley spilled over into the military arena. The New York governor objected to Shirley's request for certain artillery from New York City for the Niagara expedition and for some New York troops originally designated for Crown Point. Shirley irritated De Lancey by urging him to stop the clandestine trade between Albany and Montreal by which the French secured military information as well as goods. Shirley also objected to New York's attempt to raise its quota of troops by recruiting in Connecticut. Shirley unfortunately now became involved in a misunderstanding with Johnson over the enlistment of Indian scouts for the Niagara expedition. De Lancey quickly capitalized on their rift, turning Johnson and another Shirley aide, Thomas Pownall, against the Massachusetts governor.[31]

29. Shirley to George Clinton, 9 July 1748, George Clinton Papers, Clements Library, Ann Arbor, Mich.; John A. Schutz, *William Shirley, King's Governor of Massachusetts* (Chapel Hill, 1961), pp. 198–99; Theodore Thayer, "The Army Contractors for the Niagara Campaign, 1755–1756," *William and Mary Quarterly* 3rd ser., 14 (1957): 31–46.

30. Thayer, "Army Contractors," p. 43; Smith, *History*, 2:185n, 213; William Alexander to Peter Van Brugh Livingston, 9 July 1755, New Jersey Historical Society *Proceedings* 6(1851–53):45.

31. Gipson, *British Empire*, 6:141–47; Schutz, *Shirley*, pp. 200–02; Schutz, *Thomas Pownall, British Defender of American Liberty* (Glendale,

When Shirley's attack on Niagara stalled in the fall of 1755 because of bad weather and supply and transport problems, the anti-Shirley forces were delighted. They were overjoyed when Johnson, on 8 September 1755, repulsed an attack by French forces under Baron Dieskau at Lake George. The innocent Shirleyites were as pleased with Johnson's success as were the De Lanceys. William Livingston, in his newspaper column, praised Johnson for his "unexampled Wisdom and Valour," and Shirley's aide, William Alexander, reported that Johnson's victory had put the entire Shirley headquarters "in high spirits."[32]

The elation of the Shirleyites was short-lived as they perceived the use to which the De Lanceyites put the Johnson victory. Johnson's letter describing his success was published in New York and in colonies as far south as Virginia, setting off wild celebrations. Johnson's aide-de-camp sent it personally to De Lancey, but Shirley, who by virtue of Braddock's death was now commander-in-chief of all British forces in North America and Johnson's immediate commander, received his copy of the letter secondhand.[33]

The De Lanceys now began "industriously" propagating unfavorable "reflections" about Shirley in New York City, contrasting the failure of the Niagara campaign with Johnson's success. De Lancey, one Livingston observed, would "do all he can to ruin his [Shirley's] interest." In December 1755, both Shirley and John-

---

Calif., 1951), pp. 58–62; Smith, *History*, 2:206–07; James T. Flexner, *Mohawk Baronet* (New York, 1959), p. 127; William Alexander to Shirley, 10 May 1755, New Jersey Historical Society *Proceedings* 5(1850–51): 187–88. By May 1755, Shirley was convinced that he would have to dismiss Johnson. Shirley to Robert Hunter Morris, 2 May 1755, *Pennsylvania Archives*, 1st ser., 2(1852): 297–98.

32. *New-York Mercury*, 22 September 1755; Livingston to Rev. David Thompson, 12 January 1756, Letter Book A, Livingston Papers, Massachusetts Historical Society; William Alexander to Peter Van Brugh Livingston, 17 September 1755, New Jersey Historical Society *Proceedings* 6(1851–53):61.

33. On the letter and its effect, see Milton W. Hamilton, "Battle Report: General William Johnson's Letter to the Governors, Lake George, September 9–10, 1755," American Antiquarian Society *Proceedings* 74(1964): 19–36.

son arrived in New York City. The commander-in-chief was greeted "without shew," while Johnson received a tumultuous public reception carefully arranged, in the view of the Livingstons, "to put contempt upon Mr. Shirley." Charles Hardy, newly appointed as governor of New York, became a convert to the anti-Shirley intrigue, and the De Lanceys prepared a set of official charges against the Massachusetts general. Pownall, whose brother was secretary to the Board of Trade, agreed to carry the charges personally to London.[34]

Unaware of the plot, Shirley held a war council with the governors of New York, Maryland, Pennsylvania, and Connecticut and proposed a broad plan of hostilities against Canada in 1756, with Fort Frontenac, on the north shore of Lake Ontario, added to Niagara and Crown Point as targets. Privately Shirley confided his plans to William, Philip, and Robert R. Livingston and to William Smith, Jr. and secured promises of their public support. Governor Hardy, however, objected to Shirley's inclusion of Fort Frontenac, and the De Lanceys soon echoed the objection publicly on the ground that this fort was legitimately on French soil. The Livingston publicists took up the literary cudgels in defense of Shirley's proposal, and a bitter press war ensued.[35]

Cartography was enlisted as a weapon by both sides. In 1755 Lewis Evans, a Pennsylvania mapmaker, published a map of the northern English colonies which showed Fort Frontenac as French territory. In an *Analysis* accompanying the map, Evans criticized

34. Peter Van Brugh Livingston to William Alexander, 3 September and 25 October 1755, William Alexander manuscripts 1, New York Historical Society; Sir Charles Hardy to the Earl of Halifax, 27 November 1755, in Stanley Pargellis, ed., *Military Affairs in North America, 1748–1765* (New York, 1936), pp. 149–53; Schutz, *Pownall*, pp. 65–66; Schutz, *Shirley*, p. 221; Flexner, *Mohawk Baronet*, p. 158.

35. William Smith Diary, "December 27, 1755," "January 29, 1756," 2:398, 400, New York Public Library; Gipson, *British Empire*, 6:160–61, 177–79; Schutz, *Shirley*, pp. 222–23. On the press war, see especially *New-York Mercury* (Supplement), 23 February 1756.

Shirley's proposed attack on the fort as a clear violation of treaties then in force between Great Britain and France. The Shirley faction accused Evans of being a tool of the De Lanceys, and their suspicions seemed confirmed by Evans's dedication of his work to Thomas Pownall, one of the anti-Shirley cabal. William Smith, Jr. commented cynically that Pownall had paid fifty pistoles for the honor. William Livingston sneered that Evans's "voluminous Pamphlet" was intended to "ingratiate himself with some of our invidious Politicians." Livingston's strictures against Pownall were even more caustic: he was a politician who "would sacrifice any body to his own Interest" and who cared "for no Body any farther than he can make him subservient to his own ambition and Lust of Power."[36]

With Shirley's approval and assistance, Livingston and Smith prepared a public vindication of Shirley's proposed strategy and a violent attack on Evans's counterproposal for a campaign in the Ohio Valley. Evans replied that Shirley was sacrificing the interests of Virginia and Pennsylvania merely to promote his own fame. Shirley's aide, Alexander, denounced the Evans composition as "full of misrepresentations and falsehoods," and the Shirleyites published a rejoinder in the newspapers.[37]

Not even the best of press polemics could help Shirley, however. The Ministry's confidence in him was undermined by the De Lan-

36. Lawrence H. Gipson, *Lewis Evans* (Philadelphia, 1939), pp. 63–72; William Smith Diary, "July 8, 1756," 2:410, New York Public Library; William Livingston to William Alexander, 15 March 1756, William Alexander manuscripts 2, New York Historical Society; William Livingston to Robert Livingston, 13 June 1757, Livingston-Redmond Collection, F.D.R. Library. On the battle of the maps, see also Max Savelle, *The Origins of American Diplomacy* (New York, 1967), pp. 533–36, and Lawrence C. Wroth, *An American Bookshelf: 1775* (Philadelphia, 1934), pp. 45–53, 148–66.

37. William Smith Diary, 2:398–401, New York Public Library; *New-York Mercury*, 5 January and 2 February 1756; William Alexander to William Smith, Jr., 23 March 1756, William Alexander manuscripts, 2, New York Historical Society.

cey penmen, and early in 1756 it replaced him with a regular army officer, Lord Loudoun. Worse, from the Livingston point of view, Shirley's rival, William Johnson, was knighted, granted a £5,000 gift, and awarded a new royal commission as Secretary of Indian Affairs for the northern tribes. William Livingston made light of Johnson's "grand Commission" and deprecated the baronetcy as "but a poor thing to live upon," but the news of Shirley's recall as governor of Massachusetts as well as from the command of the American forces chastened him. The rout of the Shirleyites became apparent as each of the general's enemies received his reward: Pownall secured the Bay Colony governorship, De Lancey and Hardy became confidants of the new commander-in-chief, and Oliver De Lancey replaced Livingston and Morris as principal contractor for the British forces in America. As Peter Van Brugh Livingston surveyed the wreckage of the Shirley forces, he concluded grimly: "Some peoples ends are now fully answered with the new Alteration. The whole Clamour made about Gen[era]l Shirley and to put somebody else up in op[p]osition to him was only made to remove him in order to get into their hands what I have been about for this year past and now you will find every thing will go very smooth."[38]

The anti-Shirley faction now used its power to abuse Shirley himself and to embarrass his supporters. Loudoun ordered an examination of the Livingston-Morris supply accounts and suspended all unpaid warrants issued by Shirley. The general was accused of mismanaging funds, of leaving Oswego undefended, and of interfering with Loudoun's command. When Oswego fell to the French in August 1756, Shirley was blamed for the catastrophe, and in-

38. Schutz, *Shirley*, pp. 232–34; Gipson, *British Empire*, 6:186–91; Pargellis, *Lord Loudoun in North America* (New Haven, Conn., 1933), pp. 39–42, 76–77, 137–39, 167, 262; Arthur Pound, *Johnson of the Mohawks* (New York, 1930), pp. 229–30; William to Robert Livingston, 11 February 1756, Peter to Robert Livingston, 23 June 1756, Livingston-Redmond Collection, F.D.R. Library.

stead of receiving the promised governorship of Jamaica he was threatened with a London court martial.[39]

Shirley and his partisans sought to counter the De Lancey attack by private letters to British officials. The triumvirate tried to get the New York Assembly to present an address of appreciation to Shirley before his departure for England, only to see the effort thwarted by the De Lanceys, who terminated the house's sessions before it approved the address. But the Shirleyites most ambitiously defended the general in the public prints. William Smith, Jr. used his history of New York, published in 1757, to minimize Johnson's victory at Crown Point, laud Shirley's plans for the Niagara campaign, and criticize De Lancey for his petty obstructionism. William Alexander, who accompanied Shirley to London, prepared—probably in conjunction with the general himself—a lengthy, documentary vindication of the unsuccessful Niagara effort.[40]

William Livingston, the chief of the triumvirate, exploited Alexander's official data to the best advantage and penned the most sensational and controversial defense of Shirley. Titled *A Review of the Military Operations in North America*, it was published anonymously in London in the spring of 1757 and in a Dublin edition a few months later.[41] The pamphlet, nominally an account

39. Thayer, "Army Contractors," pp. 45–46; Schutz, *Shirley*, pp. 234–42; Gipson, *British Empire*, 6:209–10; Pargellis, *Loudoun*, ch. 5; Pargellis, ed., *Military Affairs in North America*, pp. 223–30, 239–43, 313–14.

40. William Smith Diary, "August 22, 1756," 2:415, New York Public Library; Shirley to Secretary of War Henry Fox, 15, 16 September 1756, in *The Correspondence of William Shirley*, ed. Charles H. Lincoln, 2 vols. (New York, 1912), 2:564, 566–76; "Draft of an Address from the Assembly of New York," [1756], William Smith Papers, Box 207–14, New York Public Library; William Alexander to Robert Hunter Morris, 11 July 1756, Robert Hunter Morris Papers, 2:76, New Jersey Historical Society; Smith, *History*, 2:214–17, 220, 241; *The Conduct of Major Gen. Shirley, late General and Commander in Chief of his Majesty's Forces in North America* (London, 1758).

41. For a full bibliographical discussion, see Wroth, *American Bookshelf*, pp. 167–71.

of the first three years of the war in the colonies, was in fact a devastating assault on De Lancey and the entire anti-Shirley clique.

Much in the booklet's 144 pages was judicious, impartial, public-spirited, and imperial-minded. It called attention to the importance of the American colonies in the European balance of power: "if France rule[s] the ocean, her resources will enable her to subject all Europe to her despotic sway," and if the American colonies fell under French control, "such will be the accession to their already extended commerce and marine strength, that Great Britain must not only lose her former lustre, but . . . cease to be any longer an independent power." It contrasted French unity with British division and pleaded for union along the lines of the Albany Plan: "The strength of our colonies is divided; . . . Jealous are they of each other. . . . Without a general constitution for warlike operations, we can neither plan nor execute. We have a common interest, and must have a common council, one *head*, and one *purse*." The Albany Plan, with its common fund to defray all military expenses, would serve the purpose. The Congress itself was likened grandiloquently to "one of the ancient Greek conventions for supporting their expiring liberty against the power of the Persian empire."[42]

Conscious of the general gloom the fall of Oswego had cast over all the colonies, the *Review* sought to stimulate flagging patriotism. Livingston conceded that the year 1755 had opened "with the fairest prospects . . . for the final destruction of the whole country of New France" but that the colonies were now "nearly exhausted," their strength divided, their farms abandoned, and "the King's subjects inhumanly butchered, or reduced to beggary" as a result of the enlistment of the Indians in the French cause. But he held out the hope of ultimate victory. "Strength sufficient have we left," with the assistance of the mother country, "to extirpate

42, Livingston, *Review*, pp. 2–3, 15, 141–42. The same theme had been expounded in *The Instructor*, 13 March 1755.

this brood of French savages from the face of the continent." The colonies would respond to a determined and well-conceived plan of action from Britain, but the home government must resolve not merely to fight a defensive war but to oust France from North America altogether: "Hitherto we have wasted our strength in lopping off branches, when the axe should have been laid to the root of the tree." It was not enough to hold existing British lines. "Canada must be demolished. Delenda est Carthago, or we are undone."[43]

These imperial and relatively nonpartisan aspects of the *Review* were obscured, however, by the intensely partisan language Livingston employed in offering his "Observations, Characters, and Anecdotes; necessary to give Light into the Conduct of American transactions in general; and more especially into the political Management of Affairs in New York." This subtitle to the *Review* gave Livingston license to intersperse with his fairly straightforward account of military operations an acrid pen portrait of Lieutenant Governor James De Lancey, only less acerb sketches of Thomas Pownall, Lewis Evans, and William Johnson, and a glowing representation of William Shirley. Readers were not deceived by Livingston's protestations that he was "unconnected with all parties" and that every line had been written "with the most sacred veneration for truth" in an effort to "discharge the office of a faithful historian." A London reviewer quickly dismissed the disclaimer of impartiality, observing that "by his vindication of every measure that Governor Shirley undertook, and by his censure of almost every measure in which this Gentleman was not concerned, we are too much led to suspect him of having an interested attachment to one party, implicitly to believe all he says against the other."[44]

43. Livingston, *Review*, pp. 107, 141–44.
44. Ibid., pp. 2, 103, 139–40; *Monthly Review* 16(1757):524–27. According to Wroth, *American Bookshelf* (p. 171), the reviewer was Oliver Goldsmith.

Livingston's review of New York politics was largely a diatribe against De Lancey, whose career was traced from his share in Cosby's "odious and turbulent" administration to his responsibility for "blowing up the coals of contention" in Clinton's governorship. Livingston even intimated that De Lancey was responsible for Sir Danvers Osborne's suicide, which permitted him to assume active direction of the government. "As it always was," Livingston commented harshly, "so it will ever continue to be, his ruling passion, and the grand engine of his politics, to crush or controul the King's governors in this province." Livingston likened De Lancey to the Dutch-born Duke of Repperda (1680–1737)—an adventurer who served Holland, Spain, and Morocco and, in the process, shifted his religious affiliation each time to suit his new employer —as a man short on talent and long on ambition, thirsting after popularity, "fastidious and fawning, supercilious and sycophantic," voluptuous and lazy, blindly opposing any measure that would diminish "his own lustre" or derogate "his own sovereign influence." "His own interest," Livingston charged, "is his idol, and every thing else made subservient to procure it veneration and esteem."[45]

On specific issues, Livingston denounced De Lancey for his "unaccountable" failure to support the Albany Plan, for appearing to follow royal instructions with regard to a permanent revenue while actually collaborating with the assembly to prevent it, and for obstructing Shirley's Niagara expedition out of jealousy of the latter's "rising reputation."[46]

Shirley's other opponents were not neglected. Livingston charged that Oliver De Lancey rescued Lewis Evans from a New York jail in order to perform the cabal's dirty work with his map and analysis. His promised reward was the surveyor-generalship of New Jersey when Pownall became governor of that province. Pownall was

45. Livingston, Review, pp. 16–23, 91–92, 117, 121–22, 127–28, 160–61.
46. Ibid., pp. 16, 33–36, 109–13.

belittled for his "loose, indigested proposals" at the Albany Congress—evidence of his desire for "galloping into preferment"—and denounced for accepting Shirley's favors and then turning on his benefactor: "he openly traduced the very man, to whom he was indebted for all his significancy amongst the provinces." William Johnson was taken to task for deliberately minimizing the role of his second in command, General Phineas Lyman of Connecticut, who, according to Livingston, was the real hero of the Battle of Lake George. Johnson was also accused of timidity for failing to pursue Dieskau's demoralized troops after the first contact between the opposing forces. Sarcastically, Livingston referred to "this fortunate general," who had "obtained laurels without earning them." His reputation, Livingston insinuated, was manufactured by the De Lanceys in order to derogate Shirley: "To the panegyrical pen of Mr. Wraxal [Peter Wraxall, Johnson's aide] . . . is to be ascribed that mighty renown, which echoed thro' the colonies, reverberated in Europe, and elevated a raw unexperienced youth into a kind of second Marlborough."[47]

All these criticisms of the De Lanceys were but backdrops to Livingston's major exposition, the defense of Shirley. Using the official information provided him by William Alexander, Shirley's secretary, Livingston undertook a detailed critique of the ill-fated Niagara offensive. He attributed its failure to the "insurmountable" physical obstacles preventing the movement of troops and supplies from Albany to Oswego, the difficulty of securing Indian scouts—largely Johnson's fault—and "the malignity of the New York faction." Livingston praised Shirley's war plan for 1756 and absolved him of responsibility for the fall of Oswego because his successors ignored his advice to reinforce the fort. Bluntly admitting his "honourable mention" of Shirley, Livingston explained it

47. Ibid., pp. 29–30, 65–72, 101–06. On the Lyman-Johnson controversy, see Delphina L. H. Clark, *Phineas Lyman, Connecticut's General* (Springfield, Mass., 1964), pp. 22–26.

by his deep conviction that the general was a "Gentleman of great political sagacity, deep penetration, and indefatigable industry," thoroughly versed in American affairs, and an ardent champion of "the commonweal of the British plantations."[48]

The *Review* created a sensation both in British circles and in the colonies shortly thereafter, and the book continued to be controversial. Livingston's harsh criticisms caused extreme agitation among the adherents of De Lancey, Pownall, and Johnson. Pownall's brother accused William Alexander, then in London, of writing the offensive work, but Alexander admitted only to carrying the manuscript to England. He said, however, that the author was his "particular friend at New York." In the colony, it was quickly deduced that the author could only be either William Livingston or William Smith, Jr., Alexander's two "particular friends" there. Copies of the pamphlet were dispatched to the New York and Pennsylvania authorities by their London agents, and by summer 1757 a few were being circulated privately in New York City.[49] The De Lanceys, "inflamed" by its aspersions on their chief, seized all copies of the *Review* in sight, threatening to sue the author, when discovered, for libel. Livingston admitted that the pamphlet was "incontestably Lybellous," but so, he remarked in oblique self-praise, were "most of the best Books I ever saw." He carefully concealed his authorship and avoided even lending the book, fearful that his enemies would allege that lending it constituted publication and would thereupon prosecute him. "As for the Author," he confided to his close friend Noah Welles, "I suppose he will not

48. Livingston, *Review*, pp. 3–6, 33–34, 42–43, 73–90, 135–36, 140–41.
49. Alexander Colden to Cadwallader Colden, 12 July and 23 September 1757, *Colden Papers*, 5:157–59, 189; Robert Charles to David Jones [Speaker of the New York Assembly], 11 May 1757, William Smith Papers, No. 191, New York Public Library; Thomas Penn to Richard Peters, 14 May 1757, Peters Papers, 4:91, Historical Society of Pennsylvania.

chuse to appear, unless he should happen to find his Ears extremely incommodious."[50]

Because of its libelous nature, neither Livingston nor Smith made public their knowledge of the *Review*'s authorship, and from their silence has arisen a debate over the writer's identity that has continued to the present. Timothy Dwight, in his famous *Travels in New England and New York*, published in 1821–22, quoted liberally from the "very able *Review*" in his account of the campaigns around Lake George and insisted that the essay was written "without any reasonable doubt by the late Governor Livingston, in concert with his two celebrated friends . . . Smith . . . and . . . Scott." Jefferson, who owned a copy of the 1770 edition, also ascribed it to Livingston.[51] In 1817, however, Samuel Jones, who had been a law clerk in Smith's office when the *Review* appeared, expressed his belief that Smith wrote the book, that he had copied it himself, allowing none of his clerks to see it, and that he had then personally nailed it up in a box and sent it to London for publication. Jones conceded, however, that the manuscript might have been furnished to Alexander in England by "Smith, or Livingston, or both" and that he could not positively identify the author unless he could see the handwriting of the manuscript.[52] Despite Jones's caution, some later historians more flatly attributed the *Review* to Smith, citing Jones as their authority and adding such circumstantial evidence as: Smith's intimacy with William Alexander; Alexander's correspondence with Smith and the trans-

50. Livingston to Noah Welles, 8 August 1757, 3 January 1758, Johnson Family Papers, Yale University; William Smith Diary, "August 5, 22, 1757," "January 18, 1758," 2:418–19, New York Public Library. According to Smith, De Lancey himself was less disturbed by his "full Length" portrait in the pamphlet than were his followers.

51. Dwight, *Travels in New England and New York* (Cambridge, Mass., 1969), 3:252, 257; E. Millicent Sowerby, comp., *Catalogue of the Library of Thomas Jefferson*, 5 vols. (Washington, D.C., 1952–59), 1:202.

52. Samuel Jones to John Pintard, 24 November and 20 December 1817, New York Historical Society *Collections*, 1st ser., 3(1821):348–49, 361.

mission of official data from Shirley's headquarters via Alexander to Smith; Smith's notation of the publication of the pamphlet in his diary; the similarity between the language of the *Review* and that of Smith's *History*; Smith's gift of a copy of the *Review* to Prince William in 1782 (hardly appropriate if the author were Livingston, since the latter was then the "rebel governor" of New Jersey while Smith was a Loyalist); and, lastly, the attestation of Livingston's authorship "only by repetition," since no manuscript of the pamphlet has ever been located.[53]

None of the circumstantial evidence for Smith's authorship is very convincing. Smith confided to his diary his authorship of numerous anonymous and pseudonymous publications, but he gave no hint in it of his connection with the *Review*. His notation of publication of the *Review* in that diary is scarcely a confession of authorship. Livingston aired his own views on the subject more fully in his letter to Welles. The gift of the *Review* to His Royal Highness in 1782 was adventitious. The real object of the Prince's interest was Smith's *History*, and the latter happened to be "bound up" with a copy of the *Review*. Significantly, when Smith sent the two publications, he referred to "my History" and to "the Review." The alleged similarities between the style and language of the two publications do not exist when both are carefully read, although the factual matter concerning New York's government and the French and Indian War is obviously much the same in both because of the collaboration between Livingston and Smith during this period. However, the *History* is much milder in its treatment

53. The reasons given are those of Leslie F. S. Upton in his *Diary and Selected Papers of Chief Justice William Smith, 1784–1793*, 2 vols. (Toronto, 1963, 1965), 1:xviiin, and in his *Loyal Whig*, pp. 36–37n, and of Beverly McAnear, "Politics in Provincial New York," pp. 900–01n, and *Papers of the Bibliographical Society of America* 44(1950):335n. Based upon McAnear's attribution, Clifford K. Shipton has listed Smith as the author of the *Review* in the *National Index of American Imprints through 1800: The Short-Title Evans*, 2 vols. ([Barre, Mass.], 1967), 2:788. O'Callaghan, in *N.Y. Col. Docs.*, 6:959, and 7:909, accepts Smith as the "supposed" author.

of the principal personalities in the Shirley controversy than is the *Review*, and the praise of the Massachusetts general is not nearly as extravagant in the first as in the second.[54] Alexander's confidential communications with Smith cannot be questioned, but the official documents transmitted from Shirley's headquarters to New York City were not for Smith alone. "No person must even know that you [have] them but yourself and W[illia]m Livingston," Alexander cautioned Smith in 1756 while sending him accounts of two councils of war held at Oswego. He added: "What I write you for the future I intend for you both, and I hope the Boss [i.e., Livingston] will take that for a sufficient apology if I don't write to him." [55]

One bit of circumstantial evidence pointing strongly to Livingston rather than Smith as the *Review's* author escaped the literary detectives: Smith was readying his *History* for the press at the very same time that the *Review* was being written. Both were published in London in 1757. Smith probably could not have penned two different and fairly extensive works concurrently. There is, however, more than inferential data for Livingston's authorship of the *Review*. His son William, Jr., contemplating a publication of his father's works in 1801, made a list of "those of the writings . . . that I at present recollect." The "Military Operations of 1753" was included among them, along with at least one other anonymous piece that a modern historian attributed to Smith. Theodore Sedgwick, Jr., Livingston's great-grandson, assembled the largest

54. William Smith Diary, "July 12, 1782," New York Public Library. Two other readings of the *History* and the *Review* have resulted in the same conclusion: Harold W. Thacher, "The Social Philosophy of William Livingston" (Ph.D. diss., University of Chicago, 1935), p. 72n, and Varga, "New York Government and Politics during the Mid-Eighteenth Century," p. 53n.

55. Evidence of Alexander's and Shirley's transmission of official data to Smith is found in the Smith Diary, entries of 11, 20 October and 27 December 1755, 29 January and 14, 17 July 1756 (2:397, 401, 410, 412, New York Public Library); Alexander to Smith, 23 March 1756, William Alexander Manuscripts 2, New York Historical Society.

available collection of Livingston manuscripts while preparing his *Memoir of the Life of William Livingston*, which appeared in 1833. Sedgwick not only listed the *Review* as one of Livingston's writings but stated that he had seen "the author's assertions, which are positive," to substantiate the attribution. Finally, Thomas Jones, loyalist historian of New York during the revolution and a contemporary of both Smith's and Livingston's, recorded that Livingston introduced the *Review* at the time of the McDougall trial in 1770, pointing out to the jury that if McDougall's alleged publication was libelous, it was no more so than the *Review*. The latter, Jones gibed, Livingston could well vouchsafe, "his friends a few years afterwards publicly acknowledging that he himself was the author."[56]

The author's anonymity only added to the interest in the *Review* in both England and America. Edwin Floyd De Lancey, a descendant of the lieutenant governor, explained that the *Review* elicited no response from his ancestors because its abundant "falsehood" did not make it "worthy of notice." The De Lanceys failed to publish a defense, more because of their disinclination to call further attention to the pamphlet, which was being passed about surreptitiously in New York, than because of their indifference to its calumnies. So effectively did the De Lanceys suppress its circulation that copies were not available to New Yorkers for purchase until 1770, when it was republished there. New Englanders had a 1758 republication, probably emanating from New Haven. Abroad, Britons could read both the 1757 London and Dublin editions, and despite the English reviewer's judgment that the author was "too warm" a partisan of Shirley, the publication was "universally read

56. William Livingston, Jr. to William Patterson, 29 May 1801, Miscellaneous Manuscripts, New York Historical Society; Sedgwick, *Memoir*, pp. 114–15, 448; Thomas Jones, *History of New York during the Revolutionary War*, ed. Edwin F. De Lancey, 2 vols. (New York, 1879), 1:29.

and talked of" in the British capital. The 1770 republication in New York was justified at the time on the ground that the sale abroad of the original had been "so rapid" that few copies reached America, where they had been "instantly bought up." One reason for its British appeal, according to its most judicious critic, was that the *Review* provided more information about the campaigns in America than did the "imperfect and desultory" news accounts.[57]

The *Review's* factual aspect has given it its enduring quality. Despite his bias, Livingston's observations on the war in New York were sufficiently astute and informed to become the basis of much later historical writing on the subject. Francis Parkman drew heavily on the work for his description of the early northern campaigns in his *Montcalm and Wolfe*, explaining that the author was "an able but somewhat caustic and prejudiced" protagonist. Justin Winsor considered Alexander's and Livingston's accounts "the best contemporary narratives in print" about Shirley's command. In our own day, Lawrence H. Gipson found the *Review* as useful as Parkman had almost a century earlier for the volume on "The Years of Defeat, 1754–57" in his monumental series on the Great War for Empire.[58]

As a literary production, the *Review* bears the familiar touches of Livingston's "talented pen": a trenchant, vigorous, acerb, at times florid and extravagant style, but never dull or equivocal. Neither Livingston's friendships nor his enmities were casual. The hostility to the De Lanceys displayed in the *Review* reflected the

57. De Lancey, "Memoir of James De Lancey," *N.Y. Doc. Hist.*, 4:1054; Wroth, *American Bookshelf*, p. 167–71; *Monthly Review* 16(1757):524–27; Smith, *History*, 2:256; *New-York Mercury*, 5 March 1770. The latest republication was in the *Collections* of the Massachusetts Historical Society, 1st ser. 7(1801, reprinted 1846):67–163.

58. Parkman, *Montcalm and Wolfe*, 2 vols. (Boston, 1885), vol. I, chs. 9, 10, 12, 13, and particularly p. 316; Justin Winsor, ed., *Narrative and Critical History of America*, 8 vols. (Boston and New York, 1884–89), 5:583; Gipson, *British Empire*, volume 6, chs. 6 and 7.

long political rivalry between the two great families that underlines so much of New York's prerevolutionary history. Livingston lost none of his contempt for Pownall; in 1759 he expressed it again in a burlesque of one of the Massachusetts governor's addresses to the legislature. His hatred for Johnson extended even to the second generation; Livingston as late as 1787 declined a favor for Johnson's son because the father "was ever an enemy of mine" and the Johnsons undoubtedly bore "the same like enmity to every human creature by the name of Livingston."[59]

In its immediate political impact, Livingston's literary effort was only half-successful. Shirley was vindicated in England, although by his own defense as much as by the appearance of the *Review*, and received a new commission as governor of the Bahamas. At home, the elections of 1758 gave the Livingstons some victories over the De Lanceys but not the ascendancy they sought. But for Livingston, the contest was always worth as much as the prize. In the *Review* he had made a contribution to both colonial and imperial politics and had written a history of interest in his own day and of continuing value to a later age.

59. For a literary evaluation, see Moses Coit Tyler, *History of American Literature, 1607–1765*, 2 vols. (New York, 1897), 2:222. The Pownall burlesque appeared in Weyman's *Gazette* for 26 March 1759. Livingston confessed his authorship to Noah Welles, 21 March 1759, Johnson Family Papers, Yale University. On Johnson, see William Livingston to William Livingston, Jr., 6 March 1787, Livingston Papers, Box 15, Massachusetts Historical Society.

6.

Thomas Jefferys's *History of the French Dominions*

JOHN M. BUMSTED

In September 1759, Wolfe and Montcalm sealed the fate of the French Empire in America on the Plains of Abraham. The British victory did not end the fighting, but it clearly indicated to Britons that French America was theirs if they wanted it. Eighteenth-century wars were fought, not for ideological or nationalistic reasons, but for the results at the conference table when gains and losses were totalled up. In this war Britain would have far more gains than losses. Britain's ruling classes sought to become familiar with the new territories which might become parts of the expanding British Empire, and they soon discovered *The Natural and Civil History of the French Dominions in North and South America,* published in January 1760. Although in preparation for some time, *The Natural and Civil History* had hastily been given an addendum describing the fall of Quebec and was brought on the market to meet the anticipated demand for information about the French colonies. Based as it was on the best French sources available—indeed, in many places, it merely translated the French text into English—and containing eighteen maps and charts drawn by some of Britain's finest cartographers, it admirably filled the function for which it was intended.

Thomas Jefferys, compiler or editor of *The Natural and Civil History* (he never claimed to be its author), was one of the most fascinating figures in British publishing in the mid-eighteenth century.[1] The place and date of his birth are uncertain, although it appears doubtful that he was born as early (1695) as some older bibliographical sources indicated. Equally mysterious is Jefferys's early career; available evidence suggests that he was trained as an engraver. Somehow he turned this engraving skill to the preparation of maps, and, beginning in 1732, he began to re-engrave maps. These early productions set the tone for much of Jefferys's subsequent career. For the most part, he copied from someone else's work, but in many cases he improved the appearance of the original. By the 1740s his skill as an engraver was widely recognized; he engraved maps for the popular *Gentleman's Magazine* and for Thomas Salmon's *A New Geographical and Historical Grammar*, one of the earliest annotated atlases. In 1746 he was appointed "Geographer" to H.R.H. Frederick, Prince of Wales, and after 1748 was styled "Geographer of Maps and Charts" to the prince.

When Jefferys married in 1750, he was ready to expand his activities. He moved to a large shop at 5, Charing Cross (facing the Strand), which served him as home and place of business until his death in 1771.[2] Here Jefferys operated a cartographer's shop and expanded his engraving and publishing business. He soon specialized in the Americas, and in the 1750s an increasing quantity of charts, maps, and books about the New World emerged from his shop. These found a ready audience because of Britain's great military and imperial struggle in America. Jefferys's principal assistant appears to have been one John Green, whose cartographical works emphasized accuracy and cross-checking of maps against literary

1. The most thorough biographical study of Jefferys is J. B. Harley, "The bankruptcy of Thomas Jefferys: an episode in the economic history of eighteenth century map-making," *Imago Mundi* 20 (1966): 27–48.

2. R. A. Skelton, ed., *James Cook Surveyor of Newfoundland. Being A Collection of Charts of the coasts of Newfoundland and Labradore, &c. Drawn From Original Surveys Taken by James Cook and Michael Lane. London, Thomas Jefferys, 1769–1770* (San Francisco, 1965), pp. 20–21, 28.

and other sources.[3] After Green's death in 1757, Jefferys did not always live up to Green's standards, but his reputation was made, and Jefferys's best work had as its hallmarks accuracy, completeness, and careful draftsmanship. As his business expanded, Jefferys undoubtedly did less and less of the work himself and left increasing amounts to underlings. It appears certain that by the time of the publication of *The Natural and Civil History* in 1760, assistants did virtually all of Jefferys's work.

Much of the expansion of Jefferys's business can probably be attributed to his increasingly close connection with the Office for Trade and Plantations, a relationship which began about the same time as the publication of *The Natural and Civil History* and can perhaps be associated with his patron's accession to the throne. Although Jefferys held no monopoly of cartographic services for the lords commissioners, his work was recognized as authoritative, particularly on the Americas. He received access to public documents and drafts, which he re-engraved for publication. Private persons connected with the government turned to him as well. The first important chart by the great explorer and surveyor James Cook was a Jefferys publication, and when Cook completed the charts of his survey of the coasts of Newfoundland in 1766, Jefferys was one of the publishers.[4] By 1768, Jefferys had acquired the rights to the charts from Cook, who thus indicated his respect for the "Geographer to the King."

Unfortunately for Jefferys, either his very successful American business did not appear sufficiently profitable or it gave him delusions of grandeur. The close of the Anglo-French wars may have led him to believe that the demand for American items would decrease. He would not predict, of course, that colonial rebelliousness would keep British North America in the public eye. In any case,

3. G. R. Crone, "The Retiring Mr. Green. In Search of an Eighteenth-Century Cartographer," *Geographical Magazine* 25(1952–53):539–41.
4. Skelton, *James Cook Surveyor of Newfoundland*, pp. 27ff.

in the early 1760s Jefferys expanded into another area, that of carefully surveying English counties as a preliminary to publication of
a detailed (one inch equal to one mile) map. Unlike his New
World productions, which were based largely on other people's
work and hence relatively inexpensive, county surveying involved
large expenditures of money in advance. Like others in the same
business, Jefferys advertised for subscribers and hoped to obtain the
premium of £100 offered by the Society of Arts in 1759 for any
original one-inch-to-one-mile county survey. Nevertheless, skilled
surveyors and equipment in the field for several months, as well as
transcription and engraving expenses, became expensive. There
were other dangers as well. One of Jefferys's completed maps, "being examined by many gentlemen, was found to be very incorrect."[5] Apparently overcommitted in various ventures, especially
the county surveys, Jefferys was forced into bankruptcy in November 1766.

The bankruptcy did not put Jefferys out of business, since his
creditors did not dispute his honesty and, as he wrote, "some
Friends . . . have been compassionate enough to reinstate me in
my Shop."[6] But although Jefferys continued to publish maps,
atlases, and other cartographic items until his death in 1771, his
last years were spent in relative penury. Perhaps even more tragic
for a man who prided himself on the quality of work produced by
the "Geographer to the King," he lost personal control of his stock
and engravings. As a result, the market became flooded with works
bearing the name of Thomas Jefferys which were little more than
collections of out-of-date material. In a sense, it was a tribute to
the man's reputation that his charts were still being published and
sold under his name until the end of the century. But there can
be no doubt that the high point of Thomas Jefferys's personal
career as a cartographer and geographer was reached about 1760

5. J. B. Harley, "The re-mapping of England, 1750–1800," *Imago Mundi*
19(1965):56–67. Harley, "The bankruptcy of Thomas Jefferys," pp. 43–44.
   6. Harley, "The bankruptcy of Thomas Jefferys," p. 28.

and can probably be associated, symbolically if not actually, with the publication of *The Natural and Civil History*. Certainly that work embodied all the strengths and weaknesses of eighteenth-century British cartography and geography, of which Jefferys was an acknowledged leader.

Jefferys's issuance of a general survey of French America was a natural outgrowth of his activities during the 1750s. In 1754 he had published a pamphlet entitled *The Conduct of the French, with Regard to Nova Scotia; from its First Settlement to the Present Time*. Possibly authored by John Green, this anti-French tract had gone through several editions, had been translated into French by G. M. Butel-Dumont (one of the leading French geographers of the time), and had even evoked a French response, *La Conduite des Français Justifiée*.[7] Green was clearly responsible for *The New Map of Nova Scotia, and Cape Britain* (1755) and its accompanying "Explanation" evaluating sources. This map became a standard part of British assertions of territorial claims in the northern maritime area of North America.[8] Jefferys (or those in his shop) was therefore familiar with French sources and was actively producing and publishing relevant North American maps and charts, some of which British forces undoubtedly employed when sailing up the St. Lawrence to besiege Quebec City in 1759.[9] Indeed, all the North American maps and charts which appeared in

7. The French translation, *Conduite des Français, par rapport à la Nouvelle Ecosse, depuis le premier établissement de cette colonie jusqu'à nos jours*, was published "à Londres" in 1755; the rebuttal, written by Gilbert Arnaud François Simon de La Grange de Chessieux, was published "à Utrecht, et se trouve à Paris, chez Le Breton" in 1756.

8. G. R. Crone, "John Green. Notes on a neglected Eighteenth Century Geographer and Cartographer," *Imago Mundi* 6(1949):85–91 (especially pp. 90–91).

9. A British intelligence report of 1757, entitled "A Description of the Town of Quebeck its Strength and Situation," noted: "I observed only two difficulties in the Navigation of this River [the Saint Lawrence], which are pointed out in the Chart lately published by Mr. Jefferies. . . ." Stanley Pargellis, ed., *Military Affairs in North America 1748–1765: Selected Documents from the Cumberland Papers in Windsor Castle* (New York, 1936), p. 414.

The Natural and Civil History had been previously published separately by Jefferys. New maps and charts on the French Antilles
were prepared especially for the *History*. In almost all cases, Jefferys
based his work on French sources, although he was by far a better
draftsman than they.

The *History* was intended primarily as a showpiece for the
cartography, which was, after all, Jefferys's principal business. Contemporaries recognized this. One reviewer wrote, "Maps are commonly made for the book, but here the book is made for the maps";
another commented, "The work seems to have been compiled
chiefly with a view to recommend and illustrate the . . . Maps
and Plans, most of which have been already offered separately to
the public."[10] These were not unfair assessments. Jefferys may have
decided that he could make money from a book about French
America, particularly since he had relevant maps with which to
illustrate it, and he accompanied the illustrations with a few
hundred pages of text. There was nothing prescient about recognizing the need and demand for such a work; the newsprints and
magazines of the 1750s were full of British activities in French
territory and background material (taken from French sources)
to clarify the news.[11] Jefferys fortunately had the work well into
production when news of the conquest of Quebec arrived in London, and he hastened to bring the book out early in 1760 to take
advantage of the public stir produced by Wolfe's exploits. Thus,
although *The Natural and Civil History* was not a polemic, it was
very much a work of the moment.

The text which accompanied the maps contained nothing original or even synthetic. *The Natural and Civil History* was an English compilation of the best and most up-to-date French sources
on the French Empire in America. In some places, the text was

10. *The Critical Review For the Month of January 1760* 9:47; *The Monthly
Review For February 1760* 22:82.
11. An example is *The London Magazine, Or, Gentleman's Monthly
Intelligencer* 28(1759).

simply a translation of the French original; in others, it was a condensation. Jefferys did not scrupulously identify his sources, but neither did he disguise his reliance upon them. Contemporary reviewers in both *The Critical Review* and *The Monthly Review* recognized that the text was extracted almost bodily from French sources and named the authors employed. Neither reviewer indicated any moral distress over the semipirated nature of the production, although both complained of its implications. One was upset that in relying on French authors (mostly Jesuit missionaries), Jefferys "injudiciously preserved all those idle encomiums on the Jesuits and Priests, and the discipline of their Church, with which those Writers have so extravagantly interlarded their several relations." *The Critical Review* protested that "every thing relating to differences between the English and French, is represented in the most uncandid and fallacious light, to the disadvantage of our own country. . . . In all American contests between the two nations, the English are described as fools, knaves, brutes, and cowards." Moreover, French nomenclature, which the reviewer thought "arbitrary" (apparently because it did not agree with his own), was frequently employed.[12]

In Jefferys's defense, it must be said that authors of almost every "history" or "geography" at the time shamelessly borrowed from other writers without any acknowledgment. Even in so-called "first-hand" accounts, much of the text was commonly cribbed from somewhere else. The complicated borrowing of information on America, frequently through several languages and over several centuries, has received too little attention from scholars. Moreover, as even his critics acknowledged, Jefferys did employ the best French sources.[13] The section on Canada (New France and

12. *Critical Review,* 9:47–58; *Monthly Review,* 22:81–96.
13. The reviewer in *The Critical Review* commented that "it must be owned, in favour of this compilation, that the best and almost only materials we have for a natural history of North-America, are those published by French writers" (9:48).

Acadia) was based on the writings of Pierre François Xavier de
Charlevoix; that on Louisiana relied on Antoine Simon Le Page
du Pratz's *Histoire de la Louisiane,* published in 1758; the section
on Santo Domingo was based on Charlevoix's edition of Father
Jean LePers's manuscripts entitled *Histoire de l'Isle Espagnole,
ou de S. Domingue;* units on the remaining French Antilles came
largely from two works of Jean Baptiste Labat: *Nouveau Voyage
aux Isles de l'Amérique* (1722) and *Voyage du Chevalier Des
Marchais en Guinée, Isles Voisines, et à Cayenne* (1731). Other
works employed more peripherally included Jean Baptiste du
Tertre's *Histoire Générale des Isles de S. Christophe, de la Guadeloupe, de la Martinique, et autres dans l'Amérique* (1654) and
Histoire Générale des Antilles Habités par les Français (1667–71),
as well as Sir Hans Sloane's *A Voyage to the Islands Madera, Bar-
bados, Nieves, S. Christophers, and Jamaica, with the Natural History . . . of the Last of Those Islands* (1707–25). Although parts
of Charlevoix and Le Page du Pratz were published in English translation in 1761 and 1763 respectively, Jefferys could claim credit
for first making these two authors available to an English audience
in substantial form.[14] On the French Antilles, Jefferys remained
the best text in English throughout the century, since none of his
sources were ever translated. Because of the importance of the
French texts for *The Natural and Civil History,* we must turn to
an analysis of the French authors, their writings, and the use Jefferys made of them.

14. Extracts from Charlevoix were available in both England and America
soon after the publication of his history of New France. An anonymous
pamphlet published in Boston in 1746 and entitled *An Account of the French
Settlements in North America: Shewing from the latest Authors, the Towns,
Ports, Islands, Lakes, Rivers, &c. of Canada* included an appendix, "Giving
a more particular and exact Account of Quebec, with its Inhabitants and their
Manner of Living. By P. Charlevoix." Various magazines also carried extracts
in the 1750s. For Charlevoix's history, see W. F. E. Morley, "A Bibliographical
Study of Charlevoix's *Histoire et Description Générale de la Nouvelle France,*"
Bibliographical Society of Canada Papers (1963), pp. 21–45.

Pierre Charlevoix (1682–1761) was born in Picardy and entered the Jesuit order at the age of sixteen.[15] He went to New France in 1705 and taught at its Jesuit college until 1709, when he was recalled to France to teach at the Collège Louis le Grand. One of his pupils was the young Voltaire. Because of his familiarity with New France, his order sent him in 1720 on an inspection tour of Jesuit missionary activities in the New World. The French government issued him secret instructions as well. He devoted a good deal of his attention to the western country, and he traveled through the Great Lakes down the Mississippi to Louisiana and back to France via Santo Domingo. Back home, Charlevoix reported on the West to the French government and recommended increased French activity in the Sioux country.[16] Although the government did decide to move into the West, it did not accept Charlevoix's offer to begin a mission among the Sioux.

After his American tour, Charlevoix settled down to teaching and writing, and he became a principal eighteenth-century chronicler of and apologist for French Jesuit missionary activities. As early as 1715 he had produced the standard work on Christian missions in Japan.[17] Following his return from the New World, he wrote a popular biography of the great Ursuline missionary in New France, Marie de l'Incarnation, edited Father LePers's notes for the *Histoire de l'Isle Espagnole*, revised his *Histoire de Japon*, and in 1744 published his major work, the *Histoire et Description Générale de la Nouvelle France* in three volumes.[18] Included in this work was a journal of his trip to North America in 1720–22,

15. For biographical details, see Léon Pouliot, *François Xavier Charlevoix, S. J.* (Sudbury, Ont., 1957).

16. Louise Phelps Kellogg, ed., *Journal of a Voyage to North America. Translated from the French of PIERRE FRANÇOIS XAVIER DE CHARLEVOIX* (Chicago, 1923), pp. xi–xxviii.

17. Pierre Charlevoix, *L'Histoire et l'Établissement, des Progrès et. de la Décadence du Christianisme dans l'Empire du Japon* (Rouen, 1715).

18. The *Histoire* was not translated into English until John Gilmary Shea prepared a six-volume edition between 1866 and 1872.

written as a series of letters to a French noblewoman. Here Charlevoix presented lengthy descriptive sections on the country, its natural resources, and its inhabitants, both European and Amerindian. These letters, the *Journal of a Voyage to North America*, contained the fullest and most up-to-date descriptive material available on Canada, and Jeffery pillaged them extensively for *The Natural and Civil History*. Omitting most of Charlevoix's daily travel itinerary, Jefferys included virtually all the Jesuit's descriptive material, somewhat rearranged and occasionally condensed. Thus the section of *The Natural and Civil History* entitled "A Description of New France" is basically lifted from Charlevoix's *Journal of a Voyage*. The historical section is condensed from Charlevoix's larger *Histoire de la Nouvelle France*, and the letters from Canada by British officers in 1759 are taken from the *London Gazette*.

In preparing his *Histoire de la Nouvelle France*, Charlevoix assiduously consulted and cited a large number of sources; his "Critical List of Authors" remains one of the best annotated bibliographies of early writings about Canada. However, the *Journal of a Voyage* was based largely on personal observation and on Charlevoix's familiarity with the *Jesuit Relations*, written by French missionaries in the seventeenth century.[19] Thus, while Charlevoix was unquestionably one of the eighteenth century's more careful historians, Jefferys's use of his work did not emphasize his historical craftsmanship. What was relevant to Jefferys was that Charlevoix had lived in New France, had traveled widely from Acadia to New Orleans, and had developed clinical powers of observation for the country's natural and human resources. Indeed, Charlevoix pioneered the scientific, analytical description of the Amerindians which constituted over one-third of Jefferys's material on Canada.

19. J. G. Shea, ed., *History and General Description of New France*, 6 vols. (New York, 1866–72), 1:67–96; Kellogg, ed., *Journal of a Voyage*, pp. xi–xxviii.

Many Jesuit missionaries who wrote about the Amerindians lacked familiarity with the scholarly literature on the subject, while most European scholars had never seen an Indian. Charlevoix combined scholarship with observation. His opening chapter, "On the Origin of the Americans," summarized three centuries of scholarly debate and concluded with "at least a strong conjecture that more than one nation of America have a Scythian or Tartar original." To conclude that the Amerindians had Asian origins was not original, but Charlevoix insisted the question would not be settled without careful linguistic analysis of Indian and Asian tongues.[20] He rejected tortured Biblical proofs and literary comparisons and demanded on-the-spot study to deal with the problem (which remains unresolved). Although Charlevoix's interpretation of the Amerindians was hardly value-free, his input of information and perspective was certainly more complete than most contemporary British works could offer. Jefferys had made a good choice for his material on Canada.

For material on French Louisiana Jefferys probably chose just as well, if only a single work were to be selected. He chose the *Histoire de la Louisiane* in three volumes by Antoine Simon Le Page du Pratz. Once he had decided on du Pratz, Jefferys did not deviate from his author, even though Charlevoix's *Journal of a Voyage* also had Louisiana material which did not always agree with du Pratz's. Born in the low countries, Le Page du Pratz had emigrated to Louisiana in 1718, where he settled as a planter until he returned to LaRochelle in 1734.[21] His *Histoire* relied heavily on Dumont, Hennepin, and Charlevoix, but the descriptive passages

20. Pierre Charlevoix, *Journal of a Voyage to North-America* . . . (London, 1761), pp. 43, 49.
21. Antoine du Pratz, *Histoire de la Louisiane. Contenant la découverte de ce vaste pays, sa description géographique: un voyage dans les terres, l'Histoire naturelle, les moueurs, coutumes, et religion des Naturels avec leur origine* . . . (Paris, 1758). For biographical information on du Pratz, see *Dictionary of American Biography*.

used by Jefferys were based upon personal observation or information. Jefferys condensed, abridged, and paraphrased du Pratz.
Whether Jefferys chose the "best" work on Louisiana is a moot
question, but he picked the one which would most often be translated and reprinted over the remainder of the century. Jefferys anticipated the first English edition of du Pratz, as he had of Charlevoix.

Securing sources for Part Two of *The Natural and Civil History*, which dealt with the French Antilles, proved a bit more
difficult. It is based on a handful of French sources which Jefferys
followed closely. The general "Description of the Islands subject
to the Crown of France in the West Indies, and South America,"
as well as the material on Santo Domingo, came from Charlevoix's *Histoire de l'Isle Espagnole, ou de S. Dominigue*, which he
in turn had based on manuscript memoirs and papers of a fellow
Jesuit missionary, Father Jean LePers. Charlevoix brought a good
deal of his own point of view to LePers's material and thus constituted a bridge between Jefferys's Parts One and Two, particularly concerning climate, living conditions, and non-European
peoples.

The source for Jefferys's brief descriptions of St. Bartholomew
and Desiderada is uncertain, but the material on St. Martin,
Guadeloupe Marigalante, Los Santos, Martinico, and Grenada
was taken from the six-volume *Nouveau Voyage aux Isles de
l'Amérique* by the Dominican missionary Jean Baptiste Labat.[22]
Father Labat was in the islands from 1694 to 1705. Most of Labat's
descriptive material was firsthand, but he scattered it among accounts of journeys and missionary activities, and Jefferys turned
elsewhere for his "A Natural History of the Antilles." He used a
source upon which Labat himself had relied heavily: the four-

---

22. Published in Paris in 1722. For biographical details on Labat, see
Everild Young and Kjeld Helweg-Larsen, *The Pirates' Priest: The Life of
Père Labat in the West Indies 1693–1705* (London, 1965).

volume *Histoire Générale des Antilles Habités par les Français,* published in Paris betwen 1667 and 1671 by the missionary Jean Baptiste du Tertre.

Interestingly enough, for the section "Of the Negro Slaves of the Antilles," Jefferys turned again to Charlevoix. Except for the introductory paragraph on the Negroes, the remaining material is virtually a direct translation of Charlevoix's *Histoire de l'Isle Espagnole.* Jefferys then added to this section brief comments and quotations from du Tertre and Labat. Both the introduction and the conclusion to the brief analysis of the Negro, however, appear to be original with Jefferys and reflect his own value judgments. Jefferys's opinions on the Negro slave were summed up when he wrote, "It is impossible for a humane heart to reflect upon the servitude of these dregs of mankind, without in some measure feeling for their miseries, which end but with their lives, as if their sable complexion were the black characteristic of their misfortunes."[23]

The "Description of the Island of Cayenne," which concludes *The Natural and Civil History,* is copied mainly from the work *Voyage du Chevalier Des Marchais en Guinée, Isles Voisines, et à Cayenne, fait en 1725, 1726, & 1727,* published in 1731 by Father Labat, although the material on the local natives was taken from Pierre Barrere's *Nouvelle Relation de la France Equinoxiale* (Paris, 1743). The recognition that previous descriptive material in his *History* would not adequately cover the natives of the South American coast led Jefferys to provide his readers with a relatively sophisticated—albeit highly derivative—statement on French New World possessions. Certainly, for the reader without access to the French originals or without the time to wade through them, Jefferys provided what one contemporary reviewer accurately labeled

23. Shelby T. McCloy, *The Negro in the French West Indies* (Lexington, Kentucky, 1966); Thomas Jeffreys, *The Natural and Civil History of the French Dominions . . . ,* 2 vols. (London, 1760), 2:186.

"a very useful performance, containing a great variety of matter, much entertainment, abundance of useful instruction."[24]

Aside from its obvious utility as an English compilation of French sources on French America, did *The Natural and Civil History* have any value or significance? It would be chimerical to claim that it was a seminal work, but in several ways the *History* fit into British developments of the time. Its appearance coincided with the beginning of British debate about the disposition of newly-conquered French territory and about the nature of the British Empire. Jefferys also introduced into England French perceptions of the Amerindian which contributed to that towering concept of the eighteenth-century Enlightenment: the noble savage.

The conquest of Quebec unleashed one of the most interesting and substantial British pamphlet wars of the eighteenth century—certainly the most concentrated attention America received before the Stamp Act. Usually referred to as the "Canada Versus Guadeloupe" controversy, it was really concerned with a much larger geographical area and raised far more fundamental questions. Between 1759 and 1763, nearly one hundred pamphlets and books commented directly on British policy toward its new American conquests and discussed the whole matter of empire.[25] The basic arguments for and against retention of substantial continental North American territory and for and against expansion of West

24. *Critical Review*, 9:58.
25. See W. L. Grant, "Canada Versus Guadeloupe, An Episode of the Seven Years' War," *American Historical Review* 17(1911–12):735–43; Clarence Walworth Alvord, *The Mississippi Valley in British Politics*, 2 vols. (Cleveland, 1917); Fred J. Ericson, "British Motives for Expansion in 1763: Territory, Commerce, or Security?" *Michigan Academy of Science, Arts, and Letters Papers* 27 (1941): 581–94; Jack M. Sosin, *Whitehall and the Wilderness: The Middle West in British Colonial Policy, 1760–1775* (Lincoln, Nebraska, 1961), especially pp. 3–26; Sir Lewis Namier, *England in the Age of the American Revolution*, 2nd ed. (London, 1963), pp. 273–82; and C. E. Fryer, "Further Pamphlets for the Canada-Guadeloupe Controversy," *Mississippi Valley Historical Review* 4(1917):227–30.

Indian holdings epitomized diverse British views of empire. No one argued against an expansion of American territory; the issue was which territory and how much.

Three fundamental arguments were advanced for the retention of New France exclusive of Louisiana, and three were advanced against it. The most important argument for retention was that removal of the French was essential for the peace and security of the empire. Not to make Canada British would encourage future military conflict which was both expensive and debilitating for England and its American colonies. Moreover, removal of the French would insure free British navigation of the North Atlantic, secure the fisheries, and facilitate Anglo-American trade. A second battery of arguments dealt with the potential of the enormous territory. American colonists would have new agricultural land for expansion, thus directing their attention from manufacturing; Canada contained limitless potential raw materials, and it offered a new market for British goods.[26] A final, but less far-reaching argument, was that retention of Canada would preserve the fur trade in British hands.

Against Canada's retention, it was argued that removal of the French threat would reduce colonial dependence on the mother country and might ultimately result in American independence. Even if the colonies did not revolt, they might become so prosperous that they would be more powerful than the mother country and come to dominate it. Some suggested that Canada was sim-

26. The ablest presentation of this argument was Benjamin Franklin's, in *The Interest of Great Britain Considered, With Regard to her Colonies, and the Acquisitions of Canada and Guadeloupe* . . . (London, 1760). See Leonard W. Labaree, ed., *The Papers of Benjamin Franklin*, 14 vols. (New Haven, 1959), 9:47–100. Franklin does not cite Thomas Jefferys in the pamphlet, but during the previous year he had paid Jefferys £4.19s for "engraving, printing, and paper of the map of Pennsylvania showing Indian lands and claims," which appeared in the front of Franklin's *An Enquiry into the Causes of the Alienation of the Delaware and Shawanese Indians* (1759); see Labaree, 8:199.

ply not very valuable or promising, with its cold and forbidding climate and its production of nothing but a few beaver skins. If Canada became prosperous and productive, it would duplicate British products. Finally, what would the British do with the large number of Frenchmen in the colony? As the Earl of Hardwicke wrote to the Duke of Newcastle in 1762, "if you remove the French inhabitants, this Kingdom and Ireland cannot furnish, or procure, people enough to settle and inhabit it [Canada] in centuries to come; and, if you don't remove the French inhabitants, they will never become half subjects, and this country must maintain an army there to keep them in subjection."[27]

In favor of acquiring various West Indian islands, especially Guadeloupe, writers argued their immediate value. Sugar was a commodity of increasing demand in Europe; the islands were fertile, easily peopled, and easily defended. Equally important, the islands fit into a self-contained empire. They produced crops not possible either in Britain or North America and would serve as a market for American agricultural products which Britain did not need. Since they could not become self-sufficient, trade with the islands would require ships and offer employment for British seamen. Against acquiring the islands, two arguments were employed. The West Indies contained extremely limited amounts of land and resources, with no possibility for expansion and future development. Perhaps even more important, the islands were uncongenial to European settlement because of the debilitating nature of the climate, the presence of large numbers of Negro slaves, and the limited opportunities for employment.

A number of writers thought Louisiana important in the debate, but few knew enough about it to venture strong opinions. One relatively continual theme, however, was the retention of Louisiana along with Canada in order to eliminate the French menace from

27. Cited in Namier, *England in the Age of the American Revolution,* p. 279.

North America. To leave the French on the Mississippi would only postpone a new conflict between England and France. Curiously enough, this argument came from those who argued for a reduced share of Canada so that some islands could also be included in the settlement.

The "Canada versus Guadeloupe" debate revolved around the nature of the postwar British Empire in the New World and around the results which the various participants prophesied would follow from either of the two broad alternatives. One would maintain Britain's self-contained and self-sufficient empire in America, its expansion checked and limited by a French presence which kept colonists loyal to the mother country. The other would encourage continental expansion free of conflict between French and British. Implicit was the notion that self-sufficiency was less important than potential future markets. Unchecked American expansion would risk the Americans' becoming too independent and powerful. The government had decided to keep Canada rather than the sugar islands even before the pamphlet war really got under way—a decision based upon political and strategic considerations which had little to do with the nature of the British Empire.[28]

What was the place of *The Natural and Civil History* in the debate and the governmental decision? Technically speaking, it was not part of the pamphlet war at all, and it has never been included in scholarly consideration of the problem. Perhaps because of this, it was more influential than the cogently argued polemics. Since Jefferys claimed only to inform—on the basis of the best available sources—his work could be read by British statesmen and politicians on its "merits." Its publication early in 1760 made it available before government policy and debating blocs had solidified, and as a source of information it had no competition.

28. Sosin, *Whitehall*, pp. 3–26, and Namier, *England in the Age*, pp. 273–82, are the principal exponents of this position, which is generally accepted by other scholars.

Moreover, Thomas Jefferys was "Geographer to the King" and semi-official consultant to the Office for Trade and Plantations. It appears almost certain that interested parties within the government—perhaps even the King himself, whose preferences played an important role in the ultimate government policy—read Jefferys.

Although Jefferys did not argue the relative merits of the respective French possessions and undoubtedly did not intend to state preferences, some were nevertheless present by implication. The very amount and prominence of attention given to Canada indicated something, and Jefferys had used Charlevoix, one of that region's most enthusiastic exponents, as a major source. Moreover, by eliminating all arguments about security, strategy, and potential results for the political nature of the Empire, Jefferys reduced comparisons to climate, resources, and geo-economic potential. Jefferys countered any arguments against Canada on the grounds of climate or lack of resources. The climate was "extremely wholesome to *European* constitutions," he said. The land was rich and fertile, abounding in coal, silver, iron, and other minerals. As for the forests, "the uses they are capable of serving . . . are so many that it is impossible to enumerate them." Jefferys's use of Charlevoix's praise of the Canadians made them seem like ideal additions to any empire.[29]

Although Jefferys also thought the French Antilles would be potentially useful additions to the Empire, his words about the islands never reached the same degree of hyperbole as did those about Canada. And, unlike Canada where everything seemed highly favorable, the Antilles had disadvantages which Jefferys made clear. In his general introduction, he argued that "a man must have a very good constitution, and besides live very soberly, or else have been naturalized to this climate, to have a chance of living long in it." In the section on Guadeloupe, he noted that the

29. Jefferys, *The Natural and Civil History,* 1:2, 9, 40.

island was hot, with mosquitoes, bugs, "nauseous vermin," and "tedious and often fatal disorders."[30] Thus Jefferys provided objective information which supported and reinforced decisions made by the government for quite different reasons.

Apart from the previously unacknowledged role of *The Natural and Civil History* in the debates over British retention of conquered French territory, it strikingly presented to a British audience the French concept of "le bon sauvage." Even before the discovery of America, as Henri Baudet has noted, European attitudes toward non-Europeans displayed a marked dualism. There were concrete relations with concrete peoples, but also a realm "of the imagination, of all sorts of images of non-Western people and worlds which have flourished in our culture—images derived not from observation, experience, and perceptible reality but from a psychological urge." One persistent theme in the European's relations with other peoples was the assertion of "the natural and fundamental goodness of primitive man." The extent to which these assertions represented either imaginative constructs (myths) to suit European needs or accurate observation remains unresolved, although prevailing academic thought leans toward the former.[31] In any case, beginning with Prester John in the fourteenth century (or even earlier), Europeans have explained non-European man in various ways, although inevitably in European terms. After the discovery of the New World, the Amerindian became the most

30. Ibid., 2:5, 80.
31. Henri Baudet, *Paradise on Earth: Some Thoughts on European Images of Non-European Man* (New Haven, 1965), pp. 6, 10. For the French contribution to this theme, consult Gilbert Chinard, *L'Amérique et la Rêve Exotique dans la Littérature, Française au XVII et au XVIII Siècle* (Paris, 1913). For a discussion of the dimensions of the problem, I am indebted to an unpublished paper by Wilcomb E. Washburn, "Relations Between Europeans and Amerindians During the Seventeenth and Eighteenth Centuries: The Epistemological Problem," delivered at the International Colloquium in Early North American History, Ottawa, Canada, November 1969.

common non-European subject of discussion until the nineteenth century.[32]

While European interpreters of the Amerindian did not present a monolithic view, the British tended to be less sympathetic to the Indian than the French. This probably results from the fact that the French were not settlement-oriented and saw the Indian as an object of missionary activity, while the British viewed the native as an obstacle to settlement. Even those British authors most sympathetic to the natives, like Cadwallader Colden or James Blair, left a picture which at best presented attractive characteristics of an otherwise brutish and savage existence.[33] French Jesuit missionaries, however, exalted the Indian for what might otherwise be seen as his defects. The high point of this view among Jesuits was reached by Charlevoix, Jefferys's basic source for material on the Indians. As one commentator has noted, Charlevoix "occasionally conveyed the impression that it was the Indians themselves, not the missionaries, who established the moral standards. Americans, he wrote, scorned French riches and conveniences because they wished to show that they were the true philosophers."[34] Long before Rousseau, the French Jesuits had created the concept of the noble savage, and *The Natural and Civil History* introduced this view to most English readers.

While Charlevoix used the Indians to chastise his European readers for their departure from the simple Christian life urged by Jesuit missionaries, this did not automatically make his presentation "mythological." Certainly he had more contact with the natives than did most who wrote about them, and he did not

32. Bois Penrose, *Travel and Discovery in the Renaissance 1420–1620* (Cambridge, Mass., 1952). Howard Mumford Jones, *O Strange New World* (New York, 1967), pp. 1–70.

33. Benjamin Bissell, *The American Indian in English Literature of the Eighteenth Century* (New Haven, 1925), pp. 1–77.

34. J. H. Kennedy, *Jesuit and Savage in New France* (New Haven, 1950), p. 101.

hesitate to criticize their bad points. But at the same time, his conclusions, which Jefferys translated verbatim for British readers, can scarcely be matched in any previous writings in English about the Amerindians before *The Natural and Civil History*. Although British popular thought before 1760 paid little attention to primitive peoples and simple living, the next few years saw an explosion of interest on these topics. To writings about the Indians was added a sizable literature on the South Seas islanders, so that by 1770 James Boswell could write that "the difference between the savage and civilised state of man has been much considered of late years."[35] Jefferys's work contributed to this interest in primitivism; in this respect, as in its geographical subject matter, *The Natural and Civil History* was published on a rising tide of public interest in Britain.

The *History* managed to thrust itself into the mainstream of debate and discussion, both political and intellectual, in Britain in the early 1760s. While some of his contemporaries severely criticized it, Jefferys's work could not be ignored.

---

35. Lois Whitney, *Primitivism and the Idea of Progress in English Popular Literature of the Eighteenth Century* (Baltimore, 1934); Bissell, *The American Indian*, pp. 77ff.; Chauncy Brewster Tinker, *Nature's Simple Plan: A Phase of Radical Thought in the Mid-Eighteenth Century* (Princeton, New Jersey, 1922), p. 1.

7.

Samuel Smith's *History of Nova-Caesaria*

CARL E. PRINCE

Samuel Smith was an early example of the historian-activist. This enlightened and benevolent scion of Quaker gentry collected his data and wrote his history while he functioned at the top level of colonial politics. For a quarter-century before the revolution, Smith the politician engaged in a running battle with the Crown; his *History of the Colony of Nova-Caesaria, or New-Jersey,* published at a high point in the struggle against England, expressed his own disenchantment with overseas control of colonial fortunes. This is the key to the book. New Jersey historians have long depended on Smith's volume and recognized both his pre-eminence as a contributor to the historical guild and his significant and Quakerlike efforts on behalf of New Jersey's Indians and slaves. What has never been acknowledged is the reflection in both his life and his writings of the mounting tensions of the third quarter of the eighteenth century—tensions which culminated in the War for Independence.

More than a half-century ago, one historian not unfairly encapsulated Samuel Smith as a "benevolent Quaker whose influence for good was potent in the province" of New Jersey.[1] His extensive influence was largely an accident of birth. Born 13 December 1720 into a prominent and wealthy Quaker family in West Jersey, he

1. Edgar J. Fisher, *New Jersey as a Royal Province 1738–1776* (New York, 1911), p. 69.

stood high, not only in colonial New Jersey politics, but also within the bicolonial New Jersey-Pennsylvania Society of Friends. His great-grandfather, though he remained in England, was an original proprietor of the province of West Jersey and a signer of the "Concessions and Agreement of 1677," one of the colony's earliest constitutions. Smith's grandfather did settle in New Jersey, becoming a merchant and taking his place in the emerging ruling circle as a member of the colonial Assembly. The upward curve of the family's status, as the eighteenth century progressed, was reflected in the promotion of Samuel's father, who had earned a reputation as a "flourishing merchant," from the Assembly to the Governor's Council by Lewis Morris in 1738. The Quaker historian inherited from his father not only social status and wealth but also his profession as a merchant and eventually his seat on the Governor's Council.[2]

Samuel Smith, in his turn, was well connected and prosperous. His official positions in the colony measured his associations. Like his father before him, he rose from membership in the New Jersey Assembly (1754–63) to the Council (1763–75). In addition to his legislative responsibilities, he occupied the sensitive and powerful position of Treasurer of West Jersey during the tumultuous years 1762–75.[3] The political weight and involvement of these offices was augmented by his kinship to or intimacy with important figures in New Jersey politics and in the Society of Friends.

Samuel's older brother, John Smith, was better known than he, at least in Quaker circles. Though born in New Jersey, John spent his young manhood in Philadelphia, where he augmented the family's fortune by expanding its merchant activities. Even before he left the Quaker capital in his early forties to resettle in Burling-

2. Ibid., pp. 52–53; John Jay Smith's Biographical Sketch in Samuel Smith, *The History of the Colony of Nova-Caesaria, or New Jersey* (Trenton, William S. Sharp Edition, 1877), p. v; Abstract of Samuel Smith's Will, 1776, in *New Jersey Archives*, 1st ser., 34:480–81.

3. Larry R. Gerlach, "Revolution or Independence? New Jersey 1760–1776" (Ph.D. diss., Rutgers University, 1968), pp. 752, 755.

ton, New Jersey, John had gained a reputation as a Quaker religious writer. He had married Hannah Logan, daughter of James Logan, the "most distinguished man in the province" of Pennsylvania. Through his brother and the Logans, Samuel knew many important leaders in Quaker politics, religion, and education.[4] He fused his own ties with the Pennsylvania Friends through his marriage to Jane Kirkbride, daughter of a prosperous Bucks County farmer.

Samuel's New Jersey connections were also impeccable. While he was still an adolescent, his widower father married a sister of Lewis Morris, soon to be royal governor of New Jersey and a leading representative of the first family of that colony's politics. Samuel's connection with the Morris clan through his stepmother, of course, did not hurt his political career. Smith was also a close friend of New Jersey governor Jonathan Belcher, through whom he came to know Andrew Oliver, brother-in-law of future Massachusetts governor Thomas Hutchinson and an important politico in his own right. In the decades immediately preceding the revolution, moreover, Smith enjoyed a close working relationship and personal friendship with William Franklin, New Jersey's last and most able royal governor.[5]

As Smith's political fortunes improved, so did his life style. While others suffered from the economic dislocations of the 1760s and 1770s, Samuel Smith did not. By the early 1760s the shrewd Quaker had shifted his economic focus away from trade and into

4. Frederick B. Tolles, "A Literary Quaker: John Smith of Burlington and Philadelphia," *Pennsylvania Magazine of History and Biography* 65 (1941): 303. An example was the friendship that flowered between Samuel Smith and Anthony Benezet, controversial and outspoken Quaker educator, philosopher, and philanthropist. Benezet was also an active opponent of slavery and friend to the Indians and may well have had a strong influence in these matters. See George S. Brookes, *Friend Anthony Benezet* (Philadelphia, 1937).

5. Donald L. Kemmerer, *Path to Freedom: The Struggle for Self Government in Colonial New Jersey, 1703–1776* (Princeton, 1940), pp. 226, 226n. See Jonathan Belcher to Samuel Smith, 17 March 1755, and William Franklin to Smith, 24 August 1772, Samuel Smith Papers, Rutgers University Library, New Brunswick, N.J.

land investments. Steadily adding to his holdings in the years before the revolution, he rented his land to tenant farmers and profited handsomely. Warm and compassionate in many ways, Smith was tough in matters involving money. He did not hesitate, for example, to dun his "Loving Cousin" who owed him money.[6]

Inconsistencies like those between his economic practices and Quaker injunctions in favor of charity and against worldliness—not atypical of the colonial Society of Friends—appeared in other phases of Smith's activities. Long and sometimes loudly opposed to slavery, the historian owned at least one slave himself as late as 1750. The devout Friend's clothes were far from somber, and his purchasing habits reflected no frugality. (In 1750 he bought five hats, including two rather showy beavers.) His Burlington estate had fifteen rooms, according to a 1775 inventory, ostentatiously (if graciously) furnished. Smith owned a library in excess of 250 volumes—a collection particularly rich in history, religion, and classical philosophy. Many of those volumes found their way into Smith's footnotes. After inheriting his brother's even larger library, to which he always had access, he must have owned the greatest private collection in New Jersey. That, at least, was within Quaker tradition.[7]

Also within Quaker convention was Samuel Smith's long-time opposition to black bondage and his sometimes singlehanded efforts

6. John Merrick to Samuel Smith, 25 June 1770; Memorial to John Smith, undated [1772]; Samuel Smith to his "Loving Cousin," 5 August 1773, Samuel Lundy to Samuel Smith, 20 June 1774, in Samuel Smith Papers, Rutgers University Library, New Brunswick, N.J.

7. Proof of Smith's ownership of a slave is found in receipts of 9 March 1745 and 16 May 1750 for purchases of goods required for the slave, in the Samuel Smith Papers, Rutgers University Library. For Samuel's clothing and furniture, see Samuel Smith's Account with Israel Henlings, 16 May 1750, and an inventory of household furnishings, spring 1775, Samuel Smith papers. The papers also contain a 1775 inventory of his library. See also Frederick B. Tolles, "A Literary Quaker," p. 303. The Smith brothers increased their libraries, it appears, by relieving recently widowed relatives of their deceased husbands' books. Usually, according to John, books from such sources ended up in "Sammy's" possession. "The Journal of John Smith," in Richard Morris Smith, *The Burlington Smiths* (Philadelphia, 1877), p. 132.

to improve the lot of indigenous New Jersey Indians. It may be unfair to pass judgment on his early ownership of a slave; it should not tarnish his subsequent efforts to decrease the scope of slavery in New Jersey more than a quarter-century before such efforts became common. Many attempts had been made in New Jersey to exact duties on the importation of slaves; they dated back to 1713. All had failed until, in the late 1750s, New Jersey Quaker sentiment against slavery finally crystallized. By 1762 Samuel Smith and others had taken up the anti-slavery issue. Smith led an unsuccessful Assembly fight to tax slave imports into the colony. A year later his efforts prevailed, but the duties were disallowed by the Privy Council in London. Smith's efforts to press the issue on his friend Joseph Sherwood, New Jersey's colonial agent in England, proved unavailing, at least for the time being. Not until 1767 did such a tax pass.[8]

The Quaker politician's interest in New Jersey's Indians was at once distinctive and fruitful. He pioneered in seeking an Indian accommodation with the white man—a notable effort because it occurred so early in American history. Smith was an organizer, perhaps a key planner, of "The New Jersey Association for Helping the Indians"; he also contributed generously to its endowment. In 1758 the organization founded a white-supported settlement named Brotherton, in which were relocated the remaining Lenni-Lenape Indians. Smith wrote the constitution of the Association, a document that also served as the ruling charter for this first white-endowed Indian community.[9]

8. Charles Read to Samuel Smith, 24 September 1762, Samuel Smith Papers, Rutgers University Library, New Brunswick, N.J.; Joseph Sherwood to Samuel Smith, 21 August and 7 September 1763, Joseph Sherwood Papers, New Jersey Historical Society. Richard P. McCormick, *New Jersey from Colony to State—1609–1789* (Princeton, N.J., 1964), pp. 103–04.

9. Rufus M. Jones, *The Quakers in the American Colonies* (London, 1923), p. 403; Dorothy Cross, "The Indians of New Jersey," New Jersey Historical Society *Proceedings* 70(1952):13; William E. Schermerhorn, *The History of Burlington, New Jersey* (Burlington, 1927), p. 255; McCormick, *New Jersey from Colony to State,* p. 103.

Smith's Quaker concern increasingly involved him in the colony's political affairs. As he approached middle age, one trait evident in both his politics and his writing was hostility to the British Empire. This hostility had its roots in a bitter experience Smith suffered at the hands of the Board of Trade, and events of national consequence beginning in 1763 only reinforced his prejudice against the mother country.

When Samuel Smith's father died in 1751, Governor Jonathan Belcher, a family friend, proposed to fill the vacancy on the Governor's Council by appointing the son. The elder Smith, by the time he died, had acquired a reputation as a political maverick; he "had always," it was said, "supported the people against the proprietors."[10] Samuel may have picked up this trait—or the reputation for it—which made him so unpopular in overseas ruling circles. At any rate, Belcher's nomination of Samuel Smith caused a stir both in the colony and abroad.

In 1751, when Belcher first proposed the younger Smith, the Board of Trade responded: "We have enquired into the character of Mr. Samuel Smith, whom you recommend to Us as a Proper person to supply the Vacancy in the Council." Whitehall found "that he is a Wellwisher to the Rioters and his Family active in that Faction."[11] The Lords then took after the Governor: "We cannot but express Our surprize, that, contrary to your Duty, you should thus attempt to fill the Council Board with Persons dis-

10. Fisher, *New Jersey as a Royal Province*, p. 62.
11. From 1745–51 conflicts erupted between the West and East Jersey proprietors and settlers on lands claimed by the two groups. Settlers rioted in several places in the colony against the proprietors and thus, frequently, against the legal establishment to which the proprietors had access. "The rioters soon developed a powerful organization throughout the northern counties and even extending into West Jersey as well. Jails were wrecked, sheriffs and judicial officers were threatened, armed bands took vengeance on those who held titles from the proprietors, and law enforcement agencies were quite powerless to deal with the emergency." For a succinct description and explanation see McCormick, *New Jersey from Colony to State*, pp. 77–79.

affected to His Majesty's Government, and attach'd to such as disturb the peace of the Colony entrusted to your Care. . . . You [should] give us no future Cause to animadvert upon your Conduct in this respect."[12] Samuel Smith was not appointed.

Smith's antipathy for the Crown seems to have grown out of this rejection by Whitehall in 1751. The lords had been told that Smith favored the settlers who rioted against the proprietary establishment. Although Belcher denied Smith's complicity or sympathy, Smith did not deny involvement. The young politician did sign a petition supporting the rioters' demands as just and reasonable. His accuser before the Board of Trade was James Alexander (father of "Lord Stirling" of Revolutionary War fame), who branded Smith a ringleader in defending the "wanton" acts of the "criminals." Alexander offered evidence to justify his allegations against Smith and others in West Jersey.[13]

Smith's antipathy toward the Crown's power over the colonies marked his subsequent public career. If Whitehall eventually forgot or overlooked its early mistrust of Smith, the Quaker politician never lost his animus against England. When tension between England and the colonies mounted after 1760, Smith's interest correspondingly increased. He kept himself well-informed about imperial developments and corresponded not only with his colony's agent in London but with several British Quakers and Pennsylvanians.[14]

His knowledge of imperial affairs, evident in his book, and his political acumen in dealing with imperial problems caused Gover-

12. Lords of Trade to Governor Jonathan Belcher, 27 March 1751, *New Jersey Archives*, 1st ser. 7:586.
13. James Alexander to Robert Hunter Morris, 22 and 27 October 1751, *New Jersey Archives*, 1st ser. 7:626–31. See also Fisher, *New Jersey as a Royal Province*, p. 62; *New Jersey Archives*, 1st ser. 9:394n.
14. See the Joseph Sherwood Papers, 1760–66, New Jersey Historical Society. See especially Joseph Sherwood to Smith, 6 June, 16 September, and 2 December 1761, and 17 August 1762, and Sherwood to Robert Laurence et al., 27 February 1762.

nor William Franklin in 1763 to renew Smith's nomination to the Council. "I think from his Abilities and extensive influence in the Province," Franklin wrote the Board of Trade, "he will make a very useful Member of the Council." Smith was approved without hindrance and remained in that post until poor health forced him to retire in 1775.[15] This appointment, coupled with his position as Treasurer of West Jersey, placed the eminent Quaker in the midst of his colony's drift toward independence.

He was one of the first and most vocal protesters against both the Sugar and Stamp Acts. In 1764, as a member of an official Committee of Correspondence, Smith drafted and signed a remonstrance to Whitehall denouncing the sugar duties. The protest carried the stamp of his hostility: "In the name and in the Behalf of this Colony," it said, "we look upon all Taxes laid upon us without our Consent as a fundamental infringement of the Rights and Privileges Secured to us as English Subjects." The duties "will not only cramp us in our Business with one another and the English Merchants, but Impede the Growth of the Settlement of this Province." New Jersey's London agent duly transmitted the missive to the Board of Trade. Smith also opposed the proposal for a Stamp Act and repeatedly enjoined Joseph Sherwood to voice New Jersey's displeasure with the idea.[16]

Although Sherwood was his friend, Smith grew increasingly unhappy with the agent's laxity in pressing colonial claims in London. Smith came to admire Benjamin Franklin's representation of the colonies' position, which combined firmness with tact. Governor

15. Governor William Franklin to the Lords of Trade, 10 May 1763, and Franklin to the Earl of Dartmouth, 3 October 1775, *New Jersey Archives*, 1st ser. 9:387 and 10:665 respectively.

16. Samuel Smith et al. to Joseph Sherwood, 10 September 1764, Jacob Spicer Papers, New Jersey Historical Society. Although Smith's letters have not survived, Sherwood's answers indicate clearly the tone of the Quaker's missives. See Sherwood to Smith, 13 May and 14 December 1765, and 11 January and 25 February 1766, Joseph Sherwood Papers, New Jersey Historical Society.

William Franklin wrote his father in 1767 that "our friend Samuel Smith . . . says that he thinks all the provinces in North America ought to join to make it worth your while to reside in England as long [as] you live."[17]

Smith's criticism of imperial power remained a characteristic of his until he died. He lived long enough, in fact, to exult at the Declaration of Independence; he died on 13 July 1776, less than two weeks after its promulgation. A last entry in his account book for the Treasury of West Jersey recorded a payment of £330 to the New Jersey Committee of Correspondence for expenses incurred in opposing the mother country. Technically these were Crown funds being expended to overthrow the Crown, and Smith, perhaps tongue in cheek, noted the expense with malicious detail in his ledger so that no one could mistake his satisfaction in registering it.[18] The historian in Smith survived to the end.

Not long after his death, Smith's abilities as a historian were acknowledged. His friend Anthony Benezet in 1783 singled out *Nova-Caesaria* as "candid" and "sensible." Smith carefully preserved and transmitted vital historical documents to posterity. He not only collected them assiduously, tended them with care, and passed them on to others, but he also recorded history as he saw it from these archives. As Smith himself acknowledged, he pulled together manuscripts "scattered in different provinces" and "in danger of being lost." He left his own epitaph as a historical preservationist when he noted: "Whatever success may attend this undertaking . . . 'tis some satisfaction, that the labour of collecting [the manuscripts] cannot be altogether useless."[19]

17. William Franklin to Benjamin Franklin, 10 June 1767, *New Jersey Archives*, 1st ser. 9:625.

18. Samuel Smith's Account Book, entry undated (but after 26 December 1774), New Jersey Historical Society. For Smith's feelings about the Declaration of Independence, see the introduction to the Account Book.

19. Anthony Benezet to George ———, 14 September 1783, in Brookes, *Friend Anthony Benezet*, p. 403; Samuel Smith, *The History of the Colony of Nova-Caesaria, or New Jersey* (Burlington, 1765), p. xi.

Subsequent historians have confirmed Smith's judgment. More than a century later, William Nelson, editor of the *New Jersey Archives*, summarized Smith's contribution, noting that "Mr. Smith accumulated a great deal of material for a history of New Jersey, Pennsylvania and of the Society of Friends," not all of which was published in *Nova-Caesaria* or elsewhere. In 1765, after the appearance of the New Jersey volume, Smith began a history of Pennsylvania, which he never finished.[20] He also collected and used manuscripts relating to the Society of Friends and to other religious sects in eighteenth-century New Jersey and Pennsylvania.

Donald F. Durnaugh has attested to Smith's breadth and accuracy as a historian. After examining manuscripts now in the hands of The Brethren of the Common Life that Smith had either possessed or had access to when he described the sect in his *History of the Province of Pennsylvania*, Durnaugh acknowledged that "the account of the Brethren in Smith's history is quite accurate. . . . It bears evidence of being based on firsthand information from Brethren in Pennsylvania."[21]

Wallace N. Jamison, a prominent student of American religion, noted that *Nova-Caesaria* was "still useful because of the letters, laws and other primary sources quoted extensively in it." Rufus Jones, another eminent historian of religion, acknowledged that Smith was a link in the preservation of important papers of the Quaker establishment in colonial America. After the death of John Kinsey in 1750, Smith received the papers of the Quaker yearly meetings dating back to the seventeenth century, according to Rufus Jones.[22] Some of these sources found their way into the 1765 *His-*

20. The uncompleted portion, in the possession of the Historical Society of Pennsylvania, was eventually published as *History of the Province of Pennsylvania* (Philadelphia, 1913).

21. *New Jersey Archives*, 1st ser. 9:394–95n. Donald F. Durnaugh, *The Brethren in Colonial America* (Elgin, Illinois, 1967), pp. 14–15.

22. Wallace N. Jamison, *Religion in New Jersey* (Princeton, N.J., 1964), p. 165; Jones, *The Quakers in the American Colonies*, p. 546.

tory of the Colony of Nova-Caesaria, but most, along with Smith's
notes and unpublished writings, were transmitted to Robert Proud,
who used them in his *History of Pennsylvania* before they ended
up in various archival libraries.[23]

Smith's contribution as a functioning historian has been evalu-
ated differently by two schools of thought over two centuries. A
minority view has Smith a dry, dull chronicler of little moment.
The weightier evaluations find Smith not only useful but singularly
important. Anthony Benezet set the tone for the minority in 1771
by reporting wryly that "at our last Meeting of Sufferings we were
told that Saml. Smith had lately given expectations that he would
proceed on ye History of the Province [of Pennsylvania]."[24]

Some historians would have viewed another history by Smith
as a cause for suffering. Moses Coit Tyler, writing in 1897, found
Smith "a dry, ponderous performance, a compilation of dull documents and dull facts." *Nova-Caesaria*, he concluded, was written
"doubtless with great patience, and only to be read by an abundant
exercise of the same virtue." A half-century later Tyler found some
support. Louis B. Wright found the book "so tedious that it is of
interest only to the specialist." Michael Kraus discovered "nothing

23. See Robert Proud, *The History of Pennsylvania*, 2 vols. (Philadelphia,
1797–98). Some historians have noted similarities between Proud's *History*
and manuscript drafts of Smith's that came into the former's hands. I do not
accept the allegation that Proud used Smith's notes and copy verbatim; what
Proud did use were the manuscripts dealing with Pennsylvania history that
Smith collected and that eventually came into Proud's possession. It is fair to
say, however, as Michael Kraus has noted, that "Smith's *History* was useful
to Proud." See Michael Kraus, *A History of American History* (New York,
1937), p. 121. Sydney G. Fisher, in *The Quaker Colonies* (New Haven,
Conn., 1921), p. 193, takes a very similar view. For the most damning in-
dictment of Proud, see William A. Whitehead's running commentary comparing the work, published and unpublished, of the two historians in "Minutes
of the Society," New Jersey Historical Society *Proceedings*, 1st ser., 47(1849):
102ff, 8(1856):40ff, and 9–10(1857–58): passim. See also ibid., 3rd ser.
47(1912):165–66.

24. Anthony Benezet to John and Henry Gurney, 23 December 1771, in
Brookes, *Friend Anthony Benezet*, p. 282.

exciting about Smith's narrative," concluding that the volume was
"an index to Samuel Smith's character; he disliked any disturb-
ance [! !] and expended little of himself emotionally." Homer
Hockett also found Smith's work "placid" and written with "undis-
turbed equanimity."[25] While some have found Smith dull, however, no one has ever questioned his meticulous accuracy.

For more than a century, however, other historians have sung
Smith's praises. William A. Whitehead, an important nineteenth-
century New Jersey historian, told an 1849 gathering of the New
Jersey Historical Society that "no one who attempted to study the
history of the State, could withhold the expression of his thanks for
the assistance derived from Smith's history." A half-century later,
William Nelson, editor of the *New Jersey Archives,* observed that
Smith's *History* was "the first and best History of New Jersey."
The early years of the professionalization of the historical craft
established the Quaker historian's reputation.[26]

Edgar J. Fisher considered Smith "the pioneer historian of
New Jersey," and John Spencer Bassett described Smith as "industrious and conscientious," so much so that *The History* "has not
been entirely superceded." Sydney G. Fisher, an important historian of the Quakers, felt in 1921 that among "the older histories
of New Jersey," Smith's "should have first place." Among its virtues, he observed, were the book's inclusion of "valuable original
material not found elsewhere" and "as intelligent a grasp of politi-

25. Moses Coit Tyler, *A History of American Literature During the
Colonial Time, 1677–1765,* 2 vols. (New York, 1897), 2:225; Louis B.
Wright, *The Cultural Life of the American Colonies 1607–1763* (New York,
1957), p. 165; Michael Kraus, *A History of American History,* pp. 99–101,
and *The Writing of American History* (Norman, Oklahoma, 1953); Homer
C. Hockett, *The Critical Method in Historical Research and Writing,* 3rd
ed. (New York, 1955), pp. 197–98.
26. [William A. Whitehead], "Minutes of the Society, 1849," New Jersey
Historical Society *Proceedings* 4(1849):102; William Nelson, ed., *New Jersey
Archives,* 1st ser. 24:273n.

cal events as any modern mind could show." A score of years later, Donald L. Kemmerer still felt that Smith was "the first noteworthy chronicler of New Jersey history . . . an eminently fair and broadminded gentleman."[27]

Samuel Smith's reputation has grown with time, as contemporary historians will attest. During the 1960s several historians, including Frederick B. Tolles, called for a reprinting of *The History*. Bibliographer and historian Nelson R. Burr, two hundred years after the publication of *The History of the Colony of Nova-Caesaria*, dedicated a volume of his own "to the memory of Samuel Smith, Author of the first history of New Jersey." Richard P. McCormick commented that Smith's is "a remarkable work, still worthy of study"—a book both "cultivated and learned" that "commands respect even today." It is, McCormick concluded, a fine example of the Quaker mind at work. John T. Cunningham, one of New Jersey's best-known historians, believes Smith's book to be the first "genuine" history of the colony. John E. Pomfret characterized Smith's publication as "the starting point for all later [New Jersey] histories," as a book that, uniquely for its day, "recognized the value of contemporary source materials."[28] These representative comments pay tribute to a historian who, irrespective of time and place, wrote as he lived.

27. Fisher, *New Jersey as a Royal Province*, p. 69; John Spencer Bassett, *The Middle Group of American Historians* (New York, 1917), p. 11; Sydney G. Fisher, *The Quaker Colonies* (New Haven, Conn., 1921), pp. 192–93; Kemmerer, *Path to Freedom*, p. 227n.

28. Frederick B. Tolles, "The Historians and the Middle Colonies," in Ray A. Billington, ed., *The Reinterpretation of Early American History: Essays in Honor of John Edwin Pomfret* (San Marino, California, 1966), p. 76; Nelson R. Burr, A *Narrative and Descriptive Bibliography of New Jersey* (Princeton, N.J., 1964), p. vi; McCormick, *New Jersey from Colony to State*, pp. 101, 176; John T. Cunningham, *New Jersey: America's Main Road* (Garden City, New York, 1966), p. 311; John E. Pomfret, *The New Jersey Proprietors and Their Lands* (Princeton, N.J., 1964), p. 125.

History is not often so neatly packaged, but Smith's book reflects the overriding interests of his life. His lifelong concern for the Indians is extensively mirrored in *Nova-Caesaria*. An equally pervasive theme—and perhaps one of greater significance—is his unrelenting hostility toward British colonial control. He undoubtedly directed his animosity against the empire backward into time, an animosity so evident in the 1760s that the publication date of 1765 is crucial in understanding the volume. *Nova-Caesaria* was in preparation through fifteen years of Smith's political involvement; it was published coincident with the aftermath of the Sugar Act and the beginning of the furor over the Stamp Act.

The book was a political tract for the times. It provided a reformer's manual to guide the white man in dealing with the Indians and a political lesson in the pitfalls of English hegemony over the American colonies. Every generation writes history in its own image, but this book nevertheless remains good history. It holds an important place in the literature of New Jersey; it should hold an important place in the literature of the revolution.

Samuel Smith's sensitivity to the white injustices done the Indians pervaded the book. After mentioning seventeenth-century Swedish purchases of land from "some Indians," he added with typical finesse, "but whether of such [Indians] as had the proper right to convey is not said." The historian pointed out that, in dealing with the white man, "the Indians Kept this league [treaty] faithfully." Though it was not always reciprocated, Smith said, "through a long course of experience, [the Indians] manifested an open hospitable disposition" to all white settlers.[29]

He repeatedly recounted Indian acts of kindness toward whites and challenged the credibility of accounts of occasional Lenni-Lenape acts of violence against settlers. In New Jersey, according

29. Smith, *The History of the Colony of Nova-Caesaria*, pp. 22, 33, 52.

to Smith, once the whites had paid for the lands, the Indians "became [from] a jealous, shy people, serviceable good neighbours, and though frequent reports of their coming to kill the white people, sometimes disturbed their repose, no instance occurs of their hurting [whites] in those early settlements." Smith was a literate and discerning historian; he could also reach high eloquence when he wrote about New Jersey's indigenous population. An excellent chapter on Indian civilization concludes with this combination of incisive analysis and literary grace:

From their infancy they were formed with care to endure hardships, bear derision, and even blows patiently; at least with a composed countenance: Though they were not easily provoked; it was generally hard to be appeased whenever it happened: Liberty in its fullest extent, was their ruling passion; to this every other consideration was subservient; their children were train'd up so as to cherish this disposition to the utmost . . . and they seemed to abhor a slavish motive to action, as inconsistent with their notions of freedom and independency; even strong persuasion was industriously avoided, as bordering too much on dependence, and a kind of violence offered to the will: they dreaded slavery more than death.[30]

Smith's compendium of the New Jersey Indians' treaties, mores, and character was so scrupulously detailed and carefully phrased that one feels the author wanted it all there, published and available, to remind his compatriots of their promises and to make them honor their agreements with the natives.

Smith could not force Whitehall to live up to his view of its obligations to colonial Englishmen, but he strove to set the historical record straight. He rather tartly reminded his readers of the mutuality of benefit in the colonial experience. The Quaker settlements, for example, apart from adding to the Friends' own glory,

30. Ibid., pp. 64ff, 143–44.

had contributed to "the present [1765] improvement of territory to the mother country . . . a link in the chain" of imperial growth "of some considerable importance." England too often lost sight of this perspective. Smith wrote of a pervasive feeling in the colonies of a "too general negligence [in Whitehall] as to particular rights of individuals" so that "the reputation of civil policy comes in question." Such negligence was "justly made the subject of general complaint."[31] This impressive criticism of English rule set the tone for the entire volume.

Smith's animosity toward England formed a rich vein slicing through the entire work. Commenting, by way of illustration, on the first taxes levied by the English on the new colony in 1664, Smith extemporized: "It was very early to impose such an extraordinary clog upon trade as [a] 10 per cent [impost] and no doubt hard upon the young settlers to pay it, and the reason for doing it, namely that it had been done before, seems not so well calculated to render the payment easy as might have been contrived." He spelled out the link with 1765 when he concluded that "these precedents introduced a similarity of taxation, which in time proved intolerable grievances."[32]

The Quaker historian used Governor Cornbury's reign (1703–08) to analyze the legal and moral flaws in imperial rule. Edward Hyde, Lord Cornbury, first royal governor of the colony, Smith described as one who ruled by "trick and design." "It was Cornbury's weakness," he added, "to encourage men that would flatter his vanity, and trim to his humors and measures."[33] Smith examined the surrender of New Jersey's proprietary rights in 1701 in terms of the animosities alive in the 1760s. From the inception of royal rule under Cornbury, the writer made it

31. Ibid., pp. viii–xiii.
32. Ibid., p. 56; see also pp. 116–17 and *passim*.
33. Ibid., p. 358.

clear, the Crown had consistently gone beyond its prerogatives in dealing with New Jersey.

The historian's rationalization rested on the premise that the proprietors in the first decade of the eighteenth century gave away that which was not legally theirs: "There does not appear to have been any design to abridge the privileges before enjoyed," nor could those "rights and privileges belonging to the inhabitants of New Jersey" be legally abrogated "by any of the steps taken before or in the surrender [of 1701–08]." A handful of proprietors in the colony, rather, had secured royal rule in order to protect their landed investment. That, Smith claimed, was at the root of the "surrender" to the Crown. But, he concluded, "it nowhere appears, that they [the proprietors] had any legal power to represent the settlers in general," for they were "but a small part of the proprietors, and a very small part of the settlers." In this light the Crown's instructions to Cornbury, repeated to future royal governors, were more than excessive; these instructions, Smith said, were based on purely private gain and were illegal.[34]

"Every *settler* who complied with the terms of settlement publickly established" after 1664, Smith disclosed, "as well as the *purchaser*, being entitled to the privileges purchased or settled under; it could not be lawful, that the act of any fellow proprietor to the last [purchaser] or landlord to the other [settler], should deprive them of what, by the original frame and constitutions . . . they had a share in; and had been the principal inducement of their removing hither to settle." Using history artfully, Smith supplied the clincher: "If the ideas of property in British subjects are the *same* in the colonies as in the mother country; according to these, nothing but their own act by themselves as individuals . . . could deprive them of it [their rights]; any thing less would imply an absurdity." And Smith demonstrated that the colonists' rights as

34. Ibid., pp. 261–65.

Englishmen had never been legally abrogated. Therefore, England, by its attempts at regulation since 1701, had transgressed the rights of Jerseymen and, indeed, of all Americans.[35]

From the vantage point of 1765, Smith saw no period of "salutary neglect" in American colonial history. Thus a major subtheme ran through the book: Assembly usurpation of the royal prerogative in the eighteenth century was the legislature's recapture of rights originally vested in Americans in the previous century.

Smith's useful thumbnail character sketches must be viewed in light of his anti-imperial bias. For example, he appraised Cornbury's successor, Francis Lovelace, as a man whose character "in general was rather that of an upright but timid governor and good natured man." Not so charitable, however, was Smith's description of tough and unpopular Sir Edmund Andros, of whom he wrote: "he bore the unfavourable character of an arbitrary governor, who made the will of his despotic master [James II] and not the law, the chief rule of his conduct."[36]

So it goes throughout the book. Smith made it easy for the twentieth-century reader. His prose was as pointed and candid as his politics were direct and committed. Smith was a sympathetic figure who was able to remain reflective and detached even as he immersed himself in the widespread difficulties of his day. To describe him as a typical member of the colonial landed gentry does an injustice to his vision and interests. To think of him only as a Quaker implies a political passivity that was nowhere in evidence. To write of him only as an anti-imperial historian impugns his integrity as a scholar—an integrity which at the end must be judged his greatest hallmark.

35. Ibid., pp. 265–66ff.
36. Ibid., pp. 73, 77n.

8.

John Adams vs. Daniel Leonard:
"Novanglus" Opposes "Massachusettensis"

Joseph A. Dowling

The relationship of the Adamses to their country has been one of fascinating ambivalence. With the probable exception of Charles Francis Adams, the great figures of the family—John, John Quincy, Brooks, and Henry—have all, despite heroic efforts, found themselves ill at ease in their native land. They have applied their critical intelligences and severe moral standards to American society—from John's *The Defence of the Constitution of the United States* to Henry's *The Degradation of the Democratic Dogma*—they have said things that many Americans preferred not to hear, and they have fastened on themselves a general reputation of gloomy, eccentric brilliance.[1]

The Adams' passionate, searching thought has been too often lost in their reserved, aloof life style. Despite many studies to the contrary, our second President conjures up the image of an honest, intelligent, but dull "Puritan" who served as "caretaker" between the deified Washington and the brilliant Jefferson. To the general public, John Adams is the dullest of the founding fathers.[2] Without questioning his services and his brilliance, they cannot

---

1. Charles A. Beard, Introduction to Brooks Adams, *The Law of Civilization and Decay* (New York, 1955), p. vii.
2. Zoltan Haraszti, *John Adams and the Prophets of Progress* (New York, 1964), p. 1.

accept or understand his emotional and moral commitment to his fledgling country. As he himself prophetically commented, "I have a very tender, feeling heart . . . this country knows not, and never can know, the torments I have indured for its sake."[3] Nor could many contemporaries who knew the lacerating tongue but not the "feeling heart" fully appreciate the man who could give them no more rest than he could give himself.[4]

Perhaps John Adams's position as the eldest of three sons intensified his drive to succeed while it increased his adherence to his parents' standards of abstemiousness and restraint.[5] Certainly his diary shows a youth caught with more than usual intensity in the conflicting drives of adolescence. His family, although prominent in Braintree, did not rank with the wealthy of the province, and John's tremendous capacity for work can be attributed in part to his desire to make his mark. At Harvard, which he entered in 1750, Adams did well enough to be named senior sophister at graduation and to win him a job as schoolmaster in Worcester. After considering various professions and tormenting himself with doubts concerning his future, Adams studied law with his rather nonchalant Worcester friend James Putnam. Acutely aware of people and events, Adams gained much insight into the ways of the town and was urged to stay. Possessed with ambition, he decided in 1758 to study law further in Boston. He sought help from the doyen of the Boston legal profession, Jeremiah Gridley, with whose support he was admitted to practice before the Superior Court.

Thus Adams was well launched on the career which would earn him both fame and notoriety and which helped determine the nature and method of his political theory. Law was particularly congenial to Adams since it developed from concrete cases, in-

3. Page Smith, *John Adams*, 2 vols. (New York, 1962), 1:261–62.
4. Haraszti, *John Adams*, pp. 2–5.
5. For biographical data on John Adams see Smith, *John Adams*; Catherine Drinker Bowen, *John Adams and the American Revolution* (Boston, 1950); Gilbert Chinard, *Honest John Adams* (Boston, 1933).

volved hard data, and moved to abstraction only from specifics. Adams's works were marked by their abundant supporting arguments, as well as by a pithy and earthy style. Unfortunately, he so successfully buried the style under massive documentation that the casual reader might easily conclude that Adams plagiarized most of his works.

Adams struggled hard in the early years to establish himself, but he often despaired in a society overcrowded with aspiring young lawyers and established amateurs whom John called "pettifoggers." Nevertheless, he did begin to make some mark—albeit a limited one—in the world. His father's death in the influenza epidemic of 1761 brought to John Adams both property and a more substantial position in Braintree. Despite his enhanced status, Adams was still haunted by his failure to live up to his own internalized standards, and he felt that his attempt to make a position for himself in the world was proceeding at an agonizingly slow pace. Certainly, as both Bernard Bailyn and Page Smith have pointed out, there was much in Adams that was neurotic.[6] His ". . . corrosive anxieties, hostilities and aggressions" and his impulsive actions might suggest paranoid tendencies. Whatever Adams's psychology, his marriage to Abigail Smith on 25 October 1764 provided him with a reservoir of sympathy and understanding. A woman of sense and sensibility, Abigail was not above pricking the pompous bubbles of male vanity. Her ready grasp of ideas and events provided Adams with an intellectual as well as an emotional refuge from his controversy-ridden life. She was the sheet anchor of his emotional stability.

Although Adams complained that troubles with the British blocked his rise in the world, the events that catapulted him to fame began almost simultaneously with his marriage. In 1763 the

6. Smith, *John Adams*, 1:70–71. Bernard Bailyn, "Butterfield's Adams: Notes for a Sketch," *William and Mary Quarterly*, 3rd ser. 19(1962):238–56.

Great War for Empire ended, and the British found themselves heavily indebted. To ease the crushing tax burden in Britain and to distribute the cost of their vast empire, the British cast about for colonial revenues. It seemed only fair that American colonists, who had gained so much from the costly war with the French, should pay their just share. Thus in 1764, the year of Adams's marriage, Parliament passed the American Revenue Act (known as the Sugar Act) and began the long struggle over taxation, parliamentary authority, and related topics.

The story of the developments leading to the American Revolution has been told many times and need not detain us here.[7] Suffice it to say that Adams, for personal and ideological reasons, had been long converted to the Whig cause. His experience with provincial politics and his resentment of leading families who used official positions to entrench themselves and their relatives convinced Adams that "radical" Whig fears of a conspiracy against the rights and liberties of Englishmen was no chimera.[8] Otis's argument against the writs of assistance in 1761 was, as Adams testified fifty-seven years later, the birth of American independence: "Every man of an immense crowded audience appeared to me to go away as I did, ready to take up arms against writs of assistance."[9] Soon

7. John C. Miller, *Origins of the American Revolution* (Boston, 1943), Lawrence Henry Gipson, *The Coming of the Revolution* (New York, 1954), Lawrence H. Leder, ed., *The Meaning of the American Revolution* (Chicago, 1969).

8. For a discussion of the development of the Whig belief in a conspiracy see Bernard Bailyn, *The Ideological Origins of the American Revolution* (Cambridge, 1967), pp. ix, 94–159.

9. Letter from John Adams to William Tudor, 29 March 1818, reprinted in *Novanglus and Massachusettensis; or Political Essays, Published in the years 1774 and 1775, on the Principal Points of Controversy, Between Great Britain and Her Colonies* (Boston, 1819), p. 246 (hereafter referred to as *Novanglus*). For a less idealistic version of Otis's motivation, see John J. Waters and John A. Schutz, "Patterns of Massachusetts Colonial Politics: The Writs of Assistance and the Rivalry Between the Otis and Hutchinson Families," *William and Mary Quarterly*, 3rd ser. 24(October 1967):543–67.

after, Adams himself joined the propaganda battle in defense of American rights.

Parliament, despite protests and petitions, decided to raise taxes directly in America by requiring a stamp on newspapers, pamphlets, legal documents, and other items. Thus began one of the most remarkable prerevolutionary events in America. To the general uproar and opposition, Adams contributed what appears to be a scholarly treatise but is essentially a Whig tract. "A Dissertation on Canon and Feudal Law" appeared in the radical *Boston Gazette* in 1765. Adams traced the development of human liberty from the assault of church reformers on the despotism of medieval canon law through the successive struggles against the oppression of feudal law and princes. This struggle was now transferred to America where Adams's ancestors had come to escape the tyranny of church and state. Only education and a free press could preserve the rights of Americans.[10] Adams's warning of the necessity of eternal vigilance was a hallmark of Whig thinking. Immediate danger did not really frighten them; the plans and motivations that lay behind it did. It is ironic that the attempt of eighteenth-century thinkers to raise politics to a science (thereby implying determinable actions and motives) led so easily to the conspiracy theory of history.[11] Adams shortly thereafter drew up instructions for the Braintree representative to the General Court in which he attacked the Stamp Act as unconstitutional, denounced the Admiralty Courts, and warned that America would not submit to invasion of its rights and consequent enslavement.[12]

Despite these declarations, Adams was not the true revolu-

10. [Adams], "Dissertation on the Canon and Feudal Law," in Charles Francis Adams, ed., *The Works of John Adams, Second President of the United States: With a Life of the Author,* 10 vols. (Boston, 1850–56), 3:448–64.

11. Gordon S. Wood, *The Creation of the American Republic* (Chapel Hill, 1969), pp. 40–43.

12. [Adams], "Instructions of the Town of Braintree to their Representative, 1765," in Adams, ed., *Works of John Adams,* 3:465–68.

tionary as was his cousin Sam. John's adoption of the pseudonym Clarendon[13] testified to his moderate position, as did the attempt of the royal government to woo him with the important and lucrative post of advocate general of the Court of Admiralty. Recognizing this as a bribe, Adams flatly refused the offer tendered through his old friend and protagonist Jonathan Sewall and thereby cast his lot with the patriots. The press of events and the conviction that Hutchinson and the junto were engaged in a conspiracy to corrupt the freedom of the province kept Adams on a revolutionary course.[14]

His propensity to extrapolate his political theory from his immediate personal experience can be seen in his reaction to the "thaw" between James Otis and Hutchinson after the latter's governorship. The seeming reconciliation mystified him, and he remained convinced that Hutchinson was dedicated to feathering his own nest and selling out the province to the Crown. His suspicion of the junto was vindicated by Hutchinson's preemptory lecture to the General Court and by the revelation of letters written by Oliver and Hutchinson to friends in England. These letters, leaked by Franklin to the colonists, reinforced Whig belief in ministerial corruption and conspiracy.[15]

Against this background of mistrust and suspicion, Boston acted out the famed Tea Party. Adams felt dumping the tea was a justifiable defense of colonial rights. Every step had been taken to

13. [Adams], "The Earl of Clarendon to William Pym," in Adams, ed., *Works of John Adams*, 3:469–83. The Earl of Clarendon, a moderate in the English Civil War, had tried to control the extremists. Exiled during Cromwell's rule, he later aided in the restoration of Charles II.

14. The sweep of events that carried men along in directions not altogether seen or desired is considered in Bailyn, *Ideological Origins*, p. v, and in Gordon S. Wood, "Rhetoric and Reality in the American Revolution," *William and Mary Quarterly*, 3rd ser. 23(1966):3–32.

15. See Smith, *John Adams*, 1:143–44, for an account of the "leaking" of the letters. There is some suspicion that Franklin may have sent the letters to increase his stock with patriot forces.

avoid landing the tea and paying the tax, but when all had failed, only force remained. As his defense of the British soldiers in the so-called Boston Massacre testified, John Adams did not worship the mob—an attitude that came more naturally to Sam Adams. Nevertheless, there were times, he believed, when legal redress became impossible and when enforcing unconstitutional laws became law-breaking—a point he emphasized in the Novanglus papers. He realized, however, that this reasoning would not appeal to British rulers, who would look upon destruction of the tea as an outrage against property—a serious crime in British eyes. And so it was.

On 1 June 1774, the British punished the unruly colonists by closing Boston harbor. This act, soon followed by further restrictions, rallied the other colonies to the defense of Massachusetts. The most obvious sign of colonial solidarity against Parliament was the First Continental Congress assembled in Philadelphia on 5 September 1774. John Adams and his cousin Sam had been elected Massachusetts delegates, along with Robert Treat Paine and Thomas Cushing. Both of the Adamses served on the grand committee to delineate American rights. The Congress's adoption of the Suffolk Resolves indicated its feeling that no compromise should be made with Parliament. Regardless of the basis of their claims for American rights—the British constitution, charter rights, or the laws of nature—the delegates felt that firmness, like that with which the colonists had faced the Stamp and Townshend Acts, would bring a reconsideration on Britain's part.[16]

John Adams returned from the Congress considerably heartened

16. For discussions of American political ideology see: Bailyn, *Ideological Origins*; Wood, *The Creation of the American Republic*; Lawrence H. Leder, *Liberty and Authority: Early American Political Ideology, 1689–1763* (Chicago, 1968); H. Trevor Colbourn, *The Lamp of Experience: Whig History and the Intellectual Origins of the American Revolution* (Chapel Hill, 1965); Caroline Robbins, *The Eighteenth-Century Commonwealthman: Studies in the Transmission, Development, and Circumstances of English Liberal Thought from the Restoration of Charles II until the War with the Thirteen Colonies* (Cambridge, 1959).

by the efforts toward colonial unity, which he hoped would bring Britain to its senses. The barrage of Tory propaganda which then swept the colonies dismayed him. Particularly irritating to Adams were the skillful and persuasive essays appearing in the *Massachusetts Gazette* under the pseudonym of "Massachusettensis." Convinced that they were the work of his old antagonist Jonathan Sewall (the Tory writer was later discovered to be Daniel Leonard, a Taunton lawyer)[17] and fearful that Tory arguments would undo the work of the patriots, Adams entered the lists against "Massachusettensis" in the more radical *Boston Gazette*. Thus began one of the more important exchanges of prerevolutionary debate.

One difficulty in discussing the coming of the revolution is escaping identification with one side or another in the contest.[18] Despite the brilliance of the new historical analysis of the Revolution, the neo-Whig interpretation of history has subtly reargued the merits of the patriot case. On the other hand, earlier attempts to dismiss the ideological struggle as simply a rationalization of economic, familial, and religious animosities distracted us from what men thought and said about the difficulties and problems they faced. Whatever the larger forces working on an individual, his perception and conception of social reality must be used by the historian to understand any historical phenomenon.

Both Adams and Leonard raise the question of motivation. Whether the claims of either are objectively true is less important than their belief in the truth of their respective statements of events. Thucydides pointed out long ago that the historian's key

17. Daniel Leonard (1740–1829) came from a socially prominent family which had made its fortune in ironworks. Originally of whiggish persuasion, Hutchinson converted him to the Tory cause. His "apostasy" irked his neighbors and Leonard had to seek refuge behind British lines in Boston. After the revolution, Leonard served as Chief Justice of Bermuda and then became a prominent lawyer in London. He died, somewhat mysteriously, of a pistol wound in his ninetieth year.

18. Wood, "Rhetoric and Reality," pp. 3–32.

to understanding events is what men *believe* to be true and act upon. Thus, in capsule form, Adams and Leonard present us with the problems of interpreting the coming of the revolution. Considering the colonists' genuine admiration for the British constitution—and no one admired it more than John Adams—and the fact that in confrontation after confrontation the Americans had had a reasonable amount of success, why were they so incensed and fearful of the loss of their liberties? Or, put another way: what possessed Americans to take on the most powerful nation in the world on pretexts that seem to an uninvolved observer extremely slight? In brief, why a revolution?

Adams and Leonard describe the crucial actions and motivations that brought the colonies forcibly to resist Britain. They raise, in addition, theoretical questions about constitutional and legal rights, posing for us 'once again the great unsolved dilemma of when man has the "right" to oppose "legitimate" authority. As Stephen Kurtz has suggested, some modern interest in John Adams is partially explained by our concern with the phenomenon of revolution.[19] William O. Douglas has recently stated that there is no constitutional justification for revolution, but in certain instances it is justifiable. Adams and Leonard debate that very paradox.

Leonard, tracing the conflict between mother country and colonies, charged the Whig party with self-serving activities. Indeed, he dismissed Whig constitutional arguments as mere artifices to maintain and strengthen political and economic gains. "Popularity," Leonard declared, "is the ladder by which partizans usually climb. . . . If the Tories were suspected of pursuing their private interest through the medium of court favor, there was equal reason to suspect the whigs of pursuing their private interest by the means of popularity." In fact, Leonard believed that some

19. Stephen G. Kurtz, "The Political Science of John Adams, A Guide to his Statecraft," *William and Mary Quarterly*, 3rd ser. 25(1968):605–13.

Whigs owed their importance to their part in the turbulence and that without the political ferment they "must in a little time have sunk into obscurity." Opposition to the tea tax was rooted not in the violation of American rights, he said, but in the threat of cheaper tea to smuggling. This danger led the smuggler to call upon his ally, the Whig, to protect him. In Leonard's pithy phrase: "A smuggler and a whig are cousin germans, the offspring of two sisters, avarice and ambition."[20] Thus, Whig constitutional claims had little to do with actual motivation.

For Leonard, as for later commentators, British actions appeared so mild and innocuous that only individuals malevolently motivated could have misled people into believing the approach of tyranny. Whig leaders and their allies of press and pulpit so dominated the scene that they badgered everyone into accepting the Whig view. Every word and action of the government and governor had been misconstrued to justify the treasonous acts of high Whigs. "Disaffection to Great Britain being infused into the body of the people, the subtle poison stole through all the veins and arteries, contaminated the blood, and destroyed the very stamina of the constitution."[21] One means used by Whigs to spread "the subtle poison," a means which called forth Leonard's strongest invective, was the committee of correspondence, Sam Adams's brainchild. This "new, and until lately, unheard of, mode of opposition . . . is the foulest, subtlest, and most venomous serpent that ever issued from the eggs of sedition."[22]

Nor were Whigs averse to using mobs to terrorize the opposition and inflame the passions of the multitudes.[23] Despite the fact that "if any thing was in reality amiss in government, it was its be-

20. *Novanglus*, pp. 149, 161.
21. Ibid., p. 156. See letter of 6 February for a listing of treasonous acts (pp. 187–91).
22. Ibid., p. 165.
23. See Gordon S. Wood, "A Note on Mobs in the American Revolution," *William and Mary Quarterly*, 3rd ser. 23(1966): 633–42.

ing too lax," Whigs artfully contrived to keep the people in a high state of apprehension by celebrations of alleged atrocities (for example, the 5th of March celebration honoring martyrs of the Boston Massacre) and by selectively destroying symbolic buildings (like Oliver's building, rumored as a collection place for the stamp tax). To political haranguing was added the propaganda of dissenting ministers. "What effect," Leonard despairingly asked, "must it have had upon the audience to hear the same sentiments, which they had before read in a newspaper, delivered on Sundays from the sacred desk?"[24] Was it any wonder, then, a people so agitated could be led to subversion and treason?

In fact, Leonard saw the Whig position as a flattery of the peoples' desire to be independent. The Whigs were not simply Englishmen fighting for traditional rights, but revolutionaries guilty of high treason. The people of America, Leonard warned, should not be deluded by these false prophets into believing that England would sit idly by while its colonies drifted into independence. It would "as soon conquer New England as Ireland or Canada," and it had the power to do it. How could one expect undisciplined, overdemocratic colonists lacking in arms and supplies to stand up to a nation "who so lately carried her arms with success to every part of the globe, triumphed over the united powers of France and Spain and whose fleets give law to the ocean." Even if the Whigs could convince other colonies to stand with New England—a moot point indeed—within each colony there would be a large number of people loyal to the Crown. "Let me tell you, whenever the royal standard shall be set up, there will be such a flocking to it, as will astonish the most obdurate." Spelling out the terrors of civil war and the inevitable defeat of American arms did not satisfy Leonard, however; he also considered the possibility of American victory and the results of such an outcome.

24. *Novanglus*, pp. 150–51.

It would be chaos. How, Leonard asked, would Americans protect themselves from marauding European maritime powers? How protect their fisheries? On what grounds would the disparate colonists form a government, and would it not probably fall prey to some colonial Cromwell? Would not Americans faced with governing have to raise revenue, and would not subordination be as vital as in the empire? Would not Whigs, tyrants when without power, be an abomination when backed by power? "It is a universal truth, that he that would excite a rebellion, whatever professions of philanthropy he may make, when he is insinuating and worming his way into the good graces of the people, is at heart as great a tyrant as ever wielded the iron rod of oppression." Adopting a Hobbesian view of the nature of government, Leonard warned that those leading America into rebellion were advocating a path which "dissolves the social band, annihilates the security resulting from law and government; introduces fraud, violence, rapine, murder, sacrilege, and the long train of evils, that riot, uncontrolled, in a state of nature."[25]

Whig grievances simply stemmed from the colonists' failure to abide by the legitimate actions of Parliament. The necessity that the colonists bear their fair share of imperial defense costs led to various attempts at taxation—some more practical than others, but all legitimate exercises of parliamentary power. The Whigs' obdurate refusal to obey culminated in the Port Act and the Regulation Act. Certainly if the colonists could neither protect property nor control mob action, Britain in the name of orderly government must step in. As Leonard correctly observed, the crux of this debate lay in each individual's conception of the relationship of colonies to mother country. If one accepted the Whigs' position that colonies were separate or distinct states, the colonial grievances came automatically: "Could I agree with them in their first

25. Ibid., pp. 144, 145, 153, 187–88.

principle, I should acquiesce in many of their deductions: for in that case every act of parliament, extending to the colonies, and every movement of the crown to carry them into execution, would be really grievances, however wise and salutary they might be in themselves, as they would be exertions of a power that we are not constitutionally subject to, and would deserve the name of usurpation and tyranny; but deprived of this their cornerstone, the terrible fabric of grievances vanishes, like castles raised by enchantment, and leaves the wondering spectator amazed and confounded by the deception."[26]

By a judicious use of legal precedents, Leonard demonstrated prior colonial acceptance of parliamentary power to tax the colonies. The claim that the right to tax without consent would lead to slavery had little merit, he said. The right to tax for necessary, national expense was limited only by the constitution: "The supreme legislature can have no right to tax any part of the empire to a greater amount than its just and equitable proportion." An abuse of a right, Leonard warned, did not negate the right. It followed, therefore, that attacks on Bernard, Hutchinson, Oliver, and others of the "junto" were without justification. Not only had these men been acquitted of such charges, but the evidence (when not completely distorted) affirmed what was obviously the case—that Great Britain could and for certain purposes *should* tax colonies. The Continental Congress's claim that "the colonists are entitled to an exclusive power of legislation in their several provincial legislatures"[27] was a manifest revolt from the British Empire.

This persuasive and eloquent plea, in British eyes the ablest American defense of the Crown's position, hit the patriotic cause a damaging blow. Adams knew that charges of treason and accusations of conspiring for independence might frighten potential supporters. Although doubtful of a reconciliation with Britain,

26. Ibid., p. 196.
27. Ibid., p. 220.

Adams, who was convinced that there is a tide in the affairs of men, feared too precipitate action and determined to defend the legitimacy of the colonial position within a framework of loyalty to the British Crown. Choosing the pseudonym "Novanglus" (New England) Adams, while assuring readers of his Whig loyalty, launched into a most vehement attack on parliamentary authority. The temper and style of Adams was immediately evident. Despite Adams's belief that his opponent was his old friend Jonathan Sewall, he gave way to his explosive nature and violated his opening resolution not to revile his opponent; he called Massachusettensis "this angry bigot, this ignorant dogmatist, the foul mouthed scold, [who] deserves no better answer than silent contempt."[28]

Adams moved directly to the heart of the matter. The Whigs, he argued, did not pursue arcane policies; the Tories did so. The Whig argument was directed to and depended upon the people; the Tory forwarded his case by "intrigues at a distant court." Contrary to Leonard's assertion that the colonists' refusal to recognize the legitimacy of Parliament's laws forced British repression, Adams insisted that the sudden and unconstitutional assault upon traditional colonial rights produced the American response. The colonists only responded to Tory aggressions. The "latent spark" of disaffection, of which Massachusettensis complained, was the spark of liberty. "Human nature itself is evermore an advocate of liberty. There is also in human nature, a resentment of injury, an indignation against wrong. A love of truth and a veneration for virtue."[29]

The struggle, for Adams, was the resistance of human nature to oppression and enslavement. Why, therefore, fear losing; defeat meant enslavement which faced Americans anyway if they did not resist. Besides, success would fuel man's age-old drive for liberty.

28. Ibid., p. 13.
29. Ibid., pp. 10–11.

Just as Cromwell's resistance to King Charles saved science and mankind from slipping back into medieval darkness, the American struggle would preserve the possibility of a free and enlightened political society.

Undoubtedly Adams's argument will seem exaggerated and over-blown to the modern reader, but Adams wrote from his personal experience with government in Massachusetts and from a concep-tual framework which saw court politics as inevitably corrupt and conspiratorial. The revenue to be raised by these new taxes was aimed, Adams was convinced, at entrenching the "junto." Francis Bernard's plan for reconstituting the government of the American colonies, read through the eyes of a contemporary Whig, was sus-picious indeed. An American nobility, a more centralized govern-ment, a rupture of traditional American patterns awakened latent fears and anxieties in a society predisposed to believe in the malevolence of the court party. Bernard did not see his proposals as attempts to enslave America; but his ideas, shaped by the con-ception of a hierarchical society, no longer accorded with the ex-perience and genius of the American colonies.

Central to Adams's constitutional argument was his rejection of Parliament's supremacy. To the Tory insistence that America was part of the British Empire and therefore subject to its supreme legislature, Adams replied "that the terms, 'British Empire,' are not the language of the common law, but the language of news-papers and political pamphlets." He later complained in exaspera-tion, "We are to be conjured out of our senses by the magic in the words, 'British Empire' and the 'supreme power of the state.'" Britain was not an empire, Adams held, and Parliament's authority did not extend to the colonies except to regulate trade—and that only because the colonies agreed that it should. Any jurisdiction of Parliament over the colonies must, Adams insisted, be founded "upon the *compact* and *consent* of the colonies, not upon any original principle of the English constitution, not upon the principle that parliament is the supreme and sovereign legislature over them in all cases whatever."[30]

Adams's position reflected the emerging American principle that Parliament was *not* the constitution, as maintained by late eighteenth-century British theory. In the conceptual framework of developing American ideology, Parliament's actions might well be legal, but they were unconstitutional.[31] To Americans, the constitution embodied fundamental rights of man and existed superior to government or to its representatives. Since Adams would not accept the Tory premise that Parliament made the constitution, he rejected Parliament's absolute sovereignty. He argued that provincial legislatures were supreme authorities in the colonies, while Parliament had power over the oceans since nothing specified American jurisdiction in that area. American charters were, in Whig eyes, contracts between colonists and king. They were not franchises or grants to be recalled when the grantor so decided.

Adams went further than most in his assertion that colonies were distinct states "as completely so as England and Scotland were before the union." Though the provinces were united under one king, provincial allegiance to the Crown was to the king's person, not to the Crown itself, and resulted not from an act of Parliament, but from the charter and laws of the province. Adams reinforced his position by analyzing the situation of Wales and Ireland. These countries, Adams asserted, owed allegiance to the Crown but were under no obedience to Parliament. Therefore, Americans had a precedent for claiming to be loyal subjects of the king while denying parliamentary legislation, except over trade. Adams proved by lengthy legal citation that this loyalty to the king was to the natural person, "not the politick." From this argument Adams then concluded that "subjection to the king of England does not

30. Ibid., pp. 30, 78–79, 83.
31. See Wood, *The Creation of the American Republic*, ch. 7, for extended discussion of this involved development.

necessarily imply subjection to the crown of England; and that subjection to the crown of England does not imply subjection to the parliament of England." Thus, having explored all possible legal alternatives, he asserted that American laws and government were based upon "compacts with Britain and her kings, and the great legislature of the universe."[32]

The reader, however interesting or uninteresting he may find Adams's legalistic argument, will still question the reasons for the acrimonious debate over legal and constitutional differences. Obviously, legal arguments were partially *ex post facto*. The key lay in the Whig conception of events from 1764 to the eve of revolution. From the Whig standpoint, British enactments would not simply enslave and impoverish, but would begin the replacement of simple "republican" freedoms and virtues with corrupt class-ridden styles of Great Britain.

When a people becomes convinced that their government's actions are aimed not at their welfare but at their subjection, their loyalty and submission to that government wavers and the subtle ties that bind a society snap. As Adams observed in 1818, "the revolution was effected before the war commenced. The revolution was in the minds and hearts of the people."[33] In the last analysis, no government can function if it has lost credibility among its constituents. The American people, more and more convinced of British complicity, looked upon "rioters" against unpopular measures not as criminals but as heroes.

In reply to the Tory complaint that none of the Stamp Act rioters was brought to justice, Adams correctly asserted that "it is vain to expect or hope to carry on a government, against the universal bent and genius of the people, we may whimper and whine as much as we will, but nature made it impossible, when she made men." (Leonard was well aware of that fact, having been

32. *Novanglus*, pp. 40, 114, 125.
33. Letter to Hezekiah Niles, 13 February 1818, in *Novanglus*, p. 233.

driven from Taunton by irate neighbors who disapproved of his
loyalism.) Classical authority itself justified resistance to "legal"
oppression. Grotius sanctioned the waging of "some sort of private war" if "legitimate" authorities blocked justice. Locke, in a
ship metaphor so popular in the seventeenth century, agreed that
the captain can be removed if he is determined to take crew and
passengers in a direction undesired by them: "How can man any
more hinder himself from believing the captain of a ship he was in,
was carrying him and the rest of his company to Algiers, when
he found him always steering that course, though cross winds,
leaks in his ship and want of men and provisions, did often
force him to turn his course another way for some time, which he
steadily returned to again, as soon as the winds, weather, and other
circumstances would let him." Adams had no doubt that British
government policies, as Locke suggested, were tacking with the
wind but always aiming at subjecting the colonies. Since only the
people can legitimately judge whether their deputies are fulfilling
their duties, the failure of government to listen to their complaints
and to change its course means that the "very foundations of society are destroyed; the prince and people are in a state of war
with each other like two independent states."[34]

Many supporters of the Crown were themselves good enough
Whigs to agree with Adams's theoretical assumptions, but they
disagreed with Adams about the tyrannical nature of Great Britain's actions. Certainly Leonard found ludicrous the fuss about a
threepence tax on tea. But seventeenth- and eighteenth-century
intellectual traditions and the peculiar nature of American politics made it natural for the colonists, heirs to "radical" whiggery,
to see the most minor incident as part of a ministerial plot. To the
Whig it seemed apparent that the British government "was carrying him . . . and his company to Algiers."

34. Ibid., pp. 58, 62, 65–66.

men, in harmony with the views and politics of the times. In comparison, the later years seemed chaotic and dislocated. Thus Adams recalled prerevolutionary days with affectionate nostalgia and glorified the patriots. The days of the revolution and of his youth were the days before corruption. Asked why all revolutionaries of the past have failed, Adams replied, "Because human nature cannot bear prosperity. Success always intoxicates patriots as well as other men; and because birth and wealth always, in the end, overcome popular and vulgar envy, more surely than public interest."[40] Thus revolutions would always be betrayed and hopes doomed.

Nevertheless, the American Revolution was a grand assertion of the rights of man against tyranny, and Adams effectively recalled and revived the memory of the men he knew—particularly the idol of his youth, James Otis. Even near the end of his long and illustrious life, Adams was still convinced (as would be any good son of a Puritan) that only morality and respect for the rights of others makes government feasible and just: "Oh! my fellow citizens, that I had the voice of an archangel to warn you against these detestable principles. The world was not made for you, you were made for the world. Be content with your own rights. Never usurp those of others. What would be the merit, and the fortunes of a nation, that should never do or suffer wrong?"[41]

40. Letter to William Tudor, 23 April 1818, in *Novanglus*, p. 262.
41. Letter to William Tudor, 6 August 1818, ibid., p. 285.

The outbreak of hostilities shifted debate from the printed page to the battlefield, and the last few issues of the Novanglus papers disappeared in the excitement of the times. The surviving letters were probably the strongest American attack on parliamentary authority in prewar America. Along with his "Thoughts on Government," Novanglus marked the height of Adams's optimism concerning the possibility of "establishing the wisest and happiest government that human wisdom can contrive."[35]

His experiences during the 1780s on government assignments in France, Holland, and Britain eroded his belief in America's peculiar virtue and brought to the fore his sense of humanity's universal corruptibility. Adams had always been aware of the human potential for evil, and his own introspective touchiness had easily turned the disappointments of the decade into evidence of the ingratitude and malevolent machinations of his enemies. Americans were no better than others, and Adams's ambiguities and guilt about his own career made the last two decades of the century particularly trying for him. Never a blind worshipper of the people, he had from the beginning doubted whether all those who backed the revolution shared his concerns. To some, the attack on British authority was an attack upon all authority. In 1776, Adams had asserted to Mercy Warren that there was "so much rascality, so much venality and corruption, so much avarice and ambition, such a rage for profit and commerce among all ranks and degrees of men even in America" that he doubted whether there was enough virtue to support a republican government.[36]

Although Adams had argued in his "Thoughts on Government" that some "forms of government are better fitted for being well administered than others," he was nevertheless convinced that the

35. [Adams,] "Thoughts on Government," in Adams, ed., *The Works of John Adams*, 3:200.
36. Letter to Mercy Warren, 8 January 1776, Adrienne Koch and William Peden, eds., *The Selected Writings of John and John Quincy Adams* (New York, 1946), pp. 49–50.

great desideratum of politics was virtue and that the future of a republic rested on denial of self-interest. Adams had hoped to form a government dedicated to virtue and had seen in Americans a virtuousness unusual enough to make him believe that they could sustain a republic longer than one had ever been sustained in the past. Convinced of the truth of the classical theory of cyclical development, Adams believed that as societies mature and become wealthy they pursue luxury and lose the simple republican virtues of their youth. Society divides into rich and poor, few and many, aristocrats and democrats; the inevitable corruption and divisiveness leads to collapse of republican government.

Adams's isolation while he was abroad and the insults he believed Congress had meted out to him convinced him that America was declining morally at a faster pace than anyone would have expected. Shays' rebellion and similar events reinforced his pessimism about the future of the American experiment in republicanism. Professor John Howe sums up Adams's pessimism about a society dominated by conspicuous consumption and pecuniary emulation: "Characterized no longer by a great middle grouping of independent yeomen, but by extremes of wealth, it lost its social cohesion. Adams's word for the process was 'disaggregation.' From the late 1780s on, he began to describe America increasingly in these terms."[37]

Fearing destruction of the nation unless the growing conflicts were checked, Adams reaffirmed the classical belief in a balanced constitution. But this balance, which incorporated monarchic, aristocratic, and democratic elements of society, was now viewed differently by Adams. He saw the executive as mediator between warring democratic and aristocratic factions; it maintained social order only by an absolute veto. Adams's declarations that govern-

37. John R. Howe, Jr., *The Changing Political Thought of John Adams* (Princeton, N.J., 1966), p. 136.

ment needed an absolute monarchy and a standing army led many to suspect him of having monarchist propensities. His unfortunate use of terms like monarchy and aristocracy, which had precise meanings to Adams but entirely different meanings to others, set many Americans against him and increased his isolation in later years.[38]

Probably of equal significance in Adams's intellectual and personal alienation was his devotion to the ideas of the British constitution. Just as his dedication to Enlightenment political "science" had led him to statements in his *Defence* which made him the enemy of the "democracy," so too did it keep him from fully understanding the shift in political ideology represented by the American Constitution.[39] His acceptance and praise of the Constitutional Convention and its work was based on the mistaken idea that this document was a "mixed" government which balanced various factions of society. On the contrary, the Constitution (whatever its architects' motivation) was premised, not on the representation of different social orders in different branches, but on the idea that sovereignty resides in the people and that all branches of government derive their power from all the people. Society and government are not synonymous, and in America all governments are limited agencies. Division of powers in the Constitution is a parceling out of legislative, executive, and judicial functions to check an undue concentration of power; it is not and was not a reflection of the orders or estates of society.

Despite the honors that came to Adams after the revolution—minister to the Court of St. James, vice-president of the United States, and then second president—the best and happiest days of his life were those leading up to the revolution. Then he was solidly tied to his native province, admired and respected by his country

38. Haraszti, *John Adams*, pp. 37–42.
39. For a detailed discussion, see Wood, *The Creation of the America Republic*, pp. 567–617.

9.

Mercy Otis Warren's Radical View of the American Revolution

WILLIAM RAYMOND SMITH

Mercy Otis Warren's three-volume *History of the Rise, Progress and Termination of the American Revolution* offers a fascinating study of the left wing of the revolutionary generation. It represented a unique, radical point of view among early histories of the revolution.

Because of her sex, her politics, and her analysis of John Adams's character—which provoked his dictum "History is not the Province of Ladies"—Mercy Warren's work has been too often ignored. For example, Merrill Jensen's *The Founding of a Nation: A History of the American Revolution, 1763–1776* (New York, 1968) cites British divine William Gordon and South Carolina physician David Ramsay, but it does not mention Mercy Warren. Although Gordon spent the war years in America, the volumes he published in London in 1788 were little more than extracts from the *Annual Register*. Ramsay's work also leaned upon the *Annual Register* and presented a conservative view of the revolution. While Ramsay thought republican institutions developed as a reaction to unique American circumstances, Warren saw the American Revolution as the beginning of a world revolution.[1]

1. "To Elbridge Gerry," Warren-Adams Letters, Massachusetts Historical Society *Collections*, Part II, 73(1925):380; William Gordon, *The History of the Rise, Progress, and Establishment of the Independence of the United*

This advocate of revolution descended from the first families of New England. She described the first American Otis, a Glastonbury yeoman who emigrated to Massachusetts in the early 1630s, as having been "oppressed in Britain by despotic kings, and persecuted by prelatic fury," and having "fled to a distant country, where the desires of men were bounded by the wants of nature; where civilization had not created those artificial cravings which too frequently break over every moral and religious tie for their gratification." Her grandfather John (1657–1727) established the Otises at Barnstable, where he commanded the county militia and held the posts of judge and provincial councilor for many years. Her father James (1702–78), commonly called Colonel Otis, married a Plymouth Allyne, giving Mercy (1728–1814) and her elder brother James (1725–83) a complete genealogy of resistance to oppression.[2]

Like other young ladies of her time, Mercy Otis grew up without formal education. Her intellectual interests were furthered, however, by the clergyman who tutored her brother James for Harvard. After her marriage in 1754 to James Warren (1726–1808), she be-

---

States of America, 4 vols. (London, 1788). Jensen cited David Ramsay, *The History of the American Revolution*, 2 vols. (Philadelphia, 1789), although he wrote three other histories as well. For a discussion of the value of early histories of the revolution, see W. R. Smith, *History as Argument: Three Patriot Historians of the American Revolution* (The Hague, 1966), pp. 31–39.

2. Mercy Otis Warren, *History of the Rise, Progress and Termination of the American Revolution*, 3 vols. (Boston, 1805)1:5. Published sources for a life of Mercy Warren include the Warren-Adams Letters, Massachusetts Historical Society *Collections*, part I, 72(1917) and part II, 73(1925), and "Correspondence between John Adams and Mercy Warren relating to her 'History of the American Revolution,' July-August 1807," Massachusetts Historical Society *Collections*, 5th ser., 4(1878):317–491. The Massachusetts Historical Society has a collection of Mercy's papers as well as of her husband's. She has been the subject of two biographies: Allice Brown, *Mercy Warren* (New York, 1896) and Katharine Anthony, *First Lady of the Revolution: The Life of Mercy Otis Warren* (Garden City, N.Y., 1958); neither is as useful as Maud Macdonald Hutcheson, "Mercy Warren, 1728–1814," *William and Mary Quarterly*, 3d ser. 10(July 1953):378–402.

gan writing verses in the sentimental style of the eighteenth century, which turned common things like fish into "finny folk." She kept that style throughout her writing, and it no doubt accounts for some of the neglect of her work.

Mercy's marriage took her to Plymouth, where the Warrens had been established since Richard Warren signed the Mayflower Compact. The move reinforced her sense of belonging to the tradition of resistance, and she showed her pride of place by signing her history "Mrs. Mercy Warren, of Plymouth, (Mass.)." After the death of his father, James Warren entered public life by taking over his father's office of county sheriff. In the same year—1757—the first of James's and Mercy's six sons was born.

In the late 1750s, Mercy Warren's father and brother seemed headed toward membership in the provincial governing elite. The colonel was elected to the General Court from Barnstable in 1758; in 1760 he was made speaker. As a reward to his father, James Otis was appointed king's advocate general of the Vice-Admiralty Court in Boston. In this position, he prosecuted merchants accused of violating imperial trade laws.

The Otises asserted the tradition of resistance in an ambiguous manner. A new governor, Francis Bernard, took office in August 1760, and one of his first problems concerned the appointment of a new justice to the Superior Court. Colonel Otis claimed that the office had been promised him by former Governor William Shirley, and he asked the help of Lieutenant Governor Thomas Hutchinson. When Bernard appointed Hutchinson instead, the Otises took the lead in opposing the government. James resigned his post and became one of the lawyers defending the merchants. His famous 1761 speech against the Writs of Assistance was remembered by John Adams as having given birth to American independence and having sown "the seeds of patriots and heroes."[3]

3. Charles Francis Adams, ed., *The Works of John Adams*, 10 vols. (Boston, 1850–56), 10:247.

James Warren sympathized with his wife's father and brother; by the middle of the 1760s he began organizing the radicals in Plymouth County. In 1766 the county elected him to represent it in the General Court. Surrounded by political activity, Mercy Warren turned her literary attention from occasional verses on everyday life to the events of the developing revolution.

After Thomas Hutchinson became governor in 1771, Mercy Warren began the first of a series of topical, satiric plays that made her a kind of laureate for the patriot cause. The first, *The Adulateur* (1772), ridiculed Hutchinson in the role of Rapatio, the Bashaw of Servia. The publication of the Hutchinson-Oliver letters the following year provided the subject for *The Defeat*. At the suggestion of John Adams, Mercy Warren produced a poem on the Tea Party that the Boston *Gazette* printed on its front page for 21 March 1774. The Massachusetts Government Act provided the subject for *The Group*, which appeared in the Boston papers early in 1775. Two more satiric plays appeared after the war began. *The Blockheads: or the Affrighted Officers* (1776) answered Burgoyne's *The Blockade of Boston*, while *The Motley Assembly* (1779) took on the loyalists.

By the mid-1770s both Warrens had reputations as patriots. James had become a member of the inner circle of radicals where he was especially close to both Sam and John Adams. At the frequent meetings held in their Plymouth home, Mercy actively participated in the discussions. Although we only have her word in the *History* that James suggested the idea for Committees of Correspondence to Sam Adams, Warren was so well thought of that he first became president of the Massachusetts Provincial Congress and then was named speaker in the new General Court.

Both James and Mercy Warren ardently supported democratic simplicity and devoted themselves to their native soil. James accepted the post of paymaster general for the Continental Army during the siege of Boston and served as a member of the Navy

Board for the Eastern Department from 1776–81. However, his unwillingness to see a major general of the Massachusetts militia subordinated to a continental officer of lower rank led him to resign his commission in 1777 after he had excused himself from a military assignment because of ill health. John Hancock used his reticence against him, so he lost his seat in the legislature for 1778, but he was returned to office in 1779. He refused an appointment as justice of the Supreme Judicial Court of Massachusetts in 1776 and declined the lieutenant governorship in 1780, perhaps because of his notions of democratic simplicity. He was, as he wrote to Sam Adams in 1775, "content to move in a small sphere. I expect no distinction but that of an honest man who has exerted every nerve." One suspects that he gloried in a simple life lived according to his democratic principles. He wanted not too much distinction, but just enough to set him off as a man who lived by principle.[4]

Although the Warrens bought Thomas Hutchinson's confiscated estate, Milton Hill, in 1781 and lived there during most of the 1780s, they looked upon themselves as preserving the plain republican style of life that Americans began deserting after the war for such "foreign" distinctions, as membership in the Order of the Cincinnati and the inordinate pursuit of wealth. Mercy turned to "serious" writing and attempted two tragedies, *The Ladies of Castile* and *The Sack of Rome*, which she vainly hoped John Adams, as American minister in London, could get produced. James ran for governor of Massachusetts but lost because he was rumored to have favored the Shaysites. He was, however, immediately elected speaker when he returned to the House in 1787. But John Hancock once again forced Warren from active political life for advocating measures favoring debtors and for joining with Elbridge Gerry in opposition to the new Constitution. James

4. Warren-Adams Letters, part I, p. 78.

Warren was viewed as an enthusiastic democrat by old friends like John Adams. During the winter of 1787–88, he published a series of letters in the Boston papers opposing the Constitution. Mercy joined the active opposition through a pamphlet published in the spring of 1788. Her choice of *nom de guerre*, "A Columbian Patriot," successfully concealed her authorship of *Observations on the New Constitution and on the Federal and State Conventions*, which scholarship until 1930 attributed to Gerry.[5]

During the 1790s, the Warrens, once again at Plymouth, lived on the fringes of opposition politics. Although they had fallen out with Abigail and John Adams over the policies of the new federal government, Mercy listed John as a subscriber for her *Poems: Dramatic and Miscellaneous* when it appeared in 1790. In spite of James Warren's reputation, Mercy's poetry was considered apolitical enough that Robert Treat Paine asked her for a contribution to his *Federal Orrery*. She replied that politics would prevent her from signing anything she sent. (Although politically inactive, James was on the Governor's Council from 1792–94.) It was a bitter disappointment to the Warrens that politics prevented one of their sons from gaining the patronage post of collector for the port of Plymouth. Late in the decade, the Duc de la Rochefoucauld-Liancourt recorded his impressions of a visit to the Warrens. James was aging, he said, but Mercy's intellect was acute. Rochefoucauld reported that the Warrens had decided that Mercy's history should not be published while either of them still lived.[6] (They must have changed their minds, since the *History* was published in 1805.)

Mercy began writing her history as early as November 1775. She

5. Charles Warren, "Elbridge Gerry, James Warren, Mercy Warren and the Ratification of the Federal Constitution in Massachusetts," Massachusetts Historical Society *Proceedings*, 64(1932):143–64.

6. Duc de la Rochefoucauld-Liancourt, *Voyage dans les Etats-Unis d'Amérique*, 3 vols. (Paris, 1799), 3:150.

seems to have become discouraged in the summer of 1777, but when she heard that John Adams was going to France, she asked Abigail to remind him of his promise to provide accounts of European developments. She wrote to Adams in Europe several . times asking for information. While in Amsterdam in 1780, John remarked wryly in a letter to James, "I dread [Mrs. Warren's] History more than that of the Abby [Raynal]. I want to know in what Colours she will draw Brother [Arthur] Lee. He little knew what eyes were upon him." And from Paris in 1783, he wrote to Mercy, "What I said about certain Annals was no Sarcasm. I have the utmost Veneration for them, although I never was honoured with a Sight of any of them." By February 1787, Mercy had completed enough of her history to send it for criticism to James Winthrop, the Harvard librarian. Throughout the writing, she attempted to collect data from participants, including revolutionary generals Henry Knox and Benjamin Lincoln. By the end of 1787, John Adams was looking forward to the publication of the history. In a letter from London, he told Mercy that he hoped she would continue the project, "for there are few Persons possessed of more Facts, or who can record them in a more agreeable manner." Although Jefferson and the members of his cabinet subscribed for the history in 1805, Judith Sargent Murray wrote Mercy from Boston that she could not obtain many subscriptions because Marshall's "Life of Washington, it is said, forestalls, if not wholly precludes, the utility of this history; and very many urge the political principles attributed to the otherwise admired writer, as a reason for withholding their signatures." After publication, John Dickinson and James Winthrop praised the history in letters to Mercy. A long review in the Boston *Panoplist*, however, severely criticized her politics.[7]

7. Warren-Adams Letters, part I, pp. 178, 358; part II, pp. 2, 56, 81, 155, 180, 282–83, 296–98, 301, 317–18, 322, 345–47, 350–52, 378–81; *The Panoplist*, 2(January, February 1807):380–84, 429–32.

John Adams's reaction to the history opened old wounds for the Warrens. In an exchange of letters during the summer of 1807, John and Mercy renewed what had become an old argument about the principles of the revolution. As Adams pointed out errors and limitations in the history—especially those concerned with his own characterization—he became increasingly more irritated and caustic. Near the end of the exchange, he dismissed Mercy's work with the judgment that the "History has been written to the taste of the nineteenth century, and accommodated to gratify the passions, prejudices, and feelings of the party who are now predominant." The cutting blow appears to have been Mercy's assessment of him as a man of serious manner and plain habits, more adaptable to dealing with the sober Dutch than with the frivolous French. To Adams that was a "satirical sneer," and he wondered why he had been "singled out to be stigmatized as a clown?" In reply, Mercy wrote "that when I observed that Mr. Adams was no favorite of the officers and administrators of affairs at the Gallican court, and that his manners were not adapted to render him acceptable to that refined and polished nation, or that he did not appear to have much partiality for or confidence in them, I meant to convey to my readers an honorable idea of his impartiality, republicanism and independence." Adams could not be satisfied and broke off the correspondence. Not until 1813, five years after James's death, did Elbridge Gerry manage to reconcile the old friends. The following year Mercy died, leaving corrections for a second edition of her history which was never published.[8]

Given her involvement with events, one might expect Mercy's history to take the form of an apologia. In her preface, she asserted the uniqueness of her history because events were recorded "as they passed." Her account was not drawn from other histories: "Connected by nature, friendship, and every social tie, with many

8. "Correspondence between John Adams and Mercy Warren relating to her 'History of the American Revolution,' " pp. 388, 448, 463.

of the first patriots, and most influential characters on the continent; in the habits of confidential and epistolary intercourse with several gentlemen employed abroad in the most distinguished stations, and with others since elevated to the highest grades of rank and distinction, I had the best means of information through a long period that the colonies were in suspense, waiting the operations of foreign courts, and the success of their own enterprising spirit." Sex, she argued, was no barrier to one whose "mind . . . had not yielded to the assertion, that all political attentions lay out of the road of female life." Although history dictated that "characters nearly connected with the author" had to come into the narrative, she had "endeavoured, on all occasions, that the strictest veracity should govern her heart, and the most exact impartiality be the guide of her pen." Her history made "an effort to trace the origin of the American revolution, to review the characters that effected it, and to justify the principles of the defection and final separation from the parent state."[9] Mercy took a stance rather like that of Thucydides.

If her history were an apologia, it would be an apologia for the principles of the revolution rather than for the "characters nearly connected with the author." She listed her husband only twice in the index, once as originator of the idea for Committees of Correspondence and again for a letter he wrote in 1780 concerning the difficulties of financing the army. Her brother, James Otis, received more attention. His perception, she asserted, of the dangers inherent in Governor Bernard's appointment of Jonathan Sewall as "sole judge of admiralty in the Massachusetts . . . particularly when aided by writs of assistance" aroused Bernard's opposition. "By the exertion of his talents and the sacrifice of interest, [James Otis] may justly claim the honor of laying the foundation of a revolution, which has been productive of the happiest effects to

9. Warren, *History*, 1:iii, iv, vi, viii.

the civil and political interests of mankind."[10] In the context of the three-volume history, however, this boast has little to do with the direction of events.

Events, in Mercy's history, resulted from four interrelated forces: human nature, human history, divine nature, and divine history. For her, human nature was an ambiguous and paradoxical thing. All men were equal in this life, not just in the sight of God. Endowed with "restless" minds, however, men were not satisfied with their natural state. Dissatisfaction produced strong desires in every individual for personal distinction. This goad to human action could take the form of either love of fame or love of wealth. Mercy believed avarice was the stronger passion, because she had observed, at the beginning of the revolution, that when personal property was endangered a man would strike back like a predator. Man's natural ferocity had made the state of nature one of war.

But Mercy balanced this bleak view by a belief that reason and moral sense were as much part of a man's natural endowment as emotions. Although too frequently submerged in passion, reason and moral sense could turn man's desire for distinction toward social good. Reason and moral sense placed man a little above the beasts. She was not sure whether man had evil in his nature when living in the "state of nature." Once men began amassing wealth, however, the passion of avarice could turn their love of distinction toward evil ends. In her view, social improvement was possible but perfection was impossible, because property—although necessary for life—produced avarice, which overwhelmed reason and moral sense.

Mercy saw human history as a recurring fall from liberty to despotism, coupled with an advance along the scale of civilization. The advance gave the ambitious and the avaricious opportunity to destroy natural equality; thus the few gained power over the many.

10. Ibid., 4:47.

Once a particular society began to develop along one line, change of direction was unusual because inherent conservatism held men in ancestral patterns of behavior. In history Mercy saw an explanation for the fact that although men were born free and equal, in advanced societies the majority were slaves and power was held by the few.

It is difficult to say whether by the "state of nature" Mercy meant a real condition of man in some remote past or an idealized condition of men in all times as a construct for political and social theories. She clearly based her definition of man upon those characteristics she considered changeless: men were created free and equal, possessed with restless minds that sought distinction and thereby produced ambition and avarice, and endowed with reason and moral sense. The balance among these characteristics and the predominance of one of them depended upon historical circumstances. Thus, although an avaricious despotism was "natural," a society in which men lived in harmonious equality was more in accord with the "better nature" of man.

Since Mercy based her notion of history upon her concept of human nature, analysis of individual character was very important in her history. Although men had essentially the same qualities throughout history, the balance of these characteristics varied according to historical circumstances. By studying history, men might avoid past errors and might further those conditions necessary for individual and social welfare. The historian, therefore, was a teacher. For Mercy, history had two lessons to teach: that some form of government was necessary to check the ambition, avarice, and resulting ferocity of natural man; and that true religion held society together and revealed proper forms of government.

Upon true religion depended the success or failure of men, because the will of God controlled human action. God's nature, however, was beyond human grasp. Only after a particular sequence of human activity was finished could the divine direction be determined. But difficulty in distinguishing sequences made such inferences hazardous. Mercy believed that true religion revealed one aspect of divine nature: God wills human happiness.

From the human perspective, Mercy reasoned, events appeared accidental. But man was an instrument of divine history, of the Providence that shapes the course of events in accordance with the will of God. The sudden rise and fall of individuals and the progress and decline of nations revealed the natural equality of men. Providence used the nature of man, the evil intermixed with the good, to bring about the final end of human happiness.

Mercy saw the course of events depending on the nature of man as created by God. To man this nature appeared as a mixture of good and evil, but both were instruments in the workings of Providence. To his own mind, man willed his own action; but as an instrument of Providence, human will fulfilled the divine plan for man. Although on the human level man had the capacity to will action, on the divine level everything man willed contributed to the aim of Providence. While in relation to each other men acted freely, in relation to God they were acted upon. Since everything that men did contributed to the divine aim for good, Mercy concluded that even though they were naturally ferocious animals, it was doubtful that men were evil in a natural state.

Upon this basis of seventeenth-century Puritanism slightly tempered by eighteenth-century Enlightenment thought, Mercy built her history. She summed up the lesson the American Revolution taught in the final sentences of her history:

The wisdom and justice of the American governments, and the virtue of the inhabitants, may, if they are not deficient in the improvement of their own advantages, render the United States of America an enviable example to all the world, of peace, liberty, righteousness, and truth. The western wilds, which for ages have been little known, may arrive to that state of improvement and perfection, beyond which the limits of human genius cannot reach; and this last civilized quarter of the globe may exhibit those striking traits of grandeur and magnificence, which the Divine Economist may have reserved to crown the closing scene, when the angel of his presence will stand upon the sea and upon the earth, lift up his hand to heaven, and swear by Him that liveth for ever and ever, that there shall be time no longer.[11]

The expression is characteristic of the mixture of fear, hope, pride, and apocalyptic vision through which Mercy recorded the development of the revolution.

Her account of the years before the outbreak of hostilities followed the "Whig theory." The progress of colonial opinion and events between the Stamp Act and the battles of Lexington and Concord could not be attributed to any small group of professional revolutionists. It was a defense of their rights by the vast majority of Americans. Only a small minority, who received personal gain from British taxation, opposed the American cause. The movement of colonial opinion that led to the decision to fight was largely a spontaneous reaction to events that was similar in all the colonies.

The circumstances of settlement in America produced a society that forced American acceptance of the natural equality of man, based upon the genius of American political ideas brought by the first settlers to the colonies. The movement that produced revolution was an offense by Britain against colonial rights and a defense of them by the colonies. Had the British offense aimed at anything short of tyranny, however, the inherent conservatism in the nature of man would have prevented Americans from sacrificing their lives and property in order to protect their rights. They were products of a society constructed on an ideal balance between nature and civilization, so reason and moral sense occupied a more prominent place than usual in their actions. This enabled them to detect the designs of the king acting through Parliament

11. Ibid., 3:434–36.

and to resist with moderation and firmness until they were physically attacked and the war began.

In her account of the war, Mercy began to depart from the Whig theory. While other early histories of the revolution concentrated narrowly upon American events, Mercy set it in a context of a developing world war. British and American military strength depended not only on firepower, but also on diplomatic relations with Europe and on social and political developments in England and America. The outcome of naval battles influenced the intensity of military engagements in America, since the war was carried on in European waters as well as in the West Indies. Mercy developed her history of the war by paralleling military and naval actions, political and social developments, and the diplomatic relations among the several powers that influenced the war's outcome. Instead of merely telling an American story, she attempted to make her history inclusive. This scope, however, was directed toward establishing the correctness of the American Revolution.[12]

American success, in Mercy's narrative, depended more on British military, political, and social weakness than on American strength. British military action in America was pictured as inept, but the American military was shown to be pitifully weak. British government was corrupt, but Congress lost sight of principles. British national character was dominated by trade and personal pleasure, but the war brought out avarice in Americans. After Yorktown, the British successfully defended Gibraltar and de-

12. Although forty-seven percent of her history concerned military and naval operations, these were subordinated to political history (comprising thirty-three percent of the work), social history (twelve percent), and diplomatic history (seven percent). The three volumes of John Marshall's mistitled *Life of George Washington*, 5 vols. (Philadelphia, 1804–1807), which dealt with the war, devoted seventy-five percent of the space to military history, twenty-one percent to political history, and only 1 percent to diplomatic history. Most of Marshall's treatment of political history showed the connection between political and military events. The contrast points up Mercy's broader view.

feated the French at sea, but lack of supplies and men reduced the American army to immobility. America in 1782, in the picture Mercy drew, was more worn out by war than Great Britain. Peace, one might have concluded from such evidence, resulted from British boredom. Mercy, however, asserted that the American Revolution proved, no matter what the relative military strength of the contestants, the impossibility of one nation conquering another that was resolved to be free. Britain, she argued, quit the war when convinced that victory was impossible because of the depth of American determination to be independent.

In this account, national moral strength formed the basis of the determination, before hostilities, to resist encroachments of arbitrary power. When war came, however, it forced Americans from their high principles and brought out avarice. Since Mercy argued that only superior moral strength could resist superior military power, and since she saw America's moral character weakened by the war, how did she see the necessary determination maintained until the British realized the impossibility of winning?

Her answer was based, first, upon the American character: "Perhaps there are no people on earth, in whom a spirit of enthusiastic zeal is so readily enkindled, and burns so remarkably conspicuous, as among the Americans." Throughout the war, hopes were revived by the slightest military advantage. Defeat also renewed a spirit willing to suffer rather than submit. After the capture of Philadelphia in 1777, "not disheartened . . . general Washington with his brave troops, in numbers comparatively inconsiderable, kept the British army in play, until the setting in of winter." While Burgoyne was advancing from Canada, "the dangers that lowered in every quarter, seemed rather to invigorate the public mind, and quicken the operations of war." After the British victories in the South in 1780, "the people again awakened. . . . The patriotic exertions and unshaken firmness of the few in every state, again had their influence on the many, and all seemed ready to suffer anything, but a subjugation to the crown of Britain." A mutinous army and a useless currency in 1781 "were discouragements that in theory might have been thought insurmountable: but *American Independence* was an object of too great magnitude, to sink under the temporary evils, or the adventitious circumstances of war." The ability of Americans to rise above immediate difficulties in the pursuit of higher goals was, she observed, a "characteristic trait [which] may in some measure account for the rapidity with which every thing has been brought to maturity there, from the first settlement of the colonies."[13]

Enthusiasm for justice, then, was one trait that maintained American resolve. Mercy saw a second in the Congress's rejection of North's conciliation bills in 1778, when America still stood alone, not knowing that the French alliance was in effect. In the "spirited language" of this rejection, Americans showed a "due dependence on their own magnanimity and firmness; and by the dignity of their resolutions, congress manifested a consciousness of the justice of their cause, and a reliance on that providential support, they had hitherto remarkably experienced."[14]

The support of Providence was the conspicuous theme running throughout Mercy's history. It created American initiative to maintain a military force, it upheld and renewed American enthusiasm, it determined the outcome of the war. To her, this support meant, not so much that God was on the side of the Americans, but that their social and political ideas were on God's side. Providence had taken the American people and made them into an instrument in the furtherance of the divine plan. In this plan, the American Revolution advanced the world revolution in government and society that would bring about God's objective for man.

"Madam," John Adams wrote Mercy, "after the termination of

13. Warren, *History*, 1:358–59, 381; 2:11, 238–39, 286.
14. Ibid., 2:72–73.

the Revolutionary War, your subject was complete."[15] For her, however, the subject was incomplete until she had traced the effects of the revolution through the difficulties of the confederation period to the adoption of the Constitution and the establishment of the federal government in a republican direction. She looked at events during the last two decades of the eighteenth century as a fall from the revolutionary principles of republicanism. Old friends and new enemies conspired to subvert the purity of the American way. At the beginning of the nineteenth century, however, Americans again corrected their position (as they had many times during the war) and reasserted their support for republican government.

The troubles of the confederation period, in Mercy's analysis, resulted from inevitable economic difficulties produced by the war and were compounded by ineffectual national government and interstate rivalry. Because of personal difficulties and ignorance of the proper function of government, many Americans lost faith in their government. This was furthered by designing men who desired autocratic government. Finally, at the point of governmental breakdown, Americans became convinced "of the necessity of concert and union in measures that might preserve their internal peace. This required the regulation of commerce on some stable principles, and some steps for the liquidation of both public and private debts. They also saw it necessary to invest congress with sufficient powers for the execution of their own laws, for all general purposes relative to the union."[16] In Mercy's view, nothing more was necessary. The Constitution as drafted, however, went much further. It departed from the principles and precepts of republican government.

Mercy took pains to define republicanism. The concept, she asserted, was based upon four principles: (1) natural equality of

15. "Correspondence between John Adams and Mercy Warren relating to her 'History of the American Revolution,' " p. 432.
16. Warren, *History*, 3:355–56.

man; (2) national self-determination; (3) dignity of the people; and (4) popular sovereignty. From these principles, fifteen precepts of governmental operation followed: (a) respect for the general will; (b) taxation only through representation; (c) protection of freedom of conscience; (d) frequent elections; (e) rotation in office; (f) due subordination and obedience of the people to their chosen leaders; (g) economy; (h) simple manners; (i) pure morals; (j) conscientious honesty; (k) simple laws; (l) clear separation of executive, legislative and judicial powers; (m) right to jury trial; (n) protection of personal liberty; and (o) protection of private property. Both principles and precepts were based on the word of God.[17]

Until amendments were adopted, Mercy saw each step that furthered the Constitution as a departure from republicanism. The Convention exceeded its authority by drafting an entirely new structure of government. Members of the Convention were divided over many issues; some refused to sign, while others signed only because there seemed nothing better. The document itself had elements of monarchy, and the secretive drafting procedure showed a lack of respect for the general will.

Ratification also revealed lack of respect for the general will. Although advocates rammed ratification through, Mercy asserted that it was "evident that a majority of the states were convinced that the constitution, as at first proposed, endangered their liberties." She characterized the advocates as young men whose principles were aristocratic and monarchical, and as "apostate whigs" willing to exchange republican principles for European court policies. Those opposed to adopting the Constitution without amendments, however, were men who maintained the principles that had led America into the revolution. To them, she argued, "are the public indebted for the amendments and ameliorations of

17. Ibid., pp. 304–06.

the constitution, which have united all parties in the vigorous support of it."[18]

A comparison of Mercy's initial objections with the corrections made by amendments does not explain her final acceptance. Although nothing was done to remove her objections concerning term of office, separation of powers, rotation in office, Electoral College, the limited number of representatives, and congressional salaries, no Federalist exceeded Mercy's final praise: "Perhaps genius has never devised a system more congenial to their wishes, or better adapted to the condition of man, than the American constitution."[19] The explanation may be found in her distinctly Puritan concept of man. She believed that, although man was capable of reasoned action based on his moral sense, avarice and ambition severely limited this capacity. She hoped for complete implementation of republican principles in American government, but she expected that, like other peoples, Americans might sink under despotism. In being more than satisfied when the constitution after amendment lacked only a few of the elements in her definition of republicanism, Mercy was following the Puritan tradition.

Another part of that tradition made Mercy continue to cry out against the sins of her generation. George Washington, she observed, "without arrogating any undue power to himself, which success and popularity offered, and which might have swayed many more designing and interested men, to have gratified their own ambition at the expense of the liberties of America, finished his career of military glory, with decided magnanimity, unimpeached integrity, and the most judicious steps to promote the tranquility of his country." Washington's retirement from the army greatly relieved her fears of military dictatorship. She thought, however, that he should have used his prestige as a symbol of independence to unite opinion, instead of accepting the presidency where he was

18. Ibid., p. 365.
19. Ibid., p. 423.

used by his military associates to further their monarchist aims. Wary of directly criticizing him because of her maxim that "public opinion is generally grounded on truth," she tried to show how Washington fell short of what he might have done. In his farewell address he gave admirable advice concerning national unity, public economy, and foreign relations, but the advice had a hollow ring, for Americans during his administration had

split into factions; after an exotic taste had been introduced into America, which had a tendency to enhance their public and to accumulate their private debts; and after the poison of foreign influence had crept into their councils, and created a passion to assimilate the politics and the governments of the United States nearer to the model of European monarchies than the letter of the constitution, by any fair construction would admit.[20]

In her record of the years following the war, Mercy avoided political party names. Federalists were called "monarchists," while Republicans were "those who upheld the principles of the revolution" or "the advocates of republicanism." Republicans opposed the introduction of European ideas into American government, while they advocated the spread of American ideas abroad, as for example by the French Revolution. Monarchists advocated European ideas, while they opposed the spread of American ideas by becoming partisans of Britain in its war with France. While monarchists advocated a constitution without sufficient guarantees of individual rights, the funding system, Jay's treaty, and a standing army, those who upheld the revolution consistently opposed these despotic innovations. Opposition was based upon a clear set of principles and precepts, while the advocates of despotism obscured their aims to confuse the people. By her manner of characterizing the parties and by explicitly stating the basis of the Republican argument while neglecting the basis of the Federalist

20. Ibid., pp. 318, 388, 390.

argument, she made a strong case that their actions evinced a fall from republicanism.

During the Federalist administrations, Mercy saw Americans falling rapidly from the morality that must underlie republicanism. The federal financial system led to unbridled speculation and, since ambition was without hereditary titles, this furthered the growth of avarice until she "apprehended that the possession of wealth will in a short time be the only distinction in this young country." Wealth was more corrupting than titles, and its pursuit caused Americans to forget the men and the principles that had established their liberty. How, then, was she able to claim, near the end of her history, that "the illusion was however discovered, and a constitutional ardency for general freedom revived among the people?"[21]

The answer depends on Mercy's belief that republican government was based upon the rational morality of the citizens, whereas despotism could only be based on their immorality. People got the kind of government that their actions deserved. If a people behaved according to the laws of morality revealed in right religion (reformed Protestantism), they would naturally establish republicanism; but if the action of a people conformed to wrong religion (Catholicism) or if they lacked a rational religious basis for behavior (atheism or skepticism), they would find established over them an evil despotism.

In spite of the reckless speculation in virtue that ended in the establishment of a strong national government, Mercy believed that Americans still possessed a morality that made despotism unlikely and republicanism possible. As descendants of men who possessed God-given principles of religion and government and who settled in a land where natural abundance insured social equality, they inherited religious, political, and social principles and institutions that made republican government necessary and

21. Ibid., pp. 415, 430.

likely for generations to come. With their abundant morality and right principles, after a fall from republicanism as a consequence of the revolutionary war, it was possible for Americans to reassert their principles and reestablish republicanism on a sounder basis at the beginning of the nineteenth century.

In the historiography of the American Revolution, Mercy Warren's place is unique. Her work does not fit easily into the Whig interpretation, although she saw the revolution as a struggle for liberty. She used her familiarity with British politics and with events on the the continent to broaden her context, but her history does not fall into the imperial school. Economic and social considerations played a prominent role, but to other purposes than those of the progressives. For her, the revolution was not complete in the hearts and minds of men before the war began, nor could it begin once the war was over. The revolution was a result of a complex of forces acting continually upon mankind. Because of a special combination of ideas, circumstances, and environment, revolutionary activity first manifested itself in America. For success, such activity had to be constantly defended and asserted. Having begun, the revolution could end only with the Last Judgment.[22]

From our perspective, Mercy's analysis of historical forces may appear contradictory, perhaps even naïve. We might easily categorize her as a speculative philosopher of history rather than as a critical historian. Such judgments are beside the point. Mercy Warren was closely connected, from the beginning of the revolution, with the men who played an active part in Massachusetts. As the movement developed she came into contact with leaders throughout the country. Her sex barred her from those activities we call "events," but her writings helped mold opinion. What may

22. Jack P. Greene, "The Reappraisal of the American Revolution in Recent Historical Literature," in *The Reinterpretation of the American Revolution, 1763–1789* (New York, 1968), is an excellent survey of the historiography of the revolution.

have been a disadvantage for her is a boon to those trying to understand the American Revolution. Barred from events, she turned her attention to recording them. She did not record them as we would, and therein lies the peculiar value of her history. Close study of her work can provide insight into the radical point of view.

The Contributors

JOHN M. BUMSTED was educated at Tufts College and Brown University. He has taught at Tufts and McMaster University, and is presently at Simon Fraser University. A specialist in New England and Canadian history, he has published numerous articles on ecclesiastical politics and institutions. His latest work is *Henry Alline and the Beginnings of Evangelical Pietism in Canada* (Toronto, 1971).

JOSEPH A. DOWLING was educated at Lincoln Memorial University and New York University. He has taught at Shorter College, Bates College, and is presently at Lehigh University. A specialist in American intellectual history, he has published articles in that field and has recently revised *American Issues: The Social Record* (Philadelphia, 1971) in collaboration with Merle Curti, Willard Thorpe, and Carlos Baker.

DAVID FREEMAN HAWKE was educated at Swarthmore College, the University of Wisconsin, and the University of Pennsylvania. He has taught at Long Island University, Brooklyn College, and is presently at Pace College. He is the author of *In the Midst of a Revolution* (Philadelphia, 1961) and *The Colonial Experience* (Indianapolis, 1966).

MILTON M. KLEIN was educated at City College and Columbia University. He has taught and served in administrative positions at Long Island University, State University of New York College at Fredonia, and is presently at the University of Tennessee. His special area of competence is colonial politics, and he has published a number of articles on New York and has edited William Livingston's *Independent Reflector* (Cambridge, 1963).

CARL E. PRINCE was educated at Rutgers University. He has taught at Fairleigh Dickinson University and Seton Hall University, and is presently at New York University, where he has served as editor of the Albert Gallatin Papers. He has published *New Jersey's Jeffersonian Republicans* (Chapel Hill, 1967), as well as articles on New Jersey history in the late colonial and early national periods.

WILLIAM RAYMOND SMITH was educated at the University of Chicago. He has taught at Pennsylvania State University, Haverford, Scripps, and Shimer Colleges, and is presently at Reed College. He has also served as Fulbright lecturer at the Universities of Utrecht and Groningen. He has published *History as Argument* (The Hague, 1966), and *The Rhetoric of American Politics* (The Hague, 1969).

LOUIS L. TUCKER was educated at the University of Washington. He has taught at the University of California at Davis and the College of William and Mary, and has served as Director of the Historical Society of Ohio. He is presently State Historian for New York State. Among his publications are *Puritan Protagonist* (Chapel Hill, 1960) and *Cincinnati During the Civil War* (Columbus, 1962).